Italian and Italian American Studies

Stanislao G. Pugliese
Hofstra University
Series Editor

This publishing initiative seeks to bring the latest scholarship in Italian and Italian American history, literature, cinema, and cultural studies to a large audience of specialists, general readers, and students. I&IAS will feature works on modern Italy (Renaissance to the present) and Italian American culture and society by established scholars as well as new voices in the academy. This endeavor will help to shape the evolving fields of Italian and Italian American Studies by re-emphasizing the connection between the two. The following editorial board of esteemed senior scholars are advisors to the series editor.

Assassinations and Murder in Modern Italy

Transformations in Society and Culture

Edited by Stephen Gundle and Lucia Rinaldi

First published in 2007 by
PALGRAVE MACMILLAN™
175 Fifth Avenue, New York, N.Y. 10010 and
Houndmills, Basingstoke, Hampshire, England RG21 6XS.
Companies and representatives throughout the world.

PALGRAVE MACMILLAN is the global academic imprint of the Palgrave
Macmillan division of St. Martin's Press, LLC and of Palgrave Macmillan Ltd.
Macmillan® is a registered trademark in the United States, United Kingdom
and other countries. Palgrave is a registered trademark in the European Union
and other countries.

ISBN-13: 978-1-4039-8391-6
ISBN-10: 1-4039-8391-7

**Library of Congress Cataloging-in-Publication Data is
available from the Library of Congress.**

A catalogue record of the book is available from the British Library.

Design by Scribe Inc.

First edition: October 2007

10 9 8 7 6 5 4 3 2 1

Printed in the United States of America.

Contents

Contributors

Tobias Abse is Lecturer in History at Goldsmiths College (University of London) and the author of many articles on Italian history and politics.

Salvatore Coluccello is Senior Lecturer in Italian Studies at Coventry University. He is currently preparing a book on the image of the Sicilian Mafia.

Philip Cooke is Senior Lecturer in Italian at Strathclyde University (Glasgow). He is the author of *Italian Resistance Writing* (1997) and *Fenoglio's Binoculars, Johnny's Eyes* (2000).

John Foot is Professor of Italian History at University College London. His books include *Modern Italy* (2003) and *Milan Since the Miracle* (2001).

Robert Gordon is University Senior Lecturer in Italian at Cambridge University and author of *Pasolini: Forms of Subjectivity* (1996) and *Primo Levi's Ordinary Virtues* (2001).

Stephen Gundle is Professor of Film and Television Studies at Warwick University. He is the author of *Between Hollywood and Moscow: The Italian Communists and the Challenge of Mass Culture 1943–91* (2000) and *Bellissima: Feminine Beauty and the Idea of Italy* (2007), and co-author of *The Glamour System* (2006) and *Mass Culture and Italian Society from Fascism to the Cold War* (2007).

Elizabeth Leake is Associate Professor of Italian at Rutgers University. She is the author of *The Reinvention of Ignazio Silone* (2003).

Carl Levy is Reader in European Politics at Goldsmiths College (University of London). He is author of *Gramsci and the Anarchists* (1999) and editor of *Italian Regionalism* (1996).

Duncan McDonnell is Dottorando di ricerca at the Department of Political Studies, University of Turin. He has recently published on Italian local politics and the Lega Nord and is the co-editor (with Daniele Albertazzi) of *Twenty-first Century Populism: The Spectre of Western European Democracy* (Palgrave Macmillan, 2007).

David Moss is Professor of Anthropology at the State University of Milan. His best-known book is *The Politics of Left-Wing Violence in Italy 1969–84* (1989).

Ellen Nerenberg is Associate Professor of Romance Languages and Literatures at Wesleyan University and author of *Prison Terms: Representing Confinement during and after Italian Fascism* (2001).

Daragh O'Connell is completing a PhD on Sicilian literature at Strathclyde University (Glasgow) and is a temporary lecturer in Italian at University College, Dublin.

Giuliana Pieri is Senior Lecturer in Italian at Royal Holloway (University of London). She is author of *The Influence of Pre-Raphaelitism on fin-de-siècle Italy* (2006) and several articles on Italian detective fiction.

Karen Pinkus is Professor of French, Italian, and Comparative Literature at the University of Southern California. She is author of *Bodily Regimes: Italian Advertising under Fascism* (1995) and *The Montesi Scandal* (2003).

Stanislao Pugliese is Professor of History at Hofstra University and author of *Carlo Rosselli: Socialist Heretic and Anti-Fascist Exile* (1999). He has also edited volumes on Italian fascism and anti-fascism, the Jews of Italy, and Frank Sinatra.

Dana Renga is Assistant Professor of Italian at Ohio State University. She is currently preparing a book on gender and space in Italian cinema.

Lucia Rinaldi has recently completed her PhD at Royal Holloway (University of London) on postmodernism and identity in contemporary Italian crime fiction. She has published articles on popular fiction and television adaptations of detective fiction. She is at present a Teaching Fellow in Italian at the University of Exeter.

Mary Wood is Reader in European Cinema at Birkbeck College (University of London) and author of *Italian Cinema* (2005).

Introduction

Stephen Gundle and Lucia Rinaldi

Contemporary Italian history has been marked by an extraordinary series of murders. The assassination of King Umberto in 1900 by an anarchist marked a murderous reaction against what was seen as a brutal and repressive state. Although no other head of state has been murdered, many political figures have been the victims of assassination or attempted assassination. Perhaps the most famous murder of a political figure has been the killing of former Prime Minister Aldo Moro by the Red Brigades in 1978. Opponents of the government have also been frequent victims, from Giacomo Matteotti and Carlo Rosselli under fascism to the student Carlo Giuliani, who was shot by a policeman during the G8 protests in Genoa in 2001. Few killings in Italy, especially political murders, are completely clear in their causes and motives. Debate and controversy usually ensue, and this is often followed by polemical or reflective novels, plays, and films. The Moro case has given rise to numerous investigations and a web of speculation, as well as a minor industry of memoirs, reconstructions, conspiracy theories, and films. Such a varied production is not exclusive to this case. The death of the anarchist Pinelli, who allegedly threw himself from a police station window in 1969 after being accused of placing a bomb in a bank in Milan's Piazza Fontana, was blamed by the left on a police inspector, who was himself subsequently assassinated. The lack of clarity over Pinelli's death, which occurred in the context of an official attempt to blame the anarchists for a bomb that was later found to have been placed by the neo-fascist right, was taken as a sign of the complicity of the state. It was memorably satirized in Nobel prize winner Dario Fo's play *Accidental Death of an Anarchist*. Novels and films have been inspired by the execution of the anti-fascist Cervi brothers in 1944, the mafia murders of the magistrates Falcone and Borsellino, the killing of fashion designer Gianni Versace and other cases.

The purpose of this book is to explore some of the best known cases of murder and assassination in Italy and place them in their historical, political, and cultural contexts.[1] Connections are made between different facets of the cases examined, including their place in public opinion and their treatment in literature, art and film. Precisely because the cases are normally considered singly, a comparative analysis can highlight patterns and continuities. By including true crime and mafia killings, both of which have—in certain instances—given rise to controversy and debate no less than political killings, we have endeavored to ensure that the Italian culture of murder is considered in the round.

A major justification for the book lies in the fact that murder cases have provided some of the key watersheds of contemporary Italian history. They have also had a structuring effect on public opinion. In addition they have provided a cultural stimulus and an inspiration to journalists, writers, and film makers, who have used them to provide general interpretations of Italian society and its conflicts and contradictions. None of this has been fully recognized up to now, and for this reason the book aims to make a highly original contribution to the study of Italian culture and society. We hope it will provoke new ways of thinking about Italian history and culture by drawing out previously unnoticed patterns of behavior and representation.

We do not wish to overstate the uniqueness of the Italian experience of assassination and murder. This is a common failing of area studies specialists that it is important to guard against. Every country has its own specific history of crime and political murder, and these often figure prominently in national representations. The United States has witnessed more assassinations of leading political figures than Italy, and the assassination of President Kennedy is probably the single biggest generator of conspiracy theories in the world. Even in the United Kingdom, due to the contested British presence in Northern Ireland, several significant establishment figures have been assassinated. Moreover, in France and in southern Europe more generally, changes of regime, war, and foreign occupation, as well as sharp political divisions, have tended to politicize the manner in which some murders are received and remembered. Nevertheless, Italy does present certain features which, while they may not be in every respect unique, are sufficiently curious and important to warrant extended examination. It is striking, in the chapters of the book, how frequently larger forces and events seem to bear on even the most straightforward of cases. It is equally true that in many instances no solution can ever definitively satisfy the whole of public opinion. These characteristics are related to the certain specific features of Italy's political development. Democracy developed only against considerable opposition and in a context in which there was distrust of the population on the part of the state elite. The experience of dictatorship, changes of regime, civil war and sharp political conflict exacerbated this. In addition, the presence of secret state apparatuses that were not neutral but subordinate to political interests alimented the belief, which was rarely purely fantasy, that events were being manipulated from behind the scenes. This in turn fueled a taste for *dietrologia* (that is, seeing events in terms of invisible plots and conspiracies). The cumulative effects of a long series of mysteries turned this approach into the standard response to many murders.

The cases that are examined in this volume are varied and complex. It would therefore be wrong or misleading to try and reduce them to a common pattern. However, it is worth highlighting a sequence of events that seems to be present in a considerable number of them. First, the killing of a person or persons (whether well-known or unknown) has an initial impact on public opinion. This is followed by investigations that identify sooner or later a real or a possible assassin. This process is accompanied by press speculation and interpretation that leads to the adoption of positions as to the innocence or guilt of the identified assassin. These attitudes, once fixed, will outlast any verdict of the courts. The case will be then kept alive in the public mind by those who do not accept the official outcome. Among these may be writers or filmmakers, who have the power to turn a case into a cultural artifact and to explore possible solutions that go beyond the known facts. Where political factors bear on a murder, differences of interpretation are likely to be strongest.

What is often most interesting about the murder cases treated in the volume is that they do not lend themselves easily to schematic interpretation. It is impossible to identify a pattern of guilt or offer any sort of master thesis or "solution" to unsolved or problematic murders. The contributors, each an expert in his or her area, subtly draw out meanings and complexities in the cases they consider. In adopting this skeptical and open approach they draw direct or indirect inspiration from two of twentieth-century Italy's greatest writers, both of whom tackled the issue of murder and/or assassination.

Carlo Emilio Gadda's *Quer brutto pasticcaccio di Via Merulana* (*That Awful Mess in Via Merulana*) was published in installments in 1946–47 and as a novel ten years later. In it, Francesco Ingravallo, a policeman from Molise working in the capital, is called to via Merulana to investigate the robbery of some jewels in the apartment of a Signora Menegazzi and, in the same block of flats, the murder of a Signora Liliana Balducci, a dear friend of his. Ingravallo starts interviewing all the people living in the block to find clues about the robbery, and all those who were close to Liliana to solve the murder. However, despite his eagerness and personal involvement, he does not discover much. At first, Liliana's cousin, Giuliano, is arrested, but then he is released without being charged. In the meanwhile, an officer who is following one of the many lines of the investigation, recovers Signora Menegazzi's jewels in a storage depot on the outskirts of the city. In the end, no one is arrested for the crimes, and the novel finishes right in the middle of the questioning of a suspect, but without a proper solution for the cases.

In the first pages of the novel, through Ingravallo's reasoning, Gadda presents his own "theory of chaos," which is the key to understanding the work:

> He sustained, among other things, that unforeseen catastrophes are never the consequence or the effect, if you prefer, of a single motive, of a cause singular; but they are like a whirlpool, a cyclonic point of depression in the consciousness of the world, towards which a whole multitude of converging causes have contributed.[2]

In fact, already from the title the reader is informed that the novel is a *pasticcio* (a mess)—in terms of content, language, and structure. Gadda deconstructs detective fiction conventions and does not adopt a linear development for his story. The plot is rather unimportant, and the detective fails to discover the culprit(s) of the crimes. However, the *giallo* form (the term is used today in Italian to denote detective and crime fiction after the yellow covers of the publisher Mondadori's 1929 series of books; by extension it is also applied to any complex and unsolved crime case) allows him to explore notions of "truth" (an intrinsic feature of the genre) and "reality," and to demonstrate that these are complex concepts that are difficult to define objectively. Through Ingravallo, Gadda presents the notion that reason and rationality are useless for investigating reality, because normally a single cause does not lead to a single effect, but each effect is the result of several or multiple causes. Moreover, in real life events are not linked in a coherent way. In his novel, there is not a hierarchy of events, but instead a constant shifting between past and present.

In *Quer Pasticciaccio*, which is set in 1927, Gadda represented Italian society in the 1920s. He criticized the rigid, hypocritical fascist middle-class (of Rome) by emphasizing its decadence and shallowness. He believed that behind its polished facade and "myth" of the family, it concealed vice and violence. He focused on sexual relationships, but also on religion, magic, and superstition. He presented a satire of contemporary society and its contradictions.

In a strikingly similar approach, the Sicilian writer Leonardo Sciascia subverted the traditional form of the detective novel and, instead of making use of the *giallo* to represent the triumph of "law and order," he reworked its formulaic conventions to demonstrate the impossibility of attaining justice in a society (Sicilian and Italian) ruled by corrupt politicians often colluded with *mafiosi*.

Sciascia was particularly interested in politics; he actively participated in it (he was elected as city councilor in Palermo for the Italian Communist Party in 1975 and as a member of Parliament for the Radical Party in 1978) and wrote and commented extensively about it. His pointed criticism of the state of local and national politics emerges both in his non-fictional works (for example, *L'Affaire Moro* [*The Moro Affair*, 1978]), and fictional stories, which were often inspired by real events. In particular, in his detective novels, or rather anti-detective novels—*Il giorno della civetta* (*The Day of the Owl*, 1961); *A ciascuno il suo* (*To Each His Own*, 1966); *Il contesto* (*Equal Danger*, 1971); *Todo modo* (*One Way or Another*, 1974); *Il cavaliere e la morte* (*The Knight and Death*, 1988) and *Una storia semplice* (*A Straightforward Tale*, 1989)—he explored notions of "truth" and "power" while exposing the relationship between politics and organized crime. He dealt with the mafia penetration in the core of Italian institutions, the role and responsibility of the Church within Italian politics, and the long-lasting failure to reform the clientelism of the political class. Sciascia's six *gialli* span from the 1960s to the 1980s and mirror the evolution of the contemporary political situation.[3] His commitment to socio-political critique won him the reputation of an *engagé* writer, and his work has inspired several other authors, up to the present day.

The subtitle "Transformations in Society and Culture" has been employed in order to draw attention to the linkages between public events, and the publicity they receive, and the broader changes that they somehow crystallize or inadvertently reflect. However, what is fascinating about the murder cases under examination is that rarely if ever is any simple process of modernization detectable. In other words, it is difficult, if not impossible, to periodize the killings except by relation to political context and the particular configuration of the media at the moment they occurred. It is not possible to draw clear distinctions between "northern" and "southern" murder, except in so far as the mafia mainly operates on its home territory. Nor can some murders simply be labeled "primitive" and others "modern" or "advanced." Elements of peasant culture, urban underprivilege, and conventional family relations impinge even on the murders that took place in Rome or the north in the period since the 1970s. Transformations are visible in all manners of ways in the murder cases but so too are continuities, survivals, and throwbacks. Only one significant change has occurred, and this lies in the treatment of the murders. Politics is constantly present, and each case that is studied had an impact on public opinion. However, whereas in the period before the 1970s, each death was either treated on its own or in relation to a larger national or political conflict, more recent decades have witnessed a growing preoccupation with the forms and structures of murder. A significant blending of fact and fiction has occurred in the work of many younger detective writers. This is both a product of what Robert Gordon calls "post-modern *impegno*" (engagement) and of the spectacularization of murder cases as collective dramas.

The book is divided into sections that reflect the broad pattern of Italian murders. The first section considers three cases that arise from the Italian experience of fascist dictatorship and civil war in 1943–45. It begins with Stanislao Pugliese's examination of the circumstances of the killing by fascist agents of the anti-fascist Rosselli brothers in France in 1937. Elizabeth Leake then considers the singular case of Clara Petacci, Mussolini's last lover, who was killed with him in 1945 in circumstances that have never been definitively clarified. Finally, Philip Cooke explores the manifold resonances of the execution of seven brothers belonging to the Resistance. It perhaps does not need to be pointed out that these last two cases were not considered to be either assassinations or murders by everybody. They are included because they were highly resonant cases that were widely experienced by at least part of public opinion over time as unjustified killings that were tantamount to murder. Several of the assassination attempts on Mussolini himself are discussed in Carl Levy and Dana Renga's chapters in the final section.

The second section examines three cases in which there was possible involvement of the repressive apparatus of the state. The first of these is the mysterious death in an airplane crash in 1962 of the head of ENI (Italy's state-owned oil company), Enrico Mattei. This was memorably treated in Francesco Rosi's film *Il caso Mattei*, which forms the focus of Mary Wood's chapter. The defenestration of the anarchist Pinelli in Milan in 1969 offers the second case. John Foot shows that Dario Fo's famous play was by no means the only cultural comment on the case that still today forms a site of contested memory in the city. The third case is the shooting in the course of a violent demonstration in Genoa in 2001 of the student Carlo Giuliani. Duncan McDonnell's nuanced account of this event and its representation highlights the way in which photographic images can assist or distort the understanding of even the most public of killings.

The third section is devoted to two essays that interpret, from different points of view, the murder of Aldo Moro. Tobias Abse explores the conflicting

interpretations that have arisen of the murder, without doubt the most resonant of twentieth-century Italian history. He presents a selection of the
literature on the case and evaluates the strengths and weaknesses of both
the "official" version of events, championed by the authorities, the Red
Brigades and some academics, and the "alternative" accounts sustained by
members of the Moro family and several authors. For his part, David Moss
explores the reports of the parliamentary committees of inquiry that have
investigated the case.

In the fourth section, two high-profile mafia murders are evaluated.
Emanuele Notarbartolo, the director of the Bank of Sicily, was assassinated
on a train in 1893. His case is important because he was the first public figure to be killed by the mafia because he stood in the way of criminal penetration of Sicily's political and financial institutions. Salvatore Coluccello
highlights the way the case coincided with the emergence of the "mystique"
of the mafia as a centuries-old honorable society rather than a modern
criminal association. The judge Paolo Borsellino, by contrast, is one of the
most recent "excellent cadavers." He was killed in 1992, a few months after
his colleague Giovanni Falcone. Daragh O'Connell explores the murder
through its representation in the work of two of Sicily's leading writers,
Sciascia and Consolo.

The fifth section is devoted to a variety of "true crime" cases. Some of
these touched the political sphere; the resonance of others was due to the
fame of the victim, his or her lifestyle (or presumed lifestyle), or the identification of an assassin who refused to accept his or her guilt. The first of
these, the Montesi case, was a great *cause célèbre* of the 1950s, in which the
former foreign minister's son was tried and acquitted of the manslaughter
of a twenty-one-year-old carpenter's daughter. Karen Pinkus explores the
peculiarities of the case and reflects on her own investigation of it. The
murder in 1975 of the writer, film director, and polemicist Pier Paolo
Pasolini has given rise to numerous investigations in the press, literature,
and documentary films. The murder and this body of work are evaluated
by Robert Gordon in his chapter. Ellen Nerenberg explores the strange case
of the "monster of Florence," one of Italy's few serial killers, who terrorized
courting couples in the hills of Tuscany for well over a decade. She examines the figure of the presumed monster, Pietro Pacciani, and his depiction
in popular song. The murder in the mid-1990s of the last member of the
Gucci family to own a stake in the long-established company bearing its
name and of the fashion designer Gianni Versace provided a striking mixture of glamour and conspiracy. The narratives of the cases are assessed by
Stephen Gundle and Lucia Rinaldi. The final chapter of the section, by
Giuliana Pieri, examines the work of Carlo Lucarelli, a prolific writer of

detective fiction who has presented several successful television series of investigations into unsolved murders (that have also been published in book form).

The final section provides an assessment of the role and legacy of the anarchist assassin in Italian history. In a wide-ranging chapter, Carl Levy examines the historical background to, and the rise and fall of, anarchist assassinations. He compares and contrasts several killings, assassins, and mysteries. The second chapter, by Dana Renga, considers the treatment of one famous would-be assassin of Mussolini, Michele Schirru, in Lina Wertmüller's film *Amore e anarchia*.

The collection does not aspire to be an exhaustive account of murder and assassination in Italy. There are many failed assassination attempts (such as those on the Communist Party leader Togliatti in 1948 and on Pope John Paul II in 1981) that are not dealt with here. In addition there are many terrorist killings, mafia murders, and true crimes that are not included. However, we hope that we have presented a sufficiently broad range of cases for it to be possible for the reader to reflect in general on murder in Italy as well as on specific examples. If further research in this area follows, we shall have fulfilled our purpose.

Notes

1. This book is based on papers delivered at the annual conference of the Association for the Study of Modern Italy in London in 2003.
2. Carlo Emilio Gadda, *That Awful Mess on Via Merulana*, trans. William Weaver (London: Quartet, 1981), 5.
3. Anne Mullen, "Leonardo Sciascia's Detective Fiction and Metaphors of Mafia," in *Crime Scenes: Detective Narratives in European Culture since 1945*, ed. Anne Mullen and Emer O'Beirne, 88–99 (Amsterdam: Rodophi, 2000).

Part I

Fascism and Anti-Fascism

I

Revisiting an Assassination: The Death of Carlo Rosselli

Stanislao G. Pugliese

The sad death in exile according to a law that appears almost inevitable for the finest sons of Italy

—*Carlo Rosselli*[1]

Lovers of Italian film are familiar with Bernardo Bertolucci's 1970 film, *The Conformist*; some may even know that the film was based on Alberto Moravia's 1951 novel of the same title. But few know that the assassinated Professor Quadri in *The Conformist* was based on Carlo Rosselli. And although there is a street or piazza in almost every large Italian city dedicated to Carlo Rosselli and his historian brother, Nello, killed together in June 1937, few Italians are familiar with their ideas and the significance of their assassination.[2]

Carlo Rosselli (1899–1937) was one of the most charismatic and influential of European antifascist intellectuals. Born into a wealthy Jewish family, and abandoning a promising career as a professor of political economics, he devoted his considerable fortune and ultimately his life to the struggle against fascism. In 1925, he was instrumental in establishing the first underground antifascist newspaper, *Non Mollare!* While in *confino* on the island of Lipari for his subversive political activities, he wrote *Liberal Socialism*, arguing that socialism was the logical development of the principle of liberty. After a daring escape from Lipari in 1929, he made his way to Paris and became the driving force behind a new political movement, "Justice and Liberty." Rosselli was among the first to arrive in Barcelona after the outbreak of the Spanish Civil War, in which he commanded an armed column of volunteers in defense of the Republic. When Italian fascists discovered Rosselli's plot to assassinate Mussolini, they declared him the regime's most dangerous enemy and had him murdered, along with his brother, noted historian Nello Rosselli, on a country road in Normandy.

It was not only Rosselli's active participation on behalf of the Republic in the Spanish Civil War and rumored plots against il Duce that convinced the fascist regime that he had to be eliminated. Rosselli's heretical conception that the Spanish Civil War had to be expanded into a general, European-wide "preemptive strike" against fascism and Nazism sealed his fate. This conception was best expressed in his famous speech over Radio Barcelona in November 1936, "Oggi in Spagna, domani in Italia [Today in Spain, Tomorrow in Italy]."[3] Four days after this radio broadcast, a report was submitted by the fascist police: "Rosselli is the most outstanding personality of Italian antifascism in the Spanish Civil War . . . and participates in the most important executive committees. He enjoys great popularity among the antifascist soldiers who recently joined to designate him the only possible successor to Mussolini."[4]

Afflicted with a recurrence of painful phlebitis, Carlo left the Spanish front and returned to Paris in the spring of 1937. He then traveled to the mud-bath resort of Bagnoles-de-l'Orne in Normandy on May 27, taking a room at the Hôtel Cordier just outside the town of Tessé-la-Madeleine. Coincidentally (or perhaps not), the Duke of Ajmone, of the Royal House of Savoy, was also in the resort town.[5] Rosselli's wife Marion soon joined him, and his brother Nello arrived on June 6, leaving his wife, Maria, and a newborn son, Alberto, in Florence. Nello's request for a passport had been granted with such efficiency and so quickly (three days) that friends, especially Piero Calamandrei in Florence, were suspicious. Calamandrei warned Nello not to go to France, fearing that agents of the regime were following him and preparing some kind of action against the brothers. Nello could not imagine anything so dramatic; had not Gioacchino Volpe, official historian of the regime and director of the Istituto Storico in Rome, pulled some strings to get Nello permission to use the Library of the British Museum for his research? Nello was more concerned with the newborn Alberto and leaving his other children, Silvia, Paola, and Aldo. Carlo was in France, and Nello felt that both their lives had reached a crisis point; he had to speak with his older brother.[6]

The day of Nello's arrival, they visited Maison Blanche, the home of the historian Élie Halévy, with Raymond Aron.[7] Carlo had established a daily routine at the spa, taking the cure in the morning, working in his room until the late afternoon, and then going for a drive in the countryside with his Ford car that had been brought from the front in Spain. This routine was duly noted by several spies who had also arrived in the resort town soon after him.[8]

On the afternoon of the June 9, Carlo and Nello drove Marion to the train station and watched her depart for Paris where she would help celebrate the tenth birthday of their son, John. On the return trip to the hotel, the brothers usually avoided the heavy traffic of the main road and turned instead onto a side road that led past the forest at Couterne. Knowing this beforehand, the assassins had pulled over to the side of the road, giving the impression of mechanical failure. The brothers, arriving upon the "disabled" vehicle, stopped their car and approached to assist the driver. It was at this point that they were attacked and killed. Carlo was killed by four dagger thrusts, two of which severed the carotid artery; Nello was attacked by less efficient murderers, suffered many dagger wounds and appears to have resisted in some desperate attempt at defense. An autopsy later revealed bullet wounds as well. The bodies were dragged a short distance and left in the underbrush by the side of the road, a dagger nearby. The assassins drove off, taking Carlo's Ford, abandoning it several miles later. It was found the next day with a bomb, whose fuse had failed, in the back seat. The bodies were not found until two days later. There was an eyewitness: Hélène Besneux, a hairdresser, was bicycling on the road by the forest when she came upon the scene of the assassinations. Three days later, on June 12, she reported to the authorities that she had seen a pool of blood and that one of the men had seen her, given her a murderous look, and then driven off. [9]

News of the double assassination shocked and stunned the antifascist community. A crowd estimated at between 100,000 to 200,000 people attended the funeral services in Paris, and the cortege made its way to the Père Lachaise cemetery accompanied by the music of Beethoven's Seventh symphony.[10] There the brothers were laid to rest under the following inscription:

CARLO AND NELLO ROSSELLI
MURDERED TOGETHER
THE 9TH OF JUNE 1937
EXPECT TOGETHER
THAT THE SACRIFICE OF THEIR YOUTH
WILL HASTEN ...
THE VICTORY OF THEIR IDEALS
JUSTICE AND LIBERTY

On orders from the French government, which feared offending Mussolini, an ellipsis had been inserted where originally "IN ITALY" was to appear. The two words were carved into the monument only after the liberation of France. The double assassination had occurred thirteen years after the murder of the reform socialist deputy Giacomo Matteotti on June 10, 1924.[11] Two days after the Rosselli brothers' funeral, Leon Blum submitted his resignation as Premier of France.

The fascist press tried to link the assassinations to conflicts within the antifascist community, explicitly accusing the communists, anarchists, and allies of *Giustizia e Libertà*. The recent murder of the anarchists Camillo Berneri and Francesco Barbieri at the hands of Stalin's agents in Spain gave this story "credibility." Not coincidentally, the most aggressive support of this theory was taken up by *Il Telegrafo*, the daily newspaper of Livorno, under the editorship of Giovanni Ansaldo and controlled by Count Galeazzo Ciano, Minister of Foreign Affairs and Mussolini's son-in-law.[12] People, however, were not fooled. From his exile at Harvard University, historian Gaetano Salvemini, who had taught Nello and befriended Carlo, thundered that as far as guilt was concerned, "all roads lead to Rome."[13]

Although most observers immediately assumed that Mussolini was the author of this crime, there is no smoking gun to implicate him directly. There is, instead, Mussolini's cryptic comment to his secretary Yvon de Begnac in July 1937: "History will decide the reason of their fate. Power is not always able to control the apparatus that it represents."[14] Mussolini's foremost Italian biographer, Renzo De Felice, devotes a few revealing paragraphs to the Rosselli assassinations in his multi-volumed, massive biography of Mussolini. For De Felice, the Rosselli murders are merely a "parenthesis" (a word De Felice uses twice) in Mussolini's biography.[15] Instead, I would argue that the Rosselli assassinations can be read as a signifying moment, comparable to the assassination of Matteottti and Mussolini's order to execute Italian antifascists captured in Spain in the history of the regime. "The dead," Mussolini mistakenly remarked to Ciano, "tell no history."[16]

Could the Rosselli assassinations have been the work of the security apparatus without Mussolini's knowledge or approval? In his dispatches from Italy during World War II, Herbert Matthews of the *New York Times* wrote of Galeazzo Ciano's complicity in the assassinations. Upon Ciano's own execution by Mussolini's Italian Social Republic in 1944 (even after Mussolini's daughter, Edda, pleaded with her father to spare her husband's life), Marion Cave Rosselli wrote to the *New York Times* and pointed out that along with Ciano, General Emilio De Bono and Giovanni Marinelli were also executed; the latter two had been implicated in the Matteotti assassination twenty years earlier. In his refusal to show mercy to his own son-in-law and colleagues, Mussolini effectively silenced those who may have revealed his role in three assassinations twenty years apart.[17]

Despite attempts by the regime to accuse the left, proof of fascist (if not Mussolini's) authorship of the assassinations is provided by the regime itself. In the *Archivio Centrale dello Stato* in Rome, a document prepared by the Director of the Political Police Division on February 1, 1939, lists more than fifty antifascist volunteers killed in the Spanish Civil War. Listed as #12850 is "Carlo Rosselli, founder of *Giustizia e Libertà*, wounded at Monte Pelato, assassinated near Paris, *by fascists*, the 11th [sic] June 1937, with his brother Nello."[18]

In public, Amelia Pincherle Rosselli bore the deaths of her two sons with dignity and stoic resignation, yet letters to Nello's widow reveal a deep, private despair. Years later Italian President Sandro Pertini wrote that she seemed to emerge from the terrible events of June 1937 "like the heroine of a Corneille tragedy."[19] Marion lived for another twelve years, but as Salvemini wrote at her passing in 1949, after the deaths of Carlo and Nello, her life was "a painful descent toward death."[20]

It soon became clear that the assassins were members of the French *Cagoule*, a secret extreme right-wing sect known for the hooded cape of its followers; it had ties to the French secret services and the secret society CSAR (*Comité secret d'action révolutionnaire*).[21] Evidently, the assassins had been following Carlo Rosselli closely for at least several months, if not longer. On February 15, 1938, Marion Rosselli recognized one of those arrested in the case, Fernand Ladislav Jakubiez, who had posed as a traveling carpet salesman and had appeared one morning at their house in Paris during the autumn of 1936, asking suspicious questions about Carlo. In the spring of 1936, a certain Carlo Zanatta presented himself to members of *Giustizia e Libertà* in Paris, claiming to be an army deserter with information against a Communist Party member. Under questioning, it became apparent that his entire story was false; bursting into tears, he revealed that he had concealed a loaded pistol in the belt of his trousers. He had been approached by an *agent provocateur* at the Italian Consulate in Paris with instructions to assassinate Rosselli.[22]

The assassination of the Rosselli brothers forced the French authorities to investigate the *cagoulards*. Their work turned up more than one hundred individuals. On January 12, 1938, Minister of the Interior of the Blum government Max Dormoy announced the arrest of seven individuals related to the Rosselli murders: Jean Filliol, Fernand Jakubiez, Robert G. E. Purieux, Jean Marie Bouvyer, L.C. Huguet, André Tenaille and J. Foran. Five were already under arrest; Huguet and Filliol were being sought. One of the automobiles used in the assassination belonged to Eugene Deloncle, a leader of the CSAR. A serious shortcoming of the investigation was that it failed to admit that there was any Italian connection to the assassinations.

In January of 1938 the French daily *Matin* reported that Dormoy had noted that the weapons of the *cagoulards* came from beyond France's borders; another official in the French police force cited "the number of arms, rifles, machineguns of Italian manufacture" found in the investigation.[23] Soon after these announcements, the Blum government fell and was replaced in January 1938 by Daladier, who sought to appease Mussolini at all costs in the futile hope of distancing Italy from Nazi Germany. Consequently, for reasons of international politics, all future work on the assassinations and the *cagoulards* was confined within France's borders. With the fall of France and the creation of the Vichy regime, all those implicated in the assassinations were freed under Marshal Pétain. Dormoy was arrested by the Vichy regime and later killed during the night of July 25–26, 1941, by a bomb placed under his bed.

With the fall of the Pétain regime and the end of the war, a new inquiry was initiated against the *cagoulards*. André Tenaille had died fighting for the Nazis on the Russian front; for his services, he was posthumously awarded the Legion of Honor by the Pétain government.[24] Eugene Deloncle, after entering the service of the Nazis, was killed by the Gestapo; François Méténier became head of Pétain's bodyguard.[25] Méténier, Jakubiez, and Puireux were arrested and imprisoned; Filliol, Bouvyer, Foran, and Huguet could not be found. On June 6, 1945, Jakubiez revealed that Carlo was killed in an instant. His brother, gravely wounded, had fallen into the ravine. "I stabbed him two or three times with a dagger; Filliol finished him off with the pistol. . . . Filliol searched the bodies and took some papers, which were sent to Italy, as I discovered later."[26] The fate and content of the papers taken from the Rosselli brothers have never been revealed. Although Jakubiez had confessed in June 1945, the trial of the *cagoulards* did not take place until November 11–28, 1948. Jakubiez was sentenced to life at hard labor; Méténier was sentenced to twenty years hard labor; Puireux, four years of hard labor; those charged *in absentia* were sentenced to death. (Curiously and conveniently, both in France and in Italy, death sentences were usually handed down to those *in absentia*). No mention was made of Italians involved in the assassination. Yet the evidence proves that the Italian fascist police were watching Rosselli at the Hôtel Cordier.[27]

In Italy, the prosecution of those responsible for the Rosselli assassinations degenerated into absurdity. Attempts to place high fascist officials on trial were often haphazard, with some minor officials convicted while major party functionaries were either ignored or forgotten. As early as July 1944, a High Commission for Sanctions against Fascism had been established under the general direction of former Foreign Minister Carlo Sforza.

The *Decreto* that brought the High Commission into existence called for the creation of four commissions: one to deal with property seized from the Fascist Party; another to sequester fascist profits; a third, under the direction of Mario Berlinguer, concerned with prosecuting fascists; and a fourth, under Mauro Scoccimarro, to purge fascists from the government.[28] Those responsible were eventually brought to trial. The first document entered into evidence at the trial of Italian officials involved with the murders was prepared by the SIM (*Servizio Informazioni Militare*— Military Intelligence). After specifying various acts of sabotage (including germ warfare), it states simply:

> 5) Suppression of bothersome persons in various localities.
> Means: various, preferably poison.[29]

Judge Italo Robino of the High Commission for the Punishment of Fascist Crimes questioned General Cesare Amé, of SIM—the agency responsible for espionage and counterespionage under Mussolini. At one point in the interrogation, when the secretary who was recording the question was absent, Amé said to Robino, "Why don't you seek those responsible for the real and true bloody crimes committed by fascism? The Rosselli murders, for instance." Robino asked what Amé knew about the Rosselli assassinations, and the general replied, "I know nothing, but there is a certain Emanuele, I believe an official, who must know many things." "Are you trying to say," Robino asked, "that he participated?" Amé responded with a sphinx-like "Perhaps." Later, he was to deny ever saying anything of the kind, and even denied being questioned.[30]

Sante Emanuele was a retired colonel of the *carabinieri* (military police) who testified before the High Court of Justice that Colonel Paolo Angioi gave him the order to eliminate Carlo Rosselli. Emanuele passed the order to the head of the counterespionage center in Turin, Major Roberto Navale. It was Navale who contacted the French *cagoulards*. "The initiative came from Ciano."[31] Emanuele stated that he had met Ciano and Anfuso after the assassination of the Rosselli brothers and "I can say specifically that the attitude of Ciano was such as to clearly show that the decision was his. The attitude of Anfuso was that of one who cooperated."[32] Filippo Anfuso was cabinet chief at the Foreign Ministry and, as such, close to Ciano. Loyal to Mussolini after the *coup d'état* of July 24–25, 1943, he served in the Republic of Salò and was appointed ambassador to Berlin. Another high-ranking member of the fascist hierarchy to be implicated was General Mario Roatta, commander of the losing fascist side at the battle of Guadalajara and twice Chief of Staff of the Italian Army. Since 1934 he had been the head of the SIM and rumored to be involved in the assassination of King Alexander of Yugoslavia. He was the highest ranking Italian military officer in Spain helping Franco, along with his German counterpart Admiral Wilhelm Canaris.

The climax of Italian efforts to attain justice in the Rosselli affair was the trial held in Rome before the High Court of Justice for the Punishment of Fascist Crimes from January 29 to March 12, 1945, better known as the "Roatta Trial." The accused were accused of

> espionage, denunciations, and reprisals against antifascists, of shipwrecks, train wrecks, the arson of buildings, ships, and transports, of the diffusion of germs to provoke epidemics, of favoring of assassins and homicides, among them those of Bonomini and the Rosselli brothers, Carlo and Nello, the last assassinated at Bagnoles-de-l'Orne (France) the 9th June 1937.[33]

When questioned by Judge Lorenzo Maroni on January 31, 1945, Emanuele replied,

> The elimination of Rosselli was certainly not an isolated fact, but must be inserted into the matrix of actions relative to the war in Spain. The Rosselli "affair" must be considered as an act of sabotage to eliminate the activity of Carlo Rosselli who was recruiting "red" troops. I transmitted this mission to the Turin center, directed by commandant Navale. . . . It was this center that took care of all the details. Major Navale organized everything, independent from me.[34]

Emanuele's testimony implied that Ciano and Anfuso decided on Rosselli's assassination without conferring with Mussolini. Although there exists no "smoking gun" evidence, it is highly unlikely that either Ciano or Anfuso would have undertaken such an action on their own. On March 22, 1937, Navale had met with members of the *Cagoule* in Monte Carlo. The French asked for 100 Beretta semiautomatic weapons in exchange for "the suppression of troublesome persons." Anfuso admitted to participating in this meeting with Navale and Emanuele.[35] The dagger left behind by Jakubiez was used by the fascist papers to "prove" that it was an antifascist crime: fascists would not be so foolish to leave behind such evidence. Yet Vittorio Cerruti, former ambassador to Berlin and Paris, testified that when he met Ciano after the assassination, the Foreign Minister said to him, "You must admit that the idea of the dagger was really a brilliant idea." He then "deduced that the dagger was placed there, by orders of Ciano, with the intention of accusing the antifascists of the assassination."[36]

Before the sentences were handed down, Emilio Lussu, Aldo Garosci, Randolfo Pacciardi, and Piero Calamandrei were permitted to address the court.[37] On March 12 sentence was passed on all the accused: Anfuso (*in absentia*) was found guilty and sentenced to death by firing squad; Roatta, Emanuele, and Navale were all found guilty and sentenced to life in prison; their sentences were to be published in all the daily papers of Rome. Angioi was sentenced to twenty years and six months, Pariani to fifteen years, Petragnani to twelve years.[38] Only Roatta, Emanuele, and Petragnini were under arrest at the time, and the court was to "lose" Roatta in the middle of the trial. Roatta, who had been complaining of ill health, was in the military hospital on Via Giulia in Rome. On the night of March 4, he simply walked out of the hospital and disappeared. Although a halfhearted attempt was made to find the General, he easily made his way to Franco's Spain, where he found a warm welcome. Several days later, on March 7, the leftist parties organized a mass demonstration of fifteen thousand at the Coliseum; after marching up the Via dei Fori Imperiali, the crowd was fired upon by *carabinieri* "protecting" Prince Umberto at the Quirinale Palace.[39] The travesty of justice continued when the Supreme Court of Cassation annulled the sentences of Navale, Angioi, and Pariani. The Navale case was sent to the Court of Assizes of Rome, which recognized his guilt, yet reduced the sentence to seven years. Another trial in Perugia in 1949 absolved Anfuso, Emanuele, and Navale. In 1953 Anfuso was elected to Parliament as a deputy from the MSI (*Movimento Sociale Italiano*—the neo-fascist party that arose after the Second World War) and served as the editor of the party's newspaper, *Il Secolo d'Italia*. Roatta returned to Italy in the 1960s and died a free man in Rome in 1968.

Questions concerning the Rosselli assassinations surfaced again in 1951 with the publication of Alberto Moravia's *Il conformista*. Moravia, whose real last name was Pincherle, was a first cousin to the Rosselli brothers; his father Carlo was Amelia Rosselli's brother. Interviewed by the noted critic Enzo Siciliano in 1972, after Bernardo Bertolucci had directed his cinematic version of *The Conformist*, Moravia stated that his novel was based on the Rosselli assassinations.[40]

The Rosselli brothers, representing two different types of resistance, were thus inducted—with Piero Gobetti, Giovanni Amendola, Giacomo Matteotti, Antonio Gramsci and others who had refused to consider any moral compromise with the regime—into the pantheon of martyrs to fascism.

Postscript

In September 2003, Italian Prime Minister Silvio Berlusconi, in an interview published in the British journal, *The Spectator*, solemnly declared that

"Mussolini never killed anyone. Mussolini sent people on holiday in internal exile."[41]

Notes

1. "Filippo Turati e il socialismo italiano" (1932), originally in *Quaderni di Giustizia e Libertà* 3 (June 1932): 9–42; now in *Scritti dell'esilio*, vol. 1, ed. Costanzo Casucci (Turin: Einaudi, 1988), 132.

2. This essay is based on previously published work. On the assassination, see "Death in Exile: The Assassination of Carlo Rosselli," *Journal of Contemporary History* 32, no. 3 (July 1997): 305–19; for an intellectual biography, see *Carlo Rosselli: Socialist Heretic and Anti-Fascist Exile* (Cambridge, MA: Harvard University Press, 1999).

3. The speech was broadcast over Radio Barcelona (and into Fascist Italy) on November 13, 1936, and published two weeks later in Rosselli's newspaper, *Giustizia e Libertà*. It is reprinted in *Scritti dell'esilio*, vol. 2, ed. Costanzo Casucci (Turin: Einaudi, 1992), 424–28; my English translation appears in *Fascism, Anti-Fascism and the Resistance in Italy: 1919 to the Present*, ed. Stanislao G. Pugliese (Lanham, MD: Rowman and Littlefield, 2004), 221–27.

4. November 17, 1936, now in the Archivio Centrale dello Stato, Casellario Politico Centrale; quoted in Giordano Bruno Guerri, *Galeazzo Ciano* (Milan: Bompiani, 1979), 249.

5. Franco Bandini, *Il cono d'ombra: chi armò la mano degli assassini dei fratelli Rosselli* (Milan: SugarCo, 1990), 34–39. Bandini's work has been important in reconstructing the events surrounding the assassination of the Rosselli brothers, yet it often seems as though the author were more intent on character assassination than historical reconstruction.

6. Aldo Rosselli, *La famiglia Rosselli: una tragedia italiana* (Milan: Bompiani, 1983), 104.

7. Raymond Aron, "Incontro con i fratelli Rosselli", *Countrepoint* 18 (1975): 166.

8. ACS, CPC, Busta 4421, fascicolo 4.

9. Gaetano Salvemini, *Carlo and Nello Rosselli: A Memoir* (London: For Intellectual Liberty, 1937), 65–68; Gaetano Salvemini, "L'assassinio dei fratelli Rosselli," *No al fascismo*, ed. Ernesto Rossi, 255–304 (Turin: Einaudi, 1957); Gaetano Salvemini, "The Rosselli Murders," *The New Republic* 18 (August 1937); see also Charles F. Delzell, "The Assassination of Carlo and Nello Rosselli, June 9, 1937: Closing a Chapter of Italian Anti-Fascism," *Italian Quarterly* 28, no. 107 (Winter 1987): 47–64; Pierre Guillen, "La risonanza in Francia dell'azione di Giustizia e Libertà e dell'assassinio dei fratelli Rosselli," *Giustizia e Libertà nella lotta antiFascista* (Florence: La Nuova Italia, 1978), 239–60.

10. Lussu testified at the trial of General Roatta that "the day of the funerals, the immense boulevard that led to Père Lachaise cemetery was filled with more than 300,000 persons, of all countries. Not only Paris, but all of Europe was

present that day." His testimony is reproduced in *Il processo Roatta: i documenti* (Rome: Universale De Luigi, 1945), 82–84.

11. The phrase is Salvemini's, "L'assassinio dei fratelli Rosselli," 258. Twelve years later (1949) a monument was erected in the forest of Bagnoles-de-l'Orne to mark the site of the assassinations. Carlo Sergio Signori was commissioned to create the work, a stark and poignant design that was, according to the artist Gino Severini, "the first abstract monument in France. The abstraction of the forms expresses a mysterious and moving grandeur that is tied to the tragedy." Amelia Rosselli wrote that "the work [was] extremely noble and significant in its austere simplicity." See Luciano Galmozzo, *Monumenti alla libertà: antifascismo, resistenza e pace nei monumenti italiani dal 1945 al 1985* (Milan: La Pietra, 1986), 41–42.

12. On June 12, *Il Telegrafo* wrote that the assassination was the result of "suppression" due to the "hatreds among the diverse extremist sects of antifascism." Ansaldo wrote that "Rosselli, who recently had become a communist, had expressed, in private and in public, his approval of the 'suppression' of Berneri. This approval attracted the hatred of the Italian and Catalonian anarchists living in France." The next day the paper insisted that Rosselli "had fallen almost certainly because of some anarchist vendetta." Quoted in Salvemini, "L'assassinio dei fratelli Rosselli," 258–59n1.

13. Gaetano Salvemini, *Carlo e Nello Rosselli* (Paris: Edizioni di Giustizia e Libertà, 1938), 68.

14. Yvon de Begnac, *Palazzo Venezia: storia di un regime* (Rome: La Rocca, 1950), 613, quoted in Renzo De Felice, *Mussolini: il Duce*, vol. 2, *Lo stato totalitario, 1936–1940* (Turin: Einaudi, 1981), 422. De Felice writes (unconvincingly) that there may be an indirect confirmation of Mussolini's innocence in his son-in-law and Foreign Minister, Galeazzo Ciano's diary entry of September 16, 1937. Referring to a terrorist attack by the *cagoulards* of September 11, Ciano writes: "In any event, we are not involved." See Galeazzo Ciano, *Diario, 1937–1938* (Bologna: Cappelli, 1948), 37.

15. De Felice, *Mussolini il Duce*, 419–23.

16. Ciano, *Diario, 1937–1938*, 256.

17. Marion Rosselli to the Editor, *New York Times*, October 2, 1944.

18. ACS, CPC, Busta 4421, fascicolo 4. Emphasis added.

19. Presentation to Aldo Rosselli, *La famiglia Rosselli: una tragedia italiana*, p. vi.

20. See Salveminis's eloquent tribute, "Marion Rosselli," *Il Ponte* 5, no. 11 (November 1949): 1443.

21. On the *Cagoule*, see Philippe Bourdel, *Le Cagoule* (Paris: Albin Michel, 1970); and Christian Bernadac, *Dagore: Les cahiers secrets de la Cagoule* (Paris: France Empire Ed., 1977); see also J. R. Tournoux, *L'Histoire Secrete: La Cagoule, le Front Populaire, Vichy, Londres, Deuzieme Bureau l'Algérie Française, L'OAS* (Paris: Plon, 1962); and Douglas Porch, *The French Secret Services: From the Dreyfus Affair to the Gulf War* (New York: Farrar, Straus and Giroux, 1995).

22. Marion's identification of Jakubiez is recounted in Salvemini, "L'assassinio dei fratelli Rosselli," 263; the Zanatta episode is in Garosci, *Vita* II (Rome: Edizioni U, 1945), 147–48.

23. *Matin*, January 13, 1938, quoted in Salvemini, "L'assassinio dei fratelli Ross 264.

24. *La France*, September 17, 1942.

25. Salvemini, "L'assassinio dei fratelli Rosselli," 265.

26. Ibid., 293–94.

27. The document, "Highly Classified [RISSERVATISSIMA RACCOMANDA' is found in the ACS, CPC, Busta 4221, Fascicolo 4.

28. Roy Palmer Domenico, *Italian Fascists On Trial, 1943–1948* (Chapel University of North Carolina Press, 1991), x.

29. Clara Conti, *Servizio segreto* (Rome: Donatello De Luigi, 1945), 112.

30. Ibid., 22–23. Conti was the secretary of Judge Italo Robino; the two were married.

31. From the transcript of the High Court of Justice, March 12, 1945; quote Conti, *Servizio segreto*, 31; and Salvemini, "L'assassinio dei fratelli Rosselli,"

32. Testimony of Santo Emanuele at the Roatta trial, quoted in Conti, *Servizio reto*, 257–69; and Salvemini, "L'assassinio dei fratelli Rosselli," 267–69.

33. *Il processo Roatta: i documenti* (Rome: De Luigi, 1945), 12–13.

34. Ibid., 26.

35. Salvemini, "L'assassinio dei fratelli Rosselli," 279–86.

36. *Il processo Roatta: i documenti*, 77.

37. Ibid., 82–117. Calamandrei's speech before the court is partially reprinted *processo Roatta*; the entire speech was published as *Arringhe e discorsi: In me ria di Carlo e Nello Rosselli nel processo dinanzi l'Alta Corte contro Roatta* (Naples: Rispoli, 1945).

38. *Il processo Roatta: i documenti*, 183.

39. Domenico, *Italian Fascists on Trial, 1943–1948*, 134–39. The Italian penal judicial system continues to "lose" suspects and prisoners; some of the n infamous episodes include SS officer Herbert Kappler, convicted of his ro the Ardeatine Caves massacre of March 24, 1944 (supposedly spirited awa his diminutive wife in a suitcase) and Licio Gelli, leader of the murky Masonic Lodge tied to shadowy right-wing plots to destabilize the country.

40. Alberto Moravia, *Il conformista* (Milan: Bompiani, 1951). This is perhaps best psychological profile of the "fascist" mentality; in English, *The Conforn* trans. Angus Davidson (New York: Farrar, Straus, Young, 1951). Moravia rel his book to the Rosselli assassinations in Enzo Siciliano, *Moravia* (Mi Longanesi, 1971), 89. For an analysis of Bertolucci's film, see Angela D Vacche, *The Body in the Mirror: Shapes of History in Italian Cinema* (Prince NJ: Princeton University Press, 1992), 57–92; Peter Bondanella, *Italian Cine From Neorealism to the Present* (New York: Frederick Ungar, 1983), 30 Millicent Marcus, *Italian Film in the Light of Neorealism* (Princeton, Princeton University Press, 1986), 285–312.

41. "Forza Italia!" by Boris Johnson and Nicholas Farrell in *The Specta* September 6, 2003.

2

Fascists and Fetishes: Clara Petacci and the Masochistic Scene

Elizabeth Leake

Claretta's Body

Clara Petacci was Benito Mussolini's lover for twelve years, from 1933 until their deaths on April 28, 1945. In spite of the longevity of their relationship, she has historically received much less (and very different) critical attention than, say, Margherita Sarfatti.[1] Petacci seems rather to provoke a different response than Mussolini's other love interests. This may, of course, have something to do with the subject herself; for example, Petacci's character is frequently dismissed as unworthy of comment. Charitable assessments of her are few and far between: in his biography of Mussolini, Christopher Hibbert provides this not atypical, synthetic description—she sums Petacci up as "generous, hysterical, vain, obsessively sentimental and fundamentally stupid."[2] At the same time, Petacci possesses qualities that divert our attention elsewhere; indeed it is not her character but rather her *body* that interests me here, a body that this paper will scan literally from top to bottom and bottom to top: from eroticized representations of Petacci's living body to views of her corpse suspended by the heels. For in the public imagination, it was precisely this body that justified Mussolini's attraction to her, and contributed to the rhetorical construction of Mussolini as both *homo politicus* and *homo eroticus*.[3] Presented as the sum of her component parts, her body was the focus of contemporary journalistic depictions as well as a topic of unending interest to later biographers. Descriptions of her shapely legs are common, for example, and her large eyes merit regular comment. But it is her breasts, in particular, that figure so prominently in the collective imagination. Like a mermaid, perhaps, or a ship's figurehead, Clara Petacci's bountiful bust (or "enormous chest [*petto enorme*][4] or "abundant bosom" [*seno abbondante*],[5] as it is epithetized with almost Homeric regularity) is emphatically and unavoidably on discursive display. It, not the rest of her, occasions flights of fascist masculinist rhetorical fancy, insofar as it is configured as a kind of scaffolding mighty and majestic enough to serve as the monument to Mussolini's erotic prowess. Petacci's breasts were trotted out in the press in order to underscore everything from Italy's military supremacy to the importance of civic pride. Similarly, her bust serves to situate Mussolini's origins in a specific geo-social milieu: in the words of her biographer Roberto Gervaso, "her opulent bosom was the attribute that Mussolini was most struck by. As a good Romagnolo, he was particularly impressed by womanly promontories."[6]

Petacci's self-image, on the other hand, was said to be deeply ambivalent until her relationship with the dictator was firmly established. She was generally aware of the fascination she engendered but also vaguely troubled by it. It was not as a wife (she was married) but only as *il Duce*'s lover that she came to take pleasure in herself and pride in her body. Their couplings were for the most part fast and furious; apparently Mussolini was a combination of Tasmanian devil and sports announcer in bed—he yelled, cursed, thrashed around, and offered a vulgar running commentary on the process all the while.[7] But in spite of, or perhaps because of, the brutality that Mussolini often displayed with his lovers,[8] Petacci, whose crush on *il Duce* could be traced back to her early adolescence, came to conceive of her body as a sacred vessel to be consecrated exclusively to her lover's pleasure. Indeed we are told (in her diary) that she perceived not just her body but her very existence as an extension of her devotion to Mussolini. Along with her biographers, then, Petacci was also said to participate in the transmittal of her overall image as a voluptuous body to which *il Duce* had privileged access for his enjoyment. She was, in short, a self-proclaimed cipher, a body destined exclusively for manipulation by *il Duce*, the supreme embodiment of Fascism.

We can already identify two fundamental paradoxes bound up in Petacci's identity: (1) out of her very self-abnegation came her identity; and (2) her exclusivity as the supreme Fascist's lover made of her, in a sense, extremely promiscuous. Being Mussolini's lover meant being the lover of all Fascists, the screen onto which all Fascists could project their fantasies, since her body was available for visual and virtual manipulation by everyone who identified with Mussolini. The specifics of their erotic encounters reflect the condensation of gender, sex, and sexuality that prevailed during the latter portion of the Fascist *Ventennio* (twenty-year period of rule).[9] Both rhetorically and libidinally, Petacci's passivity and docility, as well as her avowed denial of any aspiration beyond those that pertain to Mussolini's carnal needs, contribute to our understanding of Mussolini as the embodiment of virility (and here my use of the term follows Barbara Spackman's).

After all, at first glance, a lover such as Petacci could only be a feather in the cap of Mussolini; she was so much more fitting, *so much less challenging* a partner than the intelligent, intellectual Margherita Sarfatti, for example. But in the public retrospection that began at the moment of her death, Petacci as the object of biography becomes surprisingly unwieldy. After all, as I mentioned, she presents not one but two aporias, both articulated around the node of sexual availability. Her unilateral monogamy created a kind of sexual satiety for all to enjoy; and her self-imposed fragmentation (as a sacred vessel and no more) led to a wholeness by way of the discursive reunion between body and character. During her *lifetime*, her fetishized representation by biographers (hers and Mussolini's) reflected her availability; Petacci's *death* would problematize that representation. In what follows I will examine how the tension, in biographers' representations of Petacci, between "sacred vessel" and the "sum of her component parts" (eyes, legs, breasts) opens up a space for female agency in Fascist-period imagination, and how that tension persists for us in the present.

Claretta's Character

Volumes have been written about the last few days of Mussolini's and Petacci's lives, volumes that indicate a certain fascination with lurid details.[10] Here again we note a biographical obsession with the corporeal in Petacci's case—was her menstrual cycle thrown off by the stress and anxiety of the times? How much of her last meal of polenta did she eat? Behind the details, however, lurks another theme that biographers are rather at a loss to countenance, because it hints at a less vacuous and considerably more courageous quality in their object of inquiry.

It is predominantly in the descriptions of her final days that alongside the titillating qualities with which her body is invested, a new attribute is acknowledged—the posthumous Petacci has character. Biographers rejoice in her many refusals to flee abroad to safety, for example, and in her spunky responses during an interrogation by partisan captors. Similarly, they admire the tenacity with which Petacci insisted on following her lover to his death, determined, if not to take his bullet, at least to be by his side when it struck. These final moments project a very different fantasy onto her screen—the fantasy of not of a sacred Fascist martyrdom but of a devoted woman dying for her man. Moreover the belated introduction of a discourse about character into her biographical representation is accompanied by a shift in tone—what was once purely pleasurable voyeurism is chastened, as it were, by new found respect. In other words, as her biographers' rendering of her final days confirm, it seems that she had now fully identified with her role as a romantic heroine; she moved from a position of carefully staged servitude to the internalization of a fiction whose strength would culminate in her self sacrifice.

That is to say, she acquires an identity (independent of that of sex-toy) at the moment she chooses to relinquish it, when she "chooses" to die. (I put the word "chooses" in quotation marks both to underscore the inauthenticity of the choice, since she had no choice, really, and to acknowledge albeit indirectly a concept that has been hovering around the margins of this study but will not be given its proper due here, namely the concept of the martyr.) Recall for a moment the first of the paradoxes I described earlier: out of Petacci's self-abnegation came her very identity. The contradictory interpellation governing the articulation between power, identity, and their lacks means, in Petacci's case, the possibility of taking passivity to its farthest extreme, of actively embracing an identity *imposed* upon her.

The Paradox of Masochism

But is this paradox specific to Petacci? Or is it not coextensive with the strategies for promoting support among all women during the Fascist era?[11] After all (as Victoria De Grazia has so compellingly demonstrated) they were subject to the same sorts of simultaneous dictates and interdictions, such as the contradictory exclusion of women from political life and touting of giving birth as a highly politicized move. And did not women supporters of Fascism derive their identities, their own personal power, from self-sacrifice for the nation as well, in the form of masochistic pleasure?[12]

In order to understand what is special to Petacci's situation, let us return our gaze, at the risk of troping exactly what I want to critique, to Petacci's body. Specifically, I want to think for a moment about what I will designate the (reciprocally or mutually) masochistic relationship (I'll return to reciprocity later) between Petacci and her biographers evident in the fetishization of Petacci's body that we observed earlier. First let me briefly rehearse Slavoj Žižek's argument on masochism. Žižek observes that while the fantasy of the masochistic encounter dictates that the balance of power be tipped exclusively in favor of the dominant partner, and that the submissive partner is identifiable and indeed definable by his or her lack of control, that fantasy disguises the paradoxical nature of the relationship insofar as it is in fact the submissive or masochistic partner who determines the nature of the encounter. She stages her own submission, entering into a contract preestablished by both parties. The illusion that must be maintained for this contract to hold is the illusion that it is the dominator who maintains mastery over the situation, when something closer to the opposite is the case.

Sometimes, that illusion disintegrates. To the dominator is revealed his objectification by the submissive partner and the discovery that the dominator is in fact merely an instrument of his partner's pleasure—in other words, the submissive partner denies the subjectivity of the dominant. As a result of that transformation (which Žižek calls the *passage à l'acte*),[13] violence previously held in abeyance becomes real, thus shifting the balance of power at the same time that the illusion of the original contract is maintained. The dominant partner "reclaims" his subjectivity, concomitantly claiming to return to the original terms established in the contract by the submissive. In the dominant's mind, we might observe the following logic: "she wanted me to hurt her, so now I am doing it."[14]

Further recall that the Petacci-Mussolini contract is not dyadic, as in the relationship described by Žižek, but rather triangulated, since the gazing public adds an additional, performative element to the supposedly private contract between the lovers. The co-presence of an additional element reassigns the logic of the dominant, previously associated with Mussolini and now appertaining to the gaze of the desiring public as mediated by Petacci's biographers.[15] In this logic, we may discern the co-presence of two conflicting "fantasy" observations that I might summarize like this:

1. Petacci is *il Duce*'s lover and as such has agreed wholly to submit to an invasive and humiliating scrutiny, for it is in her capacity as pleasure-giver to this institution (by way of its incarnation in Mussolini) that she derives her own satisfaction.
2. Petacci's selflessness (recall her self-assessment as a cipher) drives her to follow Mussolini to his death. The irony of the gaze is that it signifies both power and impotence—on the one hand, if you control the field of vision, you also bear the power.[16]

On the other hand, the gaze implies a kind of impotence as well—a witness may watch but not act. My question, specifically, is what happens when the *passage à l'acte* is witnessed, when Claretta's fetishized body (eyes, legs, breasts) is seen to submit to its own destruction, when the sacred vessel is broken?

The Guilt of the Gaze

The answer, I believe, lies in Petacci and Mussolini's climax, that is, the climax of their story, perhaps the most famous scene in which she appeared. As a result of her final interrogation by the partisans in late April of 1945, Petacci was permitted to join Mussolini, then being held prisoner. On the morning of April 28, 1945, the two were awakened at dawn, told they were about to be "liberated," and hurried out of bed. Petacci was not given time to finish dressing, and left without underwear. Taken to a deserted spot near the farmhouse where they had spent their last night, the two were shot in a manner similar to that which Petacci had already predicted two years earlier, in her diary.[17]

On April 29, 1945, the day after Petacci and Mussolini were shot, their bodies were driven to Milan's Piazzale Loreto to be displayed alongside fifteen other Fascist officials, as well as Petacci's brother Marcello.[18] An enormous, angry crowd gathered. The bodies of the pair were kicked and beaten, and Mussolini's corpse was rearranged so that his head lay on Petacci's breast, his face disfigured by an ugly open-mouth grimace. The crowd grew larger, and demanded that the bodies be raised up so that everyone could see them. Attached to a steel girder with ropes around his heels, Mussolini was the first to be hoisted up—the crowd went wild with shouts and curses. Then it was Petacci's turn. As her body, also hanging from the heels, ascended into view, and eerie silence fell over the crowd. Petacci's dress slipped down to cover her face and torso, exposing her hips and thighs. Eventually a woman made her way forward through the crowd, and tied the hem of her dress between her legs. Initially angry that their view of her body was blocked, witnesses to the scene focused, yet again, on the way her shapely legs emerged from the hem of her dress.[19] They also commented on the beauty of her face, on the modest, serene, smile that played upon her lips, and on the supernatural slowness with which her eyes finally closed.[20] Her arms, not yet rigid, opened in "an embrace, like at the beginning of a dance."[21]

Two conflicting elements are at play in this scene—the silence and the shame, on the one hand, and the continued desire to fetishize her body (eyes, legs and breasts, and now hips, thighs, and pubis). Recall the logic of the dominant about which I fantasized earlier ("submitting to the gaze is the price she had to pay for her own enjoyment" and "her selflessness drove her to death"). The co-presence of those elements in biographical mediations of the crowd's response indicates that with the spectacle of the inverted suspended corpse, the *passage à l'acte* or transformation had been experienced; the contract that once titillated now also repulsed.

For the crowd, if I understand her biographers, the significance of the transformation was the following. It destroyed the fantasy, the illusion with which the masochistic contract ensured the crowd's enjoyment (the idea that "*she* enjoyed that violence; it was part of the original deal she struck"). It substituted the illusion with an accusation of complicity, which can be articulated in my fantasy of their logic like this: "That violence has contaminated us; it has implicated us such that we cannot avoid participating in it. She has stripped us of our subjectivity by manipulating us, with the full acceptance of her role, into acts of real violence." In other words, alongside the enjoyment and the repulsion that accompany the gaze is added the guilt of the gaze. We said earlier that the gaze implies power *and* impotence; with the transformation of Petacci's selflessness from cipher to martyr comes the recognition that the gaze of the desiring spectator is perhaps less impotent bystander than it is part of the act that killed her. Granting someone the agency to choose death, it turns out, is not really granting agency. Thus, when I earlier labeled the relationship between Petacci and her biographers mutually or reciprocally masochistic, it was not my intention to imply any form of symmetry between them or to imply a zero-sum game. Rather, with these terms I wish to point to the way that the *passage à l'acte* or transformation of the contract may happen in the brief span of a few moments (such as the few excruciating moments required for the slow ascension of Petacci's body), but the leftover or residual effects are long term, evident in the biographical obsession with discursively rewinding and reviewing the climactic scene.

Petacci's Agency

In the context of Fascism in general, the broader significance of Petacci's transformation is the way it points to one of the loopholes in Fascist rhetoric, namely the way female passivity (which must be distinguished from passive resistance) can intensify, as it were, into agency. Thus Fascism contains the following dialectical thought: it demands women's passivity increasingly intensely (as in the masochistic self-sacrifice described by Spackman and Macciocchi—the sacrifice of the wedding rings, abstention from employment, and so on), and through that very passivity—which reinforces the relegation of woman to object of the gaze—a space for female agency is created.

Accounts such as Petacci's throw all stances into confusion, blurring the boundaries between support and opposition and deviating Fascist dictates from their intended course. By taking the goal of feminine passivity and self-sacrifice to its logical conclusion, Petacci, ironically, becomes less "feminine" and more "virile" in the Classical sense. What is more, in doing so, she strikes two blows against Fascism, both by invoking the guilt of the gaze among her observers and by outshining Mussolini's real wife, Donna Rachele, who could not be faulted for failing her husband except for the fact that she would not, did not, die for him. (And I suppose I should mention another way in which Petacci outdid Rachele: Recently it has been shown that Rachele conducted an extramarital affair.[22] Petacci, by contrast, devoted herself to Mussolini once her husband was sent to Japan.[23]) Petacci's story, then, inadvertently creates a reverse discourse; it is the story of a female agency defined precisely by the active choice of passivity (and in this sense borders on the territory of the voluntary martyrdom of religious suicides). This elision from "good" pro-Fascist passivity to a provocative, ultimately anti-Fascist passivity is hard, too, for observers to countenance for two reasons. First, you don't see it coming: Petacci is an unexpected source of proto-feminism, and her story lacks the road marks by which provocative oppositional arguments can usually be identified. Second, there is the question of complicity, of the guilty enjoyment that her position as object of desire so conveniently provided during its twelve years of legitimacy.

How then do we understand the continued fascination with Petacci's fetishized body on the part of her biographers, manifest fifty years later as an overdetermined erotic engagement? I believe we do so by understanding that this endless chronicling of the *passage à l'acte* is effectively a re-enactment of it, an attempt to re-assert Petacci's otherness so as to forestall the moment when the veil was lifted. The moment that the illusion of consensuality vanished, the gazing masses perceived their complicity in the masochistic scene. Forestalling that moment reinstated the original terms of the contract, restored their subjectivity and redoubled the promise of unfettered pleasure. Biographers could then return to the comfort of their observations about Clara Petacci's big breasts.

Notes

1. While there do exist biographies of Petacci, in terms of depth of engagement these are not on a par with works like Cannistraro and Sullivan's study of Sarfatti: Philip V. Cannistraro and Brian Sullivan, *Il Duce's Other Woman* (New York: William Morrow, 1993); nor is she mentioned at all in works where one might expect her to appear, such as Victoria De Grazia's *How Fascism Ruled Women: Italy 1922–1945* (Berkeley: University of California Press, 1992).
2. Christopher Hibbert, *Il Duce: The Life of Benito Mussolini* (Boston: Little, Brown, 1962), 59.

3. See for example Denis Mack Smith's *Mussolini*, which links the fact of their relationship with his reputation as a lover: "Towards the end of 1942, Mussolini's liaison with Clara Petacci, which in spite of many other infidelities had lasted for almost ten years without being generally known, became a subject of popular gossip. His sexual prowess subsequently became legendary and some of the stories may well have been true." Denis Mack Smith, *Mussolini: A Biography* (New York: Vintage Books, 1983), 285. See also Emil Ludwig, *Three Portraits: Hitler, Mussolini, Stalin* (New York: Alliance Book Publication), originally published, 1940.

4. Paolo Monelli, *Mussolini piccolo borghese* (Milan: Garzanti, 1983), 82.

5. Franco Bandini, *Claretta: profilo di Clara Petacci e dei suoi tempi* (Milan: Sugar Editore 1960), 11.

6. "[Il] seno opulento [era] l'attributo che in lei più colpiva e che più colpì Mussolini, sensibile, da buon romagnolo, ai promontorii muliebri." Roberto Gervaso, *Claretta* (Milan: Rizzoli Editore, 1982), 13.

7. He was partial to certain Italian curses in particular, such as "*porco* [pig]" this and "*boia* [executioner]" that. See Monelli, *Mussolini piccolo borghese*, 177.

8. See Mack Smith, *Mussolini*, for former lovers' as well as Mussolini's own assessment of the physical and emotional violence he displayed toward his intimates.

9. See De Grazia, *How Fascism Ruled Women*, for an overview of the changing and often contradictory attitudes toward sexuality between the years 1922–45.

10. Their titles are indicative of that taste for in extremis details; see for example Franco Bandini, *Le ultime 95 ore di Mussolini* (Milano: Mondadori, 1968); Pisanò, Giorgio, *Gli ultimi cinque secondi di Mussolini: un'inchiesta giornalistica durata quarant'anni* (Milan: Il Saggiatore, 1996); Bruno Giovanni Lonati, *Quel 28 aprile: Mussolini e Claretta: la verità* (Milan: Murisa, 1994); Alessandro Zanella, *L'ora di Dongo* (Milan: Rusconi, 1993); and Peter Whittle, *One Afternoon at Mezzegra* (London: W. H. Allen, 1969). For the posthumous fate of Mussolini, see Sergio Luzzatto's *The Body of Mussolini: Mussolini's Corpse and the Fortunes of Italy* (New York: Metropolitan Books, 2005).

11. Here again see De Grazia's definitive study of women under fascism.

12. Spackman, in her description of Maria-Antonietta Macciocchi's assessment of the "masochistic pleasure derived from sacrifices requested of them" cites the Fascist requirements of biological reproduction, the sacrifice of the *fede*, and the sacrifice of (in the form of abstention from) employment outside the home. Barbara Spackman, *Fascist Virilities: Rhetoric, Ideology, and Social Fantasy in Italy* (Minneapolis: University of Minnesota Press, 1996), 26–27.

13. Slavoj Žižek, *The Metastases of Enjoyment: Six Essays on Women and Causality* (London: Verso, 1994), 89.

14. Žižek here as elsewhere comes to this formulation through Hegel.

15. Note that her very existence as the object of such a collective gaze already places her in a sort of no-woman's land insofar as her visibility in the public sphere is problematic; it should, by current arguments, desexualize her, that is to say, remove from her the capacity to reproduce that was her sacred obligation. On the other hand, it is arguably the fact that she is not involved in economic production

or reproduction that prevents her from becoming a "sterile feminist." For a fuller discussion of these issues see Spackman, *Fascist Virilities*, 35–37.

16. Žižek, *The Metastases of Enjoyment*, 73.

17. Petacci kept a diary for thirty-seven days while she was imprisoned in Novara, August 12–September 17, 1943. In it she imagines her own death, against a wall, yelling "Per il mio *Duce*, mio solo unico amore!" Clara Petacci, *Il mio diario* (Milan: Garzanti, 1946), 52. It is an important detail insofar as it demonstrates her awareness—her agency, if you will: there was nothing last minute, unplanned, or chance about her death *with and for* Mussolini; it was pre-established by her years earlier.

18. Marcello Petacci, as well as other members of her family, was involved in a series of shady deals, but Clara's relationship with *il Duce* guaranteed their immunity from prosecution. Marcello's execution stood for the whole family. See Mack Smith, *Mussolini*, 285–86.

19. Monelli, *Mussolini piccolo borghese*, 13.

20. Hibbert, *Il Duce*, 334; Monelli, *Mussolini piccolo borghese*, 299.

21. "un abbraccio, come per un inizio di danza", Monelli, *Mussolini piccolo borghese*, 299.

22. See *Guardian Unlimited*, July 23, 2003, http://www.guardian.co.uk/Archive/Article/0,4273,4248900.00html.

23. See Mack Smith, *Mussolini*, 286, for information on Petacci's husband.

3

What Does It Matter if You Die? The Seven Cervi Brothers

Philip Cooke

On the morning of December 28, 1943, the seven Cervi brothers, along with Quarto Camurri, were executed at the firing range at Reggio Emilia.[1] Mass executions were not uncommon during the Second World War, but for complex reasons the Cervi brothers have lived on in local and national consciousness, as well as in the names of the streets and squares of central and northern Italy. In this chapter I will examine the process by which the Cervi brothers and their father, the benign patriarch Alcide, have become such a part of collective memory by focusing primarily on the role they have played in Italian culture.

The Cervi family first came to the attention of the fascist authorities in the mid-1930s when it was discovered that they had set up a people's library that distributed seditious materials. Though some members of the family were arrested, none were imprisoned or sent to *confino*. On the day that Mussolini fell, the Cervi family famously distributed a celebration dish of *pastasciutta* to the locals. After the armistice declaration of September 8, 1943, the Cervis were responsible for setting up the first partisan formation in the mountains near Reggio. This formation did not enjoy a great deal of success and was forced to cease operations shortly after its inception. Seeking other ways of contributing to the Resistance, the Cervi household offered hospitality and assistance to escaped prisoners of war. On the night of November 24, 1944, the house was surrounded, and the fascists of the RSI arrested all the male occupants. It is believed that the executions were an act of reprisal: on December 27 a fascist official, Davide Onfiani, had been killed, evidently by partisans, though no one has ever claimed or accepted responsibility for this event.

The Cervi brothers' funeral took place on October 28, 1945. In his memoir, Giannetto Magnanini describes how the seven coffins were placed on a truck and wrapped in the tricolor and red flags; they were then transported from Villa Ospizio to Campegine.[2] The crowds that followed were meant to disperse at Porta Santo Stefano in Reggio, but thousands of workers followed the coffins on their bicycles as far as Campegine. It was on this day that Alcide Cervi uttered the now famous line: "After one harvest there comes another."

Reggio Emilia is a city that has always paid a lot of attention to the victims of fascism throughout the Twentieth century, and there is no doubt that the city would have continued to pay due homage to the Cervi family. It is unlikely, though, that the Cervis would have become the national heroes that they are without some kind of state intervention. This intervention duly came on the January 7, 1947, when Alcide Cervi received seven silver posthumous medals for his sons. They were pinned to his chest (and from then on, at least in public, they remained there) by the then president of the Republic, Enrico De Nicola. The occasion for the ceremony was the 150th anniversary of the Italian tricolor invented, so it is claimed, in Reggio Emilia. In early 1947, therefore, before the fourth De Gasperi government and the expulsion of the left, the Cervi family were linked with patriotism and enjoyed privileged—iconic—status in the process of rebuilding the nation after the ravages of the war. At this stage, therefore, the Cervis and all they represented were entirely acceptable to an Italian state that was then characterized by a broad political compromise. It is inconceivable that the same honors would have been bestowed in 1948, in such a public demonstration, in the run up to the crucial elections where the cold war atmosphere polarized Italian political discourse. The posthumous fame of the Cervi is thus inextricably linked with the vicissitudes of the Resistance movement from the establishment of the Italian Republic up to the present day.

After 1947 interest in the Cervis would seem to diminish, but by 1953 the time had come to celebrate, wherever possible, the tenth anniversary of the Resistance movement. It is worth noting at this point that Ferruccio Parri successfully prosecuted the right-wing newspaper *Il Meridiano d'Italia* for defamation at the end of 1953, and that a priest from Reggio Emilia, Don Italo Paterni, was about to be prosecuted for having described the Cervi family as merchants in the black market. The Resistance then was trying to fight back. In December 1953 Italo Calvino published his article "*Nei sette volti consapevoli la nostra faticosa rinascita* [In these Seven Knowing

Faces We See Our Hard-won Rebirth]" in the partisan journal *Patria indipendente*, as well as in *L'Unità* of December 27 (thus coinciding with the tenth anniversary of their deaths). The piece starts with a carefully crafted description of the land in which the Cervi house is situated before moving on to describe the house itself and its connections with the arrest of the brothers. Calvino seems to deliberately establish himself as a kind of tourist guide for his readers, as evidenced by the frequent use of deixis: "Here from this row of trees begins the land of the seven brothers. . . . This level ground . . . these canals, this vine, everything around here, was made by the seven brothers; the story of the seven brothers took place entirely here, in this farm, on this land."[3]

The brothers, then, are firmly located by Calvino in their peasant context from the very start of his account. Calvino then goes on to describe how the family had moved to the house from Campegine and taken the unprecedented decision to level the highly uneven ground that they know lived on. The installation of a network of irrigation ditches completed the picture, setting an example for others to follow. Calvino then moves on to discuss the brothers' political proclivities as well as their business acumen. He dedicates a good deal of attention to the books that they read and to their autodidacticism. The library contains manuals on beekeeping and animal husbandry, a multivolume history of Italy, the *Divine Comedy*, the *Aeneid*, Homer, and Gorky's *The Mother*, as well as a series of journals including Einaudi's *Riforma sociale*. From these seemingly disparate titles, Calvino perceives "a culture that is felt as something absolutely concrete, which aims straight away at classic and highly specialized writings. Nothing is there by chance, everything has been sought out for a precise reason, everything has its own 'use.'"[4] In many ways the Cervi brothers' happy combination of agricultural endeavor, wide reading, and service to the community prefigure the kind of positive individual embodied by Cosimo in Calvino's novel of 1957, *Il barone rampante*. Calvino's piece continues with a brief description of the Cervis' activities during the war. The concluding paragraph reflects the key position that the Cervi family then occupied in the mentality of the Italian left:

> Everything that the people of Italy expressed so well in the Resistance, the struggle against the war, a real sense of patriotism, a new cultural direction, international solidarity, a new inventiveness of action, courage, love for the family and the land, all of this was to be found in the Cervis: so in these seven serious faces of intelligent Emilian peasants we recognize the image of our hard-won, painful rebirth.[5]

After Calvino's articles were published, he received a letter of congratulation from Piero Calamandrei, one of the architects of the Constitution. Calvino thanked Calamandrei for his kind words, saying how important it was to him that the story had been "circulated and heard and understood." Calvino then apologized for not being able to attend a ceremony at the Quirinal Palace at which Calamandrei was due to speak, but fully expected that the speech would be excellent and rhetoric free.[6]

The ceremony referred to by Calvino is one of the key events in the history of the Cervi family's fortunes in the 1950s. In January 1954 Alcide Cervi was invited to see the president, at the time Luigi Einaudi. Einaudi later published an article in *Il Mondo* (March 16, 1954) describing the meeting. Alcide Cervi was accompanied by the distinguished jurist Domenico Peretti Griva; Arrigo Boldrini, gold medal of the Resistance, PCI senator, and president of the ANPI partisan association; and Carlo Levi, who had painted a portrait of the seven brothers. Einaudi began the conversation by saying how pleased he was to discover in Calvino's article that *La riforma sociale*, a journal he once edited, was in the Cervi family library. Without any further prompting Alcide Cervi launched into a detailed account of the life of his family as the assembled guests listened awestruck. Einaudi was so taken aback by the experience that he made a series of adventurous comparisons between Alcide Cervi and other illustrious predecessors: "Was he a peasant from our lands, a Homeric hero, or a Biblical patriarch?" Einaudi himself supplies the answer: "Perhaps a bit of everything."[7]

Apart from Calamandrei's speech, and the meeting with the president, the sculptor Carlo Mazzacurati (one of the most important creators of Resistance monuments) also presented Alcide Cervi with a commemorative medal that is redolent with symbolism (an oak tree with seven boughs, seven shining stars). The iconography has its origins in a short two-stanza poem written by a Giovanni Serbardini. The poem is not a work of genius, but is instructive about how the Cervi brothers were viewed at the time:

Come la Resistenza hai resistito
Vecchia Quercia
Che i tuoi sette rami
Gagliardi d'avvenire
Opponesti alla nera tempesta
Tutti e sette insieme
In un'alba sola stroncati

Come la Resistenza hai resistito
Perchè oggi i ragazzi italiani
Sopra il tuo tronco nodoso

In uno squarcio libero di cielo
Vedano
Sette stelle d'argento

(Like the Resistance you too resisted
Old Oak
Which your seven branches
Robust with the future
Opposed the black storm
All seven together
In one single dawn broken

Like the Resistance you too resisted
So that today young Italians
Atop your knotted trunk
In a free rent in the sky
Can see
Seven silver stars.)

Sebardini's poem is just one of the many works of poetry that have been dedicated to the Cervi family. Salvatore Quasimodo, for example, wrote: "Ai fratelli Cervi, alla loro Italia [For the Cervi brothers, for their Italy]." In addition, there is a long poem by Gianni Rodari as well as countless songs.[8] But far and away the most important piece of creative writing associated with the Cervi family is *I miei sette figli*, a book published in 1955 by Editori Riuniti and written by Alcide Cervi with Renato Nicolai.[9] Nicolai was a Rome-based communist intellectual and seems to have been sent by the cultural section of the PCI to write the book.

Nicolai's method in writing the book is similar to the modern "ghost writer" of footballers' autobiographies. In a brief preface to the 1980 edition he describes how he spoke to Alcide Cervi on a number of occasions in the winter of 1944. He took notes and did not, it seems, use a tape recorder. He was unable to subject Alcide to lengthy interviews because of the state of the latter's health (he suffered from asthma). Nicolai went on to teach himself the *reggiano* dialect (an impressive feat if this is true) and, after conversations with a number of other individuals who knew the Cervi family, decided to write the book using the father as the narrator of the story.[10] The language that results is a strange mixture of artificial *reggiano* and literary Italian. The lyrical opening chapter is characterized by carefully cadenced sentences reminiscent of some of Pavese's writing. The method is, to say the least, questionable, but it does not seem to have provoked a lot of discussion when the book was first published. *Patria indipendente* did publish a review in October 1955 that is at one point critical of Nicolai's method, but in the main the reviews and the response were very positive.[11] In a short space of time the book became a publishing sensation and was translated into a wide variety of foreign languages, including Russian but not English.

The book begins with Alcide Cervi describing why he has chosen to write the book at this particular period in his life. The main reason appears to be that now he has reached eighty years of age and all his grandchildren are grown up and able to assist on the farm, so he has some time on his hands. In chapter 1 he is elected to the *comune* of Campegine and takes an unusual role, that of the individual in charge of cemeteries. He serves in the military and is converted to socialism following an encounter with Prampolini. He marries in 1899, and the first son, Gelindo, is born on 1901. In 1903 there follows a stillborn girl. Antenore is born in 1904, Diomira in 1906, Aldo in 1909, Ferdinando in 1912, Agostino in 1916, Ovidio in 1918, and, finally, Ettore in 1921. (What his wife thinks about her life during this twenty-two-year period is unknown, though Genoveffa Cervi is a "hands-on" mother who delights in reading to her children the *Promessi Sposi*, the Bible, the *Reali di Francia*, and the *Divine Comedy*. Her favorite episode is the Ugolino story, which she reads to her children before they go to bed, with unknown effects on their sensitive minds. Aldo is imprisoned for insubordination for nearly two years and freed in 1932. By the time of the establishment of the "people's library" at Campegine and the leveling of the land at the Cervi farm, Aldo has become the most politically active of the seven sons; he has fathered a child but not married the mother and is almost the chief protagonist of the book. (Aldo's centrality is brought out much more in the film, as we shall see later.) Aldo returns one day behind the wheel of a tractor, an almost unheard of piece of machinery at the time, and brings with him another purchase, a globe. If you visit the Cervi museum, a tractor and globe occupy pride of place. In chapter 7 of the book there is a description of Aldo's encounter with an anti-fascist theatre company and with the politically active actress Lucia Sarzi.

Chapters 8, 9, and part of 10 describe the activities of the sons during the period from the collapse of fascism to the executions. There is a memorable description of the *pastasciutta* episode, which has recently become a feature of the July 25 celebrations at the Cervi Museum. In the book, the Cervi's chief Resistance activity is that of providing accommodation and assistance to allied prisoners of war. The local Resistance organization (the CLN) decides that by November the numbers in the house have become dangerously high and Aldo agrees to move the majority of them to other safer locations. By this stage, however, the Cervis' secret is out and the

fascists come to arrest them. Alcide describes how the foreigners were sep-
arated from the Italians and sent to Parma.

Various plans are hatched both inside and outside the jail to free the
prisoners, but none work. One morning the guards arrive and order
the Cervi family to come with them for a trial at Parma. They leave
Alcide behind, where he encounters the future editor of *L'Espresso*, Arrigo
Benedetti.[12] Alcide is eventually freed, only to be told by his wife that all the
sons have been executed. At the end of the chapter he pronounces the
famous phrase "After one harvest there comes another. Let's keep going."[13]
This is just one example of the alteration of the reality of the Cervi story,
here purely for reasons of narrative expediency: the funeral where the
phrase was, in fact, uttered does not figure in the book.

Renato Nicolai's book has run to countless editions, all published by
Editori Riuniti. It is interesting to note that there are some significant
changes between editions. In an important article, Antonio Canovi gives a
telling example of a passage that is missing in editions published after 1980
and that contains some laudatory comments on the Soviet Union and
Stalin.[14] A close philological analysis would reveal further evidence of textual desalinization. Here is just one example: In the 1955 edition Aldo buys
the famous "globe" because Stalin had said "study the international situation." In 1980 this sentence is changed to "because the watch-word was:
study the international situation."[15] These micro textual changes reveal the
extent to which the book, as well as the Cervi story, is ineluctably bound up
with the evolving political situation. And this is even more the case if we
consider the first version of the book as a kind of vehicle for PCI political
and cultural strategy in the early 1950s. The outline of the narrative of the
story of the Cervi brothers that I have just traced corresponds, quite
closely, I would argue, to certain views on the Resistance movement and its
political utility for the PCI. It does not, I would suggest, correspond to the
historical reality of the Cervi brothers' story. There is very little in the way
of discussion or depiction of violence in the book. Fascists are disarmed in
bloodless episodes, and the main activity of the Cervis is, as we have seen,
to provide assistance to escaped foreign prisoners of war. No mention is
made of the Cervis' brief period in the hills near Reggio. The killing of the
fascist official that led to the decision to execute the Cervis as a reprisal is
also absent. Absent too is any mention of the clashes between Aldo Cervi,
the local CLN, and representatives of the PCI, who accused him of using
dangerously risky methods. Tellingly, Didimo Ferrari, one of the key figures of the Resistance movement in the Reggio area, does not even make
the briefest of appearances. Ferrari had gone to jail over the Cervi library
episode and had become one of the heroes of the Resistance movement.

But by the 1950s he was a considerable inconvenience and, at the time of the publication of the book, was living a clandestine life in Czechoslovakia, along with many other political emigrants who had been accused of postwar killings. Given the circumstances, he could not appear in the text.

From the outline of the book that I have given it is also clear that a great deal of space is given to the Cervis' role as peasants who both cultivated the land and participated in the Resistance.[16] During the 1950s the main debate about the Resistance centered on the civil war issue. The left countered this, essentially fascist, position with the argument that it was not a civil war at all, but a "second *Risorgimento*." But on this second occasion a crucial group, which was missing the first time around, according to Gramsci, participated. This group was, of course, the peasants. The Cervis then fit very conveniently into PCI strategy in the 1950s, and this is why the story is promoted over others. Their importance can be gauged by the organization of a visit by *papà* Cervi to Moscow, an account of which appeared in the PCI journal *Vie Nuove*. Alcide Cervi was also photographed standing next to Gramsci's grave.

Following the colossal success of the Nicolai book, one might have expected a film version to follow soon after. This did not happen. Cesare Zavattini had proposed a film of the Cervi story in 1954, a year before the book was itself published, but it is claimed that the proposal was blocked by the censor. Whatever the case, the film, directed by Gianni Puccini, was eventually only made in 1968.[17]

Whereas Renato Nicolai's book concentrates on the figure of *papà* Cervi, Puccini's film centers on the figure of Aldo Cervi, played by one of the stars of Italian cinema on the 1960s, Gian Maria Volonté. The film starts in 1940 with Aldo's encounter with the politically committed actress Lucia Sarzi, who is playing the role of Tosca in a play put on by a traveling theater company. The seven brothers and their father attend the play immaculately dressed, and the camera focuses on their ability to recite the actors' lines word for word. Despite their peasant background, they are clearly well-educated and culturally savvy. In the climax to the play Sarzi diverges from the script and delivers a thinly veiled anti-fascist speech about the inevitable defeat of the oppressor. Aldo realizes he has found a kindred spirit (in fact she turns out to be a communist comrade) and pays her a visit after the show has finished. He discusses the life of the Cervi family with her and, by way of a series of black and white flashbacks, Sarzi and the film's audience find out the necessary background. The information that is divulged is very similar to the content of Nicolai's book: the family moves from one farm to another following a falling out with an oppressive landowner, Aldo buys a tractor complete with *mappamondo*, and so on. Greater emphasis is placed on the Cervi brothers' loves, and there is much time devoted to Aldo's unorthodox relationship. He does not marry Verina, the woman who bears his children, and they live "in sin" in the Cervi farmhouse. Puccini's interest in this aspect of Aldo's life is part of an attempt to make the Cervis peculiarly relevant to his late 1960s audience.

This attempt to contemporize the story of the Cervis, but Aldo in particular, is even more explicit when it comes to depicting his political views and, above all, his relationship with the organized left, the PCI. The actress Sarzi organizes a meeting between Aldo and a Communist Party operative. However, it quickly becomes evident that the two have different agendas. Aldo is keen to get on with things and argues for direct action, whereas the Communist representative prefers to wait until historical conditions are right. Aldo, on the other hand, believes that history needs to be "accelerated" and suggests bombing various fascist headquarters. Sarzi has to warn him against "anarchist-style attacks," which could play into the hands of the enemy, but he is not impressed.

The strained relationship between the Cervis and the local "official left" continues after the fall of fascism and the first phase of Resistance activity in the autumn and winter of 1943. The Cervis initially organize the safe passage of former prisoners of war before taking to the hills themselves to set up their own Partisan formation. The Communist Party, in the shape of the local CLN, is not happy about their activities and asks them to leave the hills for the lower ground where, so it is claimed, they can best be employed. Following a fierce battle with German troops, the Cervis are forced to move their base and decide that their best option is to meet with the CLN at Reggio Emilia. They return home, and that same night the farm is surrounded and they are taken prisoner. Though it is never stated explicitly, Puccini almost seems to be suggesting that the PCI, by way of its gradualist strategy, was responsible for the downfall of the Cervis. The PCI, so the film suggests, was unable to cope with the new historical situation and preferred "organization" rather than "spontaneity." Of course, these kinds of discussions were the very ones that were going on in the late 1960s at the heart of the left and led to the abandonment of the PCI by countless disenchanted young communists. The analogy between the Cervi brothers and the *teste calde* (hot heads) of the late 1960s is made even more explicit in the, highly effective execution scene when, as the firing squad aims its rifles at the condemned men, one of the brothers raises his clenched fist in a final gesture of defiance.

Papà Cervi died on March 27, 1970, at the age of ninety-five. His body was put in the Chamber of the Tricolor at Reggio Emilia, and 200,000 people came to pay their last respects. He was buried a few days later, and speeches were made by the mayor, Renzo Bonazzi, Ferruccio Parri, and Giorgio Amendola, who represented the PCI.

As the 1970s proceeded, the Cervi family's legacy developed in a variety of ways and on several levels. Some elements of left-wing terrorism chose to name themselves after the Cervis—this use of Resistance-inspired titles was quite common in the early 1970s. The theme of the Cervis' "deviance" from PCI discipline resurfaced first in the translation into Italian of Anatoli Tarasov's memoir *V gorah italii*, and more explicitly in 1979 when Osvaldo Poppi, a Resistance leader from Modena, published a book-length interview in which he claimed that Aldo Cervi had described himself as an anarchist: "He considered himself an anarchist individualist who would never bow to any discipline originating in communist doctrine."[18] Poppi goes on to describe how the decision-making process in the Cervi formation was inspired by anarchist principals.[19]

More recently, the historiographical "debate" has been further developed, but certainly not enriched, by Giorgio and Paolo Pisanò, who argue, wholly unconvincingly, that the Cervi brothers were deliberately eliminated by the PCI.[20] According to the Pisanòs, the PCI were well aware that the Cervis would be executed in an act of reprisal and so, in order to rid themselves of these inconvenient mavericks, they organized the ambush of the fascists. I will not spend any more time on this preposterous argument but pass to a more important issue, the Museo Cervi.

The passing of Alcide Cervi led to the establishment of a museum. *Papà* Cervi had received during his long life countless visitors who left behind a range of gifts (including model tractors, Russian dolls, and a miniature Eiffel tower). These, and much more, are on display at the museum today. In its original concept, the museum was dedicated to the evocation of peasant life in the region. It is only over the last few years that the museum has taken on further significance by adding extra exhibition space dealing with antifascism and the Resistance. The museum has, perhaps unofficially, assumed the role of national museum of the Resistance. There is no official national Resistance museum, and the Museo Cervi seems to fill a gap. The museum also enjoys great symbolic status: when Berlusconi first came to power, the Milanese branch of Communist Refoundation organized regular bus tours.[21] In January 2004 Carlo Azeglio Ciampi visited the museum and delivered a speech praising the Cervis as "symbols of civic virtue and the choice of liberty that lies at the heart of the foundations of the Republic."

It is now more than sixty years since the seven Cervi brothers met their end. In recent years much has been written about the myth, indeed the "great lie" of the Resistance.[22] To be sure, if we dig deeply, we can find evidence of manipulation of the truth, of appropriation and cancellation of memory. Maybe the Cervis were not quite the "red heroes" they were made out to be. Nevertheless, at the core of the Cervi story lies a fundamental truth: they were executed as part of the fight against fascism, a fight that was eventually won. "What does it matter if you die?" was a line in a partisan song from 1944.[23] Perhaps the many present day detractors of the Resistance movement, whose freedom to express their views was a direct result of the commitment to liberty of the Cervis and countless others, would do well to reflect on this question.

Notes

1. I am grateful to Massimo Storchi and the staff of the ISTORECO for their invaluable help. I would also like to thank the staff at the Museo Cervi for their kindness and the British Academy for its generous financial assistance.
2. Giannetto Magnanini, *Ricordi di un comunista emiliano* (Milano: Teti, 1979), 50.
3. I quote from "La storia dei sette fratelli Cervi, " in the critical edition of Italo Calvino's works *Saggi 1945–1985*, ed. Mario Barenghi, 2171–78 (Milan: Mondadori, 1995), 2171.
4. Calvino, "La storia dei sette fratelli Cervi," 2175.
5. Ibid., 2178.
6. See Piero Calamandrei, *Uomini e città della Resistenza* (Bari: Laterza, 1955), 111–19.
7. Luigi Einaudi, "Il vecchio Cervi," in *I Cervi (scritti e documenti)*, 52–56(Reggio Emilia: ANPI, 1963), 55.
8. Gianni Rodari, *Compagni fratelli Cervi* (Reggio Emilia: No publisher, 1955). The poem begins with a description of Aldo returning with the tractor and the globe: "solenne goffo re da biblioteca / esiliato fra i campi" [solemn and awkward king of the library / in exile in the fields].
9. Alcide Cervi, *I miei sette figli*, ed. Renato Nicolai (Rome: Riuniti, 1955).
10. See Renato Nicolai, "Come è nato questo libro," in *I miei sette figli*, ed. Alcide Cervi and Renato Nicolai (Rome: Riuniti, 1980), 11–12.
11. *Patria independente*, October 16, 1955, p. 3.
12. Arrigo Benedetti gives his own account of the meeting in *Paura all'alba* (Documento—Rome: Libraio editore, 1945).
13. Cervi, *I miei sette figli*, 109.
14. Antonio Canovi, "I Cervi: un paradigma della memoria resistenziale" in *Guerra, guerriglia e comunità contadine in Emilia Romagna* (Reggio Emilia: RS libri, 1999), 295. Compare the 1955 edition (p. 100) with the 1980 edition (p. 74).
15. The references are on the same pages of the respective editions, as in the note above.
16. This view of the Cervi as ideal peasants can also be found in Roberto Battaglia, *Storia della Resistenza italiana* (Turin: Einaudi, 1964): "Far from shutting themselves away in patriarchal stasis, the families in this society act as elements of

progress and of struggle. And in this sense the family of Alcide Cervi and his seven sons . . . can stand out as *a symbol of the entire peasant Resistance* and their story embody that of hundreds of families in the Emilian plains" (123; emphasis added). It is interesting to note that this passage does not appear in the first 1953 edition of Battaglia's history.

17. For some incisive comments on the film see Lino Miccichè, *Cinema italiano: gli anni '60 e oltre* (Venice: Marsilio, 1995), 125. There is also a documentary film, *Papà Cervi*, directed by Franco Cigarini, which was made in 1968.

18. Osvaldo Poppi (Davide), *Il commissario* (Modena: ANPI, 1979), 12. Tarasov's memoir, first published in Leningrad in 1960, was partly translated in *Ricerche Storiche* 20–21 (1973): 15–44.

19. For a reply to Poppi see Gismondo Veroni, "Considerazioni sui Cervi," *Ricerche Storiche* 38–39 (1979): 117–21, which, amongst other arguments, looks at the semantics of the word *anarchico* (anarchic).

20. See Giorgio Pisanò and Paolo Pisanò, *Il triangolo della morte* (Milan: Mursia, 1992), 390–400.

21. The museum's website is at http://www.fratellicervi.it. The museum itself is run by the Istituto Alcide Cervi in Reggio Emilia, which has published a very useful guide to the museum, *Il Museo Cervi tra storia e memoria* (Reggio Emilia: Edizioni Tecnograf, 2002).

22. I refer here to Gianpaolo Pansa, *La grande bugia* (Milan: Sperling & Kupfer, 2006). The Cervis do not figure in the book.

23. The song in question is entitled "Compagni fratelli Cervi." For the full text of the song see A. Virgilio Savona and Michele L. Straniero, *Canti della Resistenza Italiana* (Milan: Rizzoli, 1985), 126–27. The collection also contains the songs "Papà Cervi raggiunge i sette figli," 305–7, and "I sette Cervi," 382–83.

Part II

State Killings

Rosi's *Il caso Mattei*: Making the Case for Conspiracy

Mary P. Wood

E nrico Mattei, the President of the Italian state hydrocarbon company ENI, died on October 27, 1962, when the Morane Saulnier executive jet carrying him, his pilot Bertuzzi, and the American journalist Andrew McHale, crashed near Milan's Linate airport. Official reports at the time failed to establish the causes of his death, as did the judicial inquiry of 1995, which reviewed allegations made during the trials of mafia inform- ers that Mattei had been killed by the mafia on American orders. This chapter will consider Francesco Rosi's cinematic investigation of the Mattei case and the visual and rhetorical strategies he uses to suggest who might have been responsible and, most importantly, why.

Rosi's film, *Il caso Mattei*, was released in February 1972, ten years after Mattei's assassination, and reflects the commercial, institutional, political, and cultural contexts of its time. It was part of an international groundswell of interest in social and political issues. From the late 1960s, American films had articulated critiques of American values and institutions.[1] The films of the "New Hollywood" borrowed some of the characteristics of European art cinema in order to represent a new conception of the world. The use of traits from different genres, jump cuts, and cinematography that drew attention to its construction mirrored the critique of dominant ideology represented in conspiracy theories. Developments in American cinema facilitated the success of films like Rosi's, which could now draw on an international educated audience. *Il caso Mattei* uses the conventions of the conspiracy thriller while resonating with Italian anxieties generated by the violence and uncertainties of the strategy of tension. Difficulties in attributing responsibility for an assassination or massacre were compounded by left- and right-wing factions constructing events to resemble the work of their political enemies and this had the effect of destabilizing Italian political life.

It is important that this film was destined for mainstream, international distribution, because by the early 1970s, the audience had changed and was now predominantly urban, educated, and middle class and therefore able to appreciate and "read" the complex narratives of conspiracy thrillers. That this audience also existed internationally meant that there was a market for political cinema, which, in turn, led to increased budgets for filmmakers who had proved themselves able to communicate ideas clearly.[2] For those who, like Francesco Rosi, were able to move into this type of international, "quality" production, the consequences were the absorption of mainstream filmic conventions.

Rosi's task was to make the complex political situation of Italy comprehensible and interesting for this audience, and his solution was to meld generic conventions in order to make his story and his message clear. With his international audience in mind, he had to structure his narrative to make the murder of an Italian state functionary interesting and comprehensible without turning it into a biopic or a didactic documentary. The very complexity of postwar Italian politics necessitated some difficult narrative choices. Explaining the different personalities and political factions in Mattei's story would have slowed the narrative down too much for the international audience, and concentration on Mattei's psychology would have diverted attention from the underlying causes of his assassination. Rosi's solution drew on his established strategy of rejecting individual psychology as an explanation of events, opting for presentation of a mosaic of journalistic inquiries, key meetings, and reconstructions that cumulatively build up a picture of a context. The new element was Rosi's presence as investigator within the film, generating a dual perspective through reenactments of events from 1945 to 1962 and an updating in 1970 of information about them.

Rosi researched in 1970 and filmed in 1971. As the published screenplay shows, Rosi and Eugenio Scalfari were interested in the multiple ambiguities around the personality of Mattei.[3] They saw him as a public servant with the attitudes of a captain of industry and who sometimes worked against the state; a Christian Democrat who conspired against his party; an honest man who actively corrupted those who stood in his path; a character who operated on the margins of acceptable behavior, whose actions were for the most part hidden from public view. Rosi and his collaborators justified their choice of Mattei as subject of the film precisely because of his emblematic nature. He stands as a metonym for his institution, ENI, and for the exercise of power without control. Several scenes allude to Mattei's running of ENI as a state within a state, threatening Italian democracy. All of Rosi's films are to some extent explorations of the nature of power, and this story is a reflection at the distance of ten years of a figure whose career coincided neatly with the early history of the Italian republic.

The film is extremely complex and presents an enormous amount of information about Italian economic development in the postwar period, and about Italy's position in the international context. To start the process of the spectator's identification of the suspects, Mattei's death is the disruption that starts the investigation, and the international dimension is raised from the beginning. A night shot of the ENI skyscraper headquarters, whose office lights gradually come on as the voices of telephonists take calls in Italian, English, French, and German, elegantly suggests the importance of both man and institution. This is reinforced through the figure of the *Time Life* journalist, Donald and, at key points, by the sequences of Mattei's meeting with the American oil man in the Hotel de Paris, his visit to the oil rig in which we see the multi-ethnic workforce and hear his views on colonialism and assistance to the Third World, his visit to Tunisia, and his flight over Yugoslavia, as well as Rosi's marshaling of French witnesses. Rosi's film is ahead of its time in linking the European colonial past and the globalization of international economies.

The film ends with a repeat of events leading up to the fatal plane crash, concluding with a voice-off as Mattei states that he will continue to fight the absurd oil monopoly and, if he does not succeed, those who have oil under their feet will do. At the end, several hypotheses are presented as "preferred explanations" of his murder. One option is that he was killed by elements within the power structure of the Italian state because his modernizing approach to running ENI was at odds with existing, clientelistic relationships. The hypothesis that he was killed by the French Secret Service because he disturbed their hegemony in North Africa is given more narrative space in sequences where Mattei talks to a journalist in Moscow's Red Square and in his private jet over Yugoslavia, as well as in Rosi's interview with the French former director of counterespionage services, Thiraud De Vosjoli. The latter establishes toward the end of the film that someone close to Mattei kept the French Secret Services informed of his movements, and that another French agent, expert on Morane Saulnier jets, was placed at Catania airport at the time of Mattei's fatal flight from Sicily to Milan.

By far the greatest number of hypotheses implicate American interests in his assassination. U.S. oil interests are identified as primary suspects because Mattei's oil explorations in Tunisia and other North African countries and proposals to work with the Russians had enormous financial and political consequences.[4] In the immediate postwar period, the Americans' main concern was that Italy should not "go communist" and any foray into Eastern Europe was regarded as a potential threat to American influence in Europe. The mafia is also implicated in Mattei's murder in two short sequences. In the first, Rosi telephones the journalist De Mauro, instructing him to research Mattei's last visit to Sicily. The second announces De Mauro's disappearance through a television news item and journalistic comments on it. The latter, as well as the long sequence in Tunisia that precedes it, contains the allegation that he was killed by the mafia, either on American instructions, or for powerful Italian right-wing reactionary elements. The interests of the mafia in keeping Sicily backward are also evoked in the sequences of Mattei's last visit to Gela, promising work and prosperity to a rapturous Sicilian population.

Rosi's films are all to some extent investigations, and he makes use of the familiar investigative structures of documentary or expository cinema, as well as of detective fiction. For a political filmmaker like Rosi, the investigative form has an epistemological function in that he is concerned to examine not only the truth of representations but also how we know what we know and, if there are gaps in our knowledge, why the truth is concealed or not plain. He uses multiple investigator figures, mainly journalists, but including himself, in order to delineate events, explore hypotheses, and produce a representation of Mattei as political operator. The predominantly linear arrangement of most mainstream narrative film is not necessary to expository film. The disposition of arguments in the latter follows the logic of persuasion so that, for example, after the plane crash and the official version that it was an accident, the narrative is concerned to reject the simple explanation and to introduce greater complexity. Considerable doubts about the official version of events are generated by flashbacks to conflicting witness statements, some of them referring to an explosion and flash of light in the air and others to this happening on the ground. The film includes historical reconstruction of periods in Mattei's life and the aftermath of his death, the testimonies of witnesses, and the opinions of experts. The film is essentially the "story" of Rosi's search for illumination, and this is what constitutes the metanarrative level and gives the film resolution.

Conventions of Italian popular detective fiction (the investigative structure) and American *film noir* (the delineation of why a crime had been committed, rather than who had committed it) are also useful in making the narrative accessible and interesting. Rosi's use of *noir* elements in *Il caso Mattei*, such as night-for-night shooting, darkness and excessive shadows, a pessimistic atmosphere, and the velocity of clues and new events in the latter half of the film, also made it a more attractive product to export to the United States. Moreover, the quality of the screenplay and cinematography, the serious nature of the subject, and the prestige and personal intervention of the director into the film lend authority to the investigation.

The agenda of revealing hidden meanings implies that *Il caso Mattei* must persuade us of its own authority and of the ethical authority of the filmmaker.[5] Rosi achieves this through the secondary text of articles and his book by stressing the work of research and the difficulties in gaining access to the truth and by positioning himself within the text. In several sequences he interviews experts and possible witnesses, and journalists report findings and opinions to him. Televised interviews, photographs, and the direct witness of Ferruccio Parri, Michele Pantaleone, Arrigo Benedetti, and Philippe Thiraud De Vosjoli give weight to the above-mentioned hypotheses. Similarly, actual black and white photographs, newspaper headlines, and reports and documentary footage are complemented by reconstructed media material. Video interviews are used in early sequences, but they feature the actor Gian Maria Volonté, who plays Mattei. Similarly, what purport to be actual photographs of Mattei and the American oilman dissolve into color re-enactments of key events. Realism is also generated by the peasants who witnessed the explosion of Mattei's plane, whose rather stiff speech signals them as "real witnesses."

Nineteen sixty-eight and the Vietnam war are among the contextual factors influencing the form of Rosi's film. Both represented political and generational conflicts, a sense that those in power were not representing the interests of the electorate and that there should be political renewal— by force, if necessary. In Italy the events of 1968 in particular led to a re-evaluation of the work of Antonio Gramsci and to the popularizing of the idea of hegemony. Rosi's interest in the processes of political hegemony is visible within the film, both through his portrayal of Mattei's interaction with those in power and through Rosi's presence on screen commenting on photographs of Italian politicians. Journalistic investigations, photographs, and video extracts function at several levels. References to the media are used to signal the presence and importance of national mass information systems, and early sequences demonstrate the politics of disinformation, as Mattei manipulates news of oil and methane deposits to justify his actions. Journalists are used as a narrative device to present information and enigmas in the investigations. They are also used to illustrate the manipulation of the media that Rosi suggests is part of the hegemonic process.

Several well-known journalists (Sennuccio Benelli, Luigi Squarzina) appear in *Il caso Mattei*, and although they are not named, their aims and opposition to Mattei's power are made obvious through the dialogue. They constitute iconic signs that refer immediately to their actual function in the world "out there" and metonymically to the news-gathering process. Rosi himself appears in the film performing analogous actions. The purpose of showing these activities is to provide a critical interpretation of the dominant version of events and, in the case of those in the *Time Life* bureau, to give the international perspective—that "the most powerful Italian since Julius Caesar" is worth a 500-word obituary. The sequences in which Mattei takes Luigi Squarzina to an ENI oilrig in the Persian Gulf and to installations in Tunisia have the narrative functions of imparting a great deal of information about Mattei's personality, his anti-colonialist politics, and of the politics of the "Seven Sisters" of the international oil cartel. Mattei is represented as an honest man, an Italian patriot, and a cynical international operator, but these sequences also have the function of illustrating how those in power attempt to use the media to reinforce dominant ideologies. Squarzina has been identified in the previous sequence of the RAI television round table discussion as critical, and Mattei works hard to present his point of view. Interestingly, in these sequences, connotations of modernity accrue around both figures, indicating visually that, for the most part, the two opponents share the same ideals.

Il caso Mattei features large numbers of television monitors within the frame, and television also plays an important part both in generating the film's "reality effect" and in illustrating the constructing of hegemony. The professional practice of media institutions tends to construct representations of the famous as powerful individuals, rather than as examples of institutional practices themselves. In Rosi's film spectacular images and visual organization that is surplus to narrative requirements, that is, visual excess, function to indicate that tensions exist between opposing views. Spectacle puts a brake on the "reality effect," drawing attention to the hegemonic process. Media sequences are invariably marked by excess: one television monitor, one photograph, or one journalist is rarely used. Banks of television monitors in darkened rooms, sheaves of photographs that then fade into or dissolve into re-enactments, and direct address to the camera by journalists and experts, all disturb the illusion of reality.

Direct address to camera by the journalist Benelli, jolts and generates unease through the effect of immediacy, which John Ellis has identified as a standard code of television news.[6] The spectator is being interpellated, called into the unfolding narrative. At points such as these the text moves onto what Jakobson designates the conative register to persuade of and cue the authenticity of the meanings uncovered by the enquiry.[7]

The film also uses frequent repetition, with important points empha-sized by slight zooms and reframings. Metaphor and metonym also enable complex ideas to be presented economically. In the short sequence where Mattei berates the banker, the character stands for his institution. The low-angle shot of his small, gnome-like, bearded figure behind a large desk gen-erates "inferential journeys" to the lack of accountability of international banking.[8] Emotional involvement is also an arm of persuasion. Again, this is generated in an early sequence of the aftermath of the crash, where the camera pans over the site, giving fragmented shots of policemen carrying a heavy white sheet, zooming in on rubber gloves, emphasizing the horror of the event. Extra-diegetic heartbeats also accompany sequences of Signora Mattei's distress, or Mattei's fear at threats to his life.

Enrico Mattei's historical significance as a modernizing agent within Italy, and as a significant figure in international oil politics, had the poten-tial to crossover from national to international audiences. Mattei's death in 1962 took place at the height of the economic boom that he himself, and ENI, had helped to create. However, by 1972, economic prosperity and the enormous social changes that went with it had exposed tensions between the demands of a modern state and a modern economy and those of the Byzantine political and social habits of a governing class. The visual organ-ization of the film encourages access to deeper levels of meaning. Rosi uses the conventions of *film noir* to indicate that the world of the film is bleak and that dark secrets exist. The color tones of the film are predominantly dark—cool blues, greys, blacks, a number of night shots punctuated by crashes, sirens, and the atonal chords of Piero Piccioni's score. Lights appear everywhere from the revolving lights of emergency vehicles to enormous ornate lamps in decorative interiors. Occasionally, the cool tones of the *mise en scène* will be relieved by splashes of yellow and gold, visually evok-ing the presence of mysteries and things to know.[9]

Contrasts between modernity and backwardness are made through the two different visual regimes that structure the film, spatial and architec-tural relationships being used to express a deeper meaning. Mattei's world is characterized by cool colors and the ordered lines of modernist architec-ture, which connote modernity. His environment is that of 1930s-style modernist offices and corridors in ordered straight lines, light, machinery, and AGIP hotels. Mattei's insistence on order, cleanliness, modern business practices, and training contrasts to his opponents' environment, character-ized by disorder, or the excessive decoration of the Baroque, representing the backwardness of the "old" Italy of clientelistic and corrupt business and political practices. Similarly, in the Sicilian sequences, Mattei is associated with his company's clean, bright hotels, in contrast to the jumbled houses of Gela, a pre-modern environment where the mafia thrives.

The complexity of the film's use of cinematic space can be seen in the sequences around the re-enactment of Mattei's negotiations with the American oil man in the Hotel de Paris, Monte Carlo. Compared to the rest of the film, these sequences are unusually static; the mobile camera that is a hallmark of Rosi's style does not feature here. Watching slides on a screen, Rosi names real people—Don Sturzo, Scelba, De Gasperi and others—without contextualizing or explaining them for a non-Italian audience. The litany of names of representative individuals makes plain the political groupings used by Mattei in the interests of building up a strong ENI, but it is suggested that Mattei was ultimately unable to combat the factions that he claimed to use like a bus, hopping on and off as it suited him. However, Rosi extends the idea of failure by introducing an international dimension, further suggesting the anachronistic nature of Italian political power. The photograph of the American oilman that fades to color and animation as it introduces the Hotel De Paris sequence is that of a large, plump, well-groomed, and supercilious man who evokes the idea "bloated capitalist." The conflict between power systems is dramatized in the negotiations, where Mattei represents Italian interests and the Italian state, and the American the powerful global interests of capitalist big business. Mattei himself stands for an entire technician class that, by virtue of its class origins is excluded from Italian governmental power, although it does wield political power at various levels, from the running of state bodies to low-level local bureaucracy. His bargaining with the American oilman is a representation of institutionalized and ritualized male conflict, illustrating that in the mid-twentieth century, the exercise of power is not simply a matter of physical constraint, limiting the freedom of others; it is about language—who controls it and who constructs definitions and meanings—and Mattei's lack of English is a factor in the failure in his negotiations. Gian Maria Volonté's performance indicates a style of power characterized by force, gesture, personality, and charm, visual correlatives of the verbal part of discourse.[10] The positioning of the characters by shots and reverse shots from opposite sides of the table expresses conflict metaphorically. They are also placed in an ornate dining room, where low-angle camera positions emphasize the visual richness of the environment, the repetition of columns supporting interlacing vaulting on the ceiling. The choice of a luxury hotel associated with wealthy aristocratic and industrialist classes who could afford a leisure lifestyle also evokes the clash of modernity and tradition by the presence in the dining room of the white collar functionaries who embody the new power order.[11] In the contemporary world status, wealth and power combine not in inheritance but in multinational corporations.

Rosi's film uses the codes and conventions of mainstream cinema to construct cinematic space but uses visual virtuosity and performative excess to subvert them and provide a critical space in which the spectator is free to make hypotheses about the wider context of events.[12] The *mise en scène* of spatial relationships becomes a code by which meanings expressed in the dialogues are repeated, or meanings not verbalized are articulated. Space is depicted primarily to facilitate the entry of the historical and cultural context into the narrative and to provide for the play of metaphorical association. Rosi is economically contrasting two dimensions of globalization, the fundamentally different aims of the political agenda of nation-states and the economic power of multinational corporations.[13]

Visual excess, visual elements that are surplus to narrative requirements, creates a sense of heightened reality. It indicates the presence of melodramatic tensions and also constitutes the directorial stylistic flourishes that indicate the presence of the director, both of which are necessary to art and quality cinema for marketing purposes.[14] In this film, visual excess is present both in environments that are coded as modern and those that are coded as traditional. Modern décors of offices, corridors, meeting rooms and mediatic spaces include beautifully composed wide-angle long shots, patternings of lights and shiny surfaces, plate glass windows, reflections, straight lines, stylish modern lights and architectural fittings, and cool color tones. Traditional décors include offices cluttered with objects connoting power and upper-class lifestyles: banks of books; ornate architectural features and lamps; baroque curls on chairs, mirrors, ceilings, and large desks; and a warm yellow color palette. Visual excess and opposing visual régimes therefore represent the tension between order and modernity, and disorder and elite interests. Internal conflicts are externalized. This conflict of visual styles has been characterized by Omar Calabrese as a neo-baroque device to indicate complex situations and the rejection of stability.[15] In this respect the neo-baroque in Italy is an expression of the postmodern undermining of the grand metanarratives. By the foregrounding of disruption and excess, doubt and ambiguity, traditional versions of social and political organization are called into question.

Fluidity, ambiguity, doubts, and excess expressed visually or in monstrous characters or in the performance of violence are all elements of the template of *film noir*. They can also be used by political filmmakers as techniques to visualize the tension between one system that aims to present itself as simple and natural, but that operates through complicated alliances of an elite class, and another that seeks for rational explanations and to discredit the other system and reveal its inner workings and true nature. Rosi signals that his own investigation is part of the rational process. Calabrese suggests that in postmodern, neo-baroque works, order and disorder, classical and Baroque, coexist as signifying systems.[16] So, in *Il caso Mattei*, there is an oscillation between simplicity and complexity as the disruptions disturb the equilibrium, the simple explanation. Understanding is achieved therefore by small steps, hypotactically, until a bigger picture is visible.

The making of *Il caso Mattei* represents a particular historical juncture when the events of ten years earlier become "infused with significance."[17] One period of enormous economic and social change, the 1960s, provided an opportunity for intellectuals in another period of political and economic upheaval (1968 to the 1970s) to identify and interpellate an educated audience and to encourage awareness of the formations of hegemonic blocs that were not in their interests. *Il caso Mattei* won the *Palme d'or* at the 1972 Cannes Film Festival, a cultural event that would ensure that it received press consideration, even if its controversial subject was not well known outside Italy. Since the corruption trials of the early 1990s, events in Italy have furnished proofs that international economic alliances whose interests are purely financial and that have no territorial allegiance exist; that alliances between the mafia and right-wing politicians in Sicily existed and continue to exist; and that the French Secret Service has employed violent means to further French ends.

The history of modern Italy has been marked by traumatic events and massive social change, events perceived as beyond individual control and profoundly threatening. Mattei's death was only one of many unexplained accidents, murders, or assassinations in Italian history. Cumulatively these events constitute constant affronts to educated or political classes who believe in democratic ideals, and they are evidence of wounds to the Italian body politic. As Susannah Radstone has argued, trauma theory is less useful as a term that "refers" to a catastrophic event than "to the revised understandings of referentiality it prompts."[18] This is especially relevant in the case of Italian cinema, with its constant references to the "real" world of Italian politics or social life, where there is perceived to be too much at stake not to attempt to make sense of everyday reality. Rosi's approach to the historical events of Mattei's assassination displays the elements identified by Humphrey as typifying trauma narratives, in which "issues of referentiality, historical memory, and authorship (even subjectivity) become spectacularly foregrounded."[19] *Noir* elements and visual excess are used to indicate a dissatisfaction with official versions of events and/or to evoke a dysfunctional world, but the codes and conventions of expository cinema are constantly used to persuade the audience of the accuracy and authenticity of Rosi's reconstruction of elements in Mattei's life.

In the 1970s Francesco Rosi was criticized for being too susceptible to Mattei's charisma to be appropriately critical of him, as well as for not naming names. In fact, Rosi's careful examination of the context of Mattei's career generates an extremely subtle analysis of why he was killed. Mattei's partisan background and desire for a modern, equitable society set him apart from the classist, corrupt, and reactionary factions in Italian society, whether those of the traditional power elite or the mafia. Both of these reacted violently to modernizing currents that threatened them. As Anthony Giddens has suggested, the postwar world required dynamic institutions with a globalizing scope.[20] Representing state industrial capitalism, Mattei's allegiance was to his country, Italy, and this ethical framework underpinned all his actions (even those condemned as unethical). He was open to alliances with other countries that he perceived as being the victims of unethical behavior by stronger nations or cartels. This inevitably brought him into conflict with the military and economic interests of another, more powerful nation-state, France. Moreover, Mattei's political agenda was both local and global, and it therefore upset the similar transnational objectives of major oil corporations. Ironically, Mattei died because of these institutional conflicts that are now recognized as the consequences of globalization. Enrico Mattei's death was traumatic precisely because he represented an attempt to introduce modern governmental practices (of all sorts) into Italian civic life. His attempt failed, and similar attempts have failed at regular intervals ever since. Francesco Rosi recognized these tensions between the local and the global, modernity and tradition, and left hypotheses open. This recognition has allowed the film to resonate further in the thirty years since it was made.

Notes

1. Michael Ryan and Douglas Kellner, *Camera Politica: The Politics and Ideology of Contemporary Hollywood Film* (Bloomington: Indiana University Press, 1988), 17.
2. Mary P. Wood, "Cultural Space as Political Metaphor: the Case of the European 'Quality' Film" (2000), http://www.mediasalles.it/crl_wood.htm.
3. Francesco Rosi and Eugenio Scalfari, *Il caso Mattei: Un 'corsaro' al servizio della Repubblica* (Bologna: Capelli, 1972).
4. There now exists a considerable range of publications devoted to identifying those responsible for Mattei's death. It is clear from these, and from "conspiracy" websites such as http://www.misteriditalia.com, the degree of research undertaken by Rosi and the level of condensation of the facts. Li Vigni, for

example, devotes a whole chapter to the sequence of Mattei's political strategy in North Africa and American reactions to it. Benito Li Vigni, *Il caso Mattei: Un giallo italiano* (Rome: Editori Riuniti, 2003), 53–107.

5. Bill Nichols, *Ideology and the Image* (Bloomington: Indiana University Press, 1981), 173.

6. John Ellis, *Visible Fictions* (London: Routledge and Kegan Paul, 1982), 134.

7. Roman Jakobson, *Selected Writings*, vol. 3, *Poetry of Grammar and the Grammar of Poetry*, ed. Stephen Rudy, 23–26 (The Hague: Mouton, 1981).

8. Umberto Eco, *Lector in fibula* 2nd ed. (Milan: Tascabili Bompiani, 1986), 111–18.

9. Italian mystery fiction has conventionally been published with yellow covers, hence the shorthand term, *giallo*. Italian *films noirs* frequently use this color to economically suggest mysteries. Mary P. Wood, "The Dark Side of the Mediterranean: Italian Film Noir," in *European Film Noir*, ed. Andrew Spicer (Manchester: Manchester University Press, 2007).

10. Norman Fairclough, *Language and Power* (London: Longman, 1989), 27.

11. Bryan S. Turner, *Status* (Milton Keynes: Open University Press, 1988), 11.

12. Ndalianis considers that the purpose of the combination of virtuosity and illusionism is precisely this critical space formed by the revelation of the constructedness of the illusion. Angela Ndalianis, *Neo-Baroque Aesthetics and Contemporary Entertainment* (Cambridge: Massachusetts Institute of Technology Press, 2004), 165–71.

13. Anthony Giddens, *The Consequences of Modernity* (London: Polity, 1991), 70–71.

14. Mary P. Wood, "Francesco Rosi: Heightened Reality," in *Projections 8*, ed. John Boorman and Walter Donohue, 272–95 (London: Faber and Faber, 1998).

15. Omar Calabrese, *Neo-Baroque: A Sign of the Times*, trans. Charles Lambert (Princeton, NJ: Princeton University Press, 1992), 25.

16. Calabrese, *Neo-Baroque*, 194.

17. Mark Fenster, *Conspiracy Theories: Secrecy and Power in American Culture* (Minneapolis: University of Minneapolis Press, 1999), 65.

18. Susannah Radstone, "Trauma and Screen Studies: Opening the Debate," *Screen* 42, no. 2 (2001): 188–92.

19. Daniel Humphrey, "Authorship, history and the dialectic of trauma: Derek Jarman's 'The Last of England,'" *Screen* 44, no. 2 (2003): 208–15.

20. Giddens, *The Consequences of Modernity*, 16.

5

The Death of Giuseppe Pinelli: Truth, Representation, Memory

John Foot

Events: A Selection

Friday, December 12, 1969, 4:37 PM. A bomb explodes in the Bank of Agriculture in Piazza Fontana, Milan. The bank is packed with clients. Fourteen people are killed immediately, two more die in hospital soon after the massacre, and eighty-eight are injured. Another bomb is found unexploded in the nearby Commercial Bank. Another three bombs explode in Rome, causing a number of injuries. Up to 4,000 leftist activists are arrested across Italy. Giuseppe "Pino" Pinelli, Milanese anarchist, is also called in for questioning to the central police station in Milan.

December 15, 1969. The funeral is held for the victims of the massacre. That same afternoon Pietro Valpreda, anarchist, is arrested in the Milanese law courts (where he had gone to answer charges of "offending the Pope") and taken to Rome for questioning about the bombs. At around midnight on December 15, Pinelli plummets from the fourth floor office window of Luigi Calabresi, the police official in charge of the investigations into the Piazza Fontana bomb. Pinelli dies on the way to a hospital.

October 1970. A libel case brought by Calabresi against the left-wing newspaper *Lotta Continua* begins in the Palazzo di Giustizia in Milan.

December 1970. Dario Fo's *Accidental Death of an Anarchist* opens in Milan.

December 12, 1970. Huge protest demonstrations are held all across Italy. The far left adopts the slogan "The massacre is by the State."

May 17, 1972. Calabresi is shot dead outside his house in Milan. In 1988 three ex-leaders of *Lotta Continua* will be arrested for the murder. After numerous trials, appeals and a re-trial, Adriano Sofri, Ovidio Bompressi and Giorgio Pietrostefani are condemned for the murder and given life sentences.

October 27, 1975. Final sentence is reached on the Pinelli case. Judge D'Ambrosio concludes that the anarchist, after three days of tense negotiations, lack of sleep, and mental torture, had suffered from an "active illness" (*malore attivo*) that had led to him "falling" from the window.

1977. A plaque is unveiled in Piazza Fontana. Its inscription reads as follows:

TO GIUSEPPE PINELLI
ANARCHIST RAILWAY WORKER
AN INNOCENT MAN KILLED IN THE POLICE STATION ON 16.12.1969
MILANESE STUDENTS AND DEMOCRATS

2006. This plaque is removed during the night by order of the Mayor of Milan, Giuseppe Albertini. The new plaque has a slightly different wording, describing Pinelli as "dead" instead of "killed." Three days later, a group of anarchists put up a copy of the old plaque next to the new one. The two plaques remain side-by-side to this day.

The Pinelli Case

Ever since Giuseppe Pinelli's death in December 1969, controversy has raged on about how he died, and why. The facts themselves have never been agreed upon. Numerous versions exist of this event, and new versions continue to appear nearly forty years after the original event. These divisions have continued to separate the ways in which Pinelli is remembered, culminating in the existence of two very similar plaques dedicated to the anarchist, in the same place, but with different messages about the circumstances of his death.

The first dividing line can be drawn between two contrasting versions of Pinelli's dramatic "fall" from the police station window in 1969. The police said immediately that Pinelli had committed suicide; they added (falsely) that he was "deeply implicated" in the Piazza Fontana bombing. Meanwhile, suspicions emerged that something different had happened. Another version took shape, which claimed that Pinelli had been murdered. The evidence for this version lay above all in the tangle of lies and jumbled versions issued by the police and in the refusal to believe that Pinelli was the type of person who would have committed suicide. Moreover, many blamed the police for Pinelli's death whether he had been murdered or not. After all, he was being held illegally for a crime he had nothing to do with, and he had been under interrogation for three days and nights. More extreme versions talk of torture of various kinds.

The last judicial word on the Pinelli case came in 1975, and it was a compromise between the two broad versions offered by the police and the

"movement." According to Italian justice, Pinelli had not committed suicide, *nor* had he been murdered. He had suffered from an "active illness," in
part due to the treatment of the police, and had "fallen" from the window
to his death. This version satisfied nobody and has been the object of
ridicule ever since. We still have no clear idea of the events in that small
police room that night. Many people know what happened, not least the
policemen who were there with Pinelli, but the truth has not materialized.
This uncertainty has only exacerbated the conflict over the memory of the
Pinelli case, symbolized by the "war of the plaques" in Milan in 2006.

Pinelli's death became a central event during the 1970s in Italy for a
number of historical and cultural reasons. First, the dramatic, almost cinematic nature of the event aroused interest and debate, as did the botched
cover-up and police lies, which were easy to rebut. Second, Pinelli's death
was intimately connected with other shocking events of that period—the
Piazza Fontana bomb for which he was arrested, but also the 1972 murder
of police inspector Luigi Calabresi, blamed by many for Pinelli's "murder."
Third, the form of the Pinelli case tapped into left-wing mythology and
history. Many drew parallels with the unexplained death of other anarchists in similar circumstances in Italy and the USA. Pinelli's "fall" was part
of a longer story that aroused memories and passions beyond the event
itself. Finally, the Pinelli case was a fascinating detective story, with
twists and turns, mysteries and misrepresentations, and a cast of shady
personalities.

The iconography of "Pinelli" was powerful, inspiring paintings, books,
films, plays, poems, and songs. Pinelli's campaign developed quickly into a
crucial component of the movement for justice (and revenge) linked to
Piazza Fontana and the "strategy of tension." Moreover, the campaign kept
the case open, leading to the creation of unforgettable images and the rak-
ing over of macabre details. A number of myths became part of left folk-
lore. The Pinelli case also contained other characters who helped the
drama of the story, above all Pinelli's wife Licia and their two young daughters.[1] Within months of his death, the Pinelli case had became part of the
very identity of the left. To position oneself politically meant taking sides
on Pinelli. There could be no grey zone here. Language itself became an
object for discussion—a dividing line between left and right. For many,
Pinelli had not just fallen; rather, he had "fallen," he had "been suicided," he
had "precipitated."

Bodies dominate the Pinelli case. Photos of Pinelli's corpse were used
in propaganda posters produced by the left. The injuries, or supposed
injuries, to Pinelli were gone over in minute detail, as were his various
fractures. One strong left myth—that Pinelli had been killed by a karate

chop—was linked to the examination of a swelling on the anarchist's shoulder. The x-rays of his back were published in the press. Everyone knew Pinelli's exact height: 1m 67cm. Pinelli's body was buried, then re-exhumed, and new autopsies were carried out; then it was re-buried, then re-exhumed, and finally re-buried in Carrara. The first exhumation was described in minute and gory detail in all the major newspapers. A dummy representing Pinelli was thrown out of a window four times in front of photographers and film cameras. Pinelli's trip to the hospital was re-run by the investigating judge. Images of Pinelli's face dominated demonstrations, posters, and obituaries for years.[2]

Representations of a "Murder": Films, Plays, Texts

Film

Pinelli's "case" inspired numerous texts, many of which were part of the campaign itself. An examination of some of these texts provides us with key information concerning the ways in which Pinelli became a posthumous political figure and helps us to understand the various versions of his death. Our first text is the least known outside of Italy and is rarely shown today. Called *Tre ipotesi sulla morte di Giuseppe Pinelli* (*Three Hypotheses Concerning the Death of Giuseppe Pinelli*) (1970) it was a militant agitprop film designed to be shown at political meetings and to provoke debate. However, it 'starred' some extremely famous actors, above all Gian Maria Volonté, one of Italian cinema's best-known performers at the time.

The film is shot in an immediate, agitprop style. We see the clapper-board, and the action seems (but isn't) unrehearsed and spontaneous. None of the actors are in costume, or wear make-up. They are all sweating. Volonté, in jeans, holds a microphone and speaks directly to the camera, and the action moves at a fast pace. Actors read from scripts and newspapers. The effect is gripping—as if the film is being created before our eyes. Unsteady zoom and close-ups are also used by the director Elio Petri. Volonté introduces the group of actors as "lavoratori dello spettacolo [worker of performance]" (and there are no real credits). The 1960s and 1970s were a time of experimentation in cinema and theater. Here there is a clear debt to Brechtian theater, communicating the political message without using props. Many actors and directors took their work out of theaters to the streets and into factories. They wanted to break down the "fourth wall" between the audience and performers. This film is an example of this kind of work applied to the cinematic form.

Three versions of Pinelli's death are portrayed in the film, with ferocious irony. The setting is claustrophobic, as it must have been for Pinelli himself. The first two versions reproduced are those given by the police. The words of the officers involved are repeated deadpan and so are emptied of all credibility. Finally—after some readings from newspapers and other texts—the Left's version is given (and shown). "Pinelli" is beaten, tortured, and thrown out of the window. Volonté concludes, with barely suppressed anger, that Pinelli was the "latest in a long line of suicided anarchists."

Produced with great skill in a kind of "directed-spontaneity." *Tre ipotesi* reflects perfectly the ways in which the lies of the state became part of the political campaign not just for "justice for Pinelli," but in general. A state that is willing to murder its citizens and then lie about it is a state that needs reforming, at the very least. Pinelli"s "murder" thus became an extremely powerful weapon in the struggle of the left in the 1970s. We have little evidence about the dissemination of the film, but it was shown at countless meetings and was still doing the rounds in the 1990s. Short and punchy, the film was intended to provoke debate, and anger. It was a perfect case of agitprop—a political "commercial," extremely modern in its style and its message.

Art

The saga of Enrico Baj's epic painting—*I funerali dell'anarchico Pinelli* (*The Funerals of the Anarchist Pinelli*) is not just a fascinating story, it also provides us with an insight into the complicated connections between art, memory, politics, and the Pinelli case. In 1971 Baj, already famous for his powerful anti-establishment work, such as *Parata a sei* (*Parade of Six Generals*, 1964), was offered the opportunity to put on a large exhibition by the *Comune di Milano*. Baj decided to accept, but with just one major new work. After discussions, this proposal was accepted. Baj started work on *I funerali* in 1971.

The origins of this painting are closely linked to the space in which it was intended to be shown. In 1953 Baj had seen Picasso's *Guernica* exhibited in the extraordinary setting of the *Sala delle Cariatidi* in Palazzo Reale in the center of Milan. This hall, formerly a luxurious ballroom, had suffered bomb damage during the war, and the statues around the walls had all lost various pieces. The *Comune* decided to leave this room with this damage "intact" as a testimony to the memory of war. This decision left the room as an extremely suggestive setting, and Baj was struck by the position of *Guernica*. In the 1970s, Baj became interested in the Pinelli case, and his long-term project to revisit the Futurist Carlo Carrà's 1911 painting, *I funerali dell'anarchico Galli* metamorphosed into a work based on Pinelli, intended for the same space where *Guernica* had been hung.

Baj's research for the painting was meticulous. He befriended the Pinelli family and borrowed books from the anarchist's library. By 1972, after seven months of work, the painting was ready. It consisted of a huge (twelve meters long and four meters high) set of thirteen jigsaw pieces that fitted together to present a series of powerful images. The painting was not of a funeral but represented a set of figures grouped around a man falling from a window. On the left, militants, journalists, and other figures (one is based on Baj himself) are crying, pointing or making clenched fist salutes. Two red and black flags, one with an anarchist sign, are flying. A small child carries a red flag and clenches her fist. Above the figures, hands stretch down, some holding bottles or knives. One is throwing a grenade. "Pinelli" is still alive and held by his foot from above.

On the right, there is a set of "Baj-like" figures similar to those used in his *I Generali* works of the 1960s. These inhuman forms, overlain with medals, bare their teeth and look ready to attack the demonstration on the left. A policeman appears to be indicating where Pinelli will fall. Other figures carry guns, truncheons, or bombs. Three figures stand in the foreground of the painting: Pinelli's daughters on the left, one of whom is covering her face, while the other holds out her hands in an expression of grief. On the right, Licia is perhaps the most Picasso-like figure of all. Naked, she is doubled over in pain. The front of the collage is covered in rags and other materials. One final detail remains—the window. At the Milan exhibition, the window was placed not over Pinelli but above the door where visitors would leave. The window contains four hands that appear to have thrown Pinelli out, and two double columns. In almost all the exhibitions since that at Milan, the window has been placed directly above Pinelli.

In the catalogue Baj included sections from books from Pinelli's library on anarchist history and a provocative essay entitled "What Is a Painting?" The essay described Pinelli as a scapegoat, and Baj concluded that he had produced a "representation . . . of the violence he was subjected to, of Licia's, Claudia's and Silvia's grief."[3] Invitations went out, posters were put up all over the city, and 2,000 copies of the catalogue were published. All seemed ready for the opening of the show, set for 5:30 PM on May 17, 1972.

That morning, police-chief Luigi Calabresi (identified by the left as responsible for Pinelli's death) was murdered in Milan outside his home. Almost immediately, the show was cancelled by the *Comune*. When Baj arrived at Palazzo Reale, he found a crowd waiting for the doors to open. A handwritten notice had been pinned to the locked doors—the exhibition could not open for "technical reasons." Baj demanded to know what these were and bombarded the *Comune* with telegrams.

The affair hit the national press, causing anger on the right and the left, though for different reasons. Far-right newspapers printed violent attacks aimed at the administration, Baj, and the picture itself (which they had only seen in photographs). Baj was associated with the so-called moral organizers of the Calabresi murder. On the left a campaign was started to "reopen" the show. Administrators were forced to admit that the "technical reasons" were an invention and that, as everyone knew, the exhibition had been canceled due to Calabresi's murder. The show never opened, and the painting became taboo in Milan. Baj was later given an exhibition in 1974 without *I funerali*.

I funerali dell'anarchico Pinelli, a work produced for the dramatic setting of the Palazzo Reale, has never been exhibited in that space. Nonetheless, it has contributed to the diffusion of the Pinelli case all around the world. To date *I funerali* has been shown in numerous cities in the United States, Europe, and Italy. Usually, in the various catalogues produced for these exhibitions, critics give a potted history of the Pinelli case and the censorship of *I funerali*.[4] At some exhibitions, *I funerali* has been the spark for further initiatives surrounding the case. In one city, extracts from Fo's *Accidental Death of an Anarchist* were read in front of the collage. At another "happening" actors and dancers dressed like the figures in the painting merged with and then came out of the area of the collage and danced around the town's streets.

I funerali has also contributed to the memory of the case in other ways, in a highly original osmosis between art and politics. Baj gave copies of some of the figures in the collage to anarchist organizations in Milan, where I discovered them hanging in late 1997, in the Giuseppe Pinelli Archive. During demonstrations these figures are often taken out and paraded. The upside-down Pinelli usually heads anniversary marches. Photos and close-ups of the characters are frequently used to illustrate articles and books on the case. The cover pages of various books carry extracts from the painting. Baj himself gave the painting to Licia Pinelli, who sold it to the Galleria Marconi in the city, whence it travels to Baj's various exhibitions all over the world. It is probably his most famous work.

This story ended in February 2000, when the Galleria Marconi in Milan decided to show *I funerali* to a Milanese public. In 2004, *I funerali* was placed in the Palazzo Brera in an extraordinary location surrounded by statues. These shows attracted little attention in the press, although many people were interested in seeing *I funerali*. The uncontroversial showing of Baj's tragic and powerful work of art, twenty-eight years after it had caused such debate and more than thirty years after the Piazza Fontana massacres, seemed to indicate that the violent divisions that had been produced by the bomb, by the Pinelli case, and by the Calabresi case had, at last, been overcome. However, this finale also showed that the memories linked to Piazza Fontana had faded into the background, and there was a real danger that the historical lessons linked to that tragic moment of Italian history had not been learned; not only that, they had not even been forgotten, they were simply being ignored.

Theater

With *Accidental Death of an Anarchist La Comune* intervened directly in the denunciation of the "state massacres," the murder of comrade Pinelli and the anti-working class plans adopted by the Italian bourgeoisie. We adopted a form of political theater intended as part of the struggle.

—Compagni senza censura, *1973*

The important thing is to move fast, to intervene as things are happening.

—*Dario Fo*[5]

Dario Fo's play *The Accidental Death of an Anarchist* is the main reason why the Pinelli case is famous throughout the world. Fo's play has been translated into many languages and produced in theaters in Europe and the United States. The play was cited when Fo was awarded the Nobel prize in 1997 and remains perhaps his most celebrated work both inside and outside Italy. Thanks to *Accidental Death*, theater audiences across the world learned of the Pinelli case, of Calabresi, of the Milan of the 1960s. I remember vividly going to visit the police station in Via Fatebenefratelli on my arrival in Milan in 1988 after seeing the play in London (twice) while I was at school.

The play was first performed on December 5, 1970, in an abandoned workshop in Via Colletta in Milan. The poster for the play consisted of an upside-down, "falling" silhouette. The ongoing Calabresi-*Lotta Continua* trial provided new material for the play that Fo inserted into the script. At every performance, Fo would introduce the play and give news on the trial and the case. A debate would usually follow each performance.[6] In Milan the show was a sellout. Over the next few years, *Accidental Death* was performed by Fo and his company at least 300 times all across Italy, often to big audiences. Fo claimed that 300,000 people had seen the play.[7] In Turin, after being refused the Theatre Duse, *Accidental Death* filled the cavernous city sports hall. The play performed a "role of counter-information and daily news," mixing moments from the case with fictional scenes invented by Fo and his collaborators. In addition, a group of journalists and lawyers passed on information to *La Comune*, some of which had not been published.

One of the main aims of the play was to expose the absurdity of the official version of Pinelli's death. In this sense the play's text is best read alongside Camilla Cederna's *Pinelli*, and the part of the journalist in the play seems inspired by Cederna herself.[8] One of the main characters in the play was clearly based on Calabresi, right down to the polo-neck sweater and "tic" noted by Cederna during the Calabresi-*Lotta Continua* trials. Fo adopted the device of "setting" the play in the 1920s, but this historical background was not sustained and just allowed for different names to be used. Yet *Accidental Death* was a real play—a work of fiction—and not the pure agitprop of later productions. This allowed the work to gain worldwide acclaim. Nonetheless, the play has quite clearly become dated and is incomprehensible to many young people today. In Fo's later play based on the Sofri case, a long prologue was added to explain the events of 1969. In 1970, his audience would have been well informed about these issues and about the main characters represented in the play.[9] *Accidental Death* is rarely seen in Italy, although Fo revived the play in defense of Pinelli's plaque in 1987, and it continues to be performed around anniversaries relating to Pinelli and Piazza Fontana.

Books

A few key books turn up in the libraries of left-wing (or formerly left-wing) Italians. One volume that everybody purchased and read in the 1970s was *Strage di Stato* (State Massacre). This short book was one of the first, and most successful, cases of "counter-information" in Italian publishing and journalistic history. It first came out in June 1970 as a supplement to the journal *Controborghese* before becoming a separate book.[10] Ten libel cases were opened against the book in the first few months, which eventually led to three trials. The legal process continued for almost ten years. The authors were anonymous and included a number of young lawyers and militants. Very little research has been done on the key texts that circulated in the 1960s and 1970s. Among this body of texts, *Strage di Stato* was interesting, in part because it was one of the few such books to be entirely Italian. (Many of the other texts were of U.S. origin, for example, the works of Marcuse and Kerouac.) Above all, *Strage di Stato* provided the movement with a well-documented series of answers to questions about the "strategy of tension." According to the book Pinelli had been murdered, and the bombs in Milan and elsewhere were the product of a complicated set of alliances between neofascists and parts of the state machine. The very title of the book became one of the key slogans of the moment. It was also a great story, full of elaborate pretense, detective-like investigation, and shady goings-on. The book uncovered fascists pretending to be anarchists and left groups infiltrated to the hilt by spies and agents. Nothing was what it seemed.

Moreover the book was well written, clear, and imaginatively marketed with modern graphic design. It was an enormous success. One hundred thirty thousand copies were sold and, a new, revised edition was produced. Pinelli appeared on the cover of the new edition, and the book was dedicated to him. Five editions had been issued by October 1971, and the book was translated into French and Swedish. *Strage di Stato* also tapped into the work of an extraordinary body of investigative journalists who dedicated themselves to the Pinelli and Piazza Fontana stories, above all Marco Nozza, Giorgio Bocca, and Corrado Stajano. The most important of this group was a woman who had previously worked in a different kind of journalism but became radicalized by the events of 1969: Camilla Cederna.

In 1970 a dramatic trial—intimately linked to the Pinelli case—opened in Milan. Following a long press campaign against him, with explicit accusations of murder, Luigi Calabresi decided to sue the leftist newspaper *Lotta Continua* for libel. The court case was seen by the left as the only way of reopening the Pinelli affair. Finally, the policemen involved could be interrogated in a public court, including Calabresi himself. Cederna followed the whole trial, making her account of it into a best-selling book. *Pinelli: Una finestra sulla strage* (Pinelli: A Window on the Massacre), came out with Feltrinelli in October 1971 and had already run to three editions by the end of that month. It was a mixture of reportage and passionate political journalism, embellished by Cederna's superb eye for detail. It read like a gripping detective story. With *Pinelli: Una finestra sulla strage*, the Pinelli campaign reached a peak, and a number of intellectuals were moved to sign a petition in *L'Espresso* calling for justice for the anarchist and his family. One of the main aims of her book was to expose the contradictions (and stupidity) of the defense adopted by the various police witnesses. In this sense the book must be compared to Fo's play. Cederna also appeared in front of Baj's painting, notebook in hand. The various texts produced from the Pinelli case tended to cannibalize each other, creating a palimpsest with layers of meaning, myth, and memory.

Conclusion: The Importance of the Pinelli Case—An Italian Dreyfus?

The Piazza Fontana massacre is an upsetting novel, full of bodies, half-invented personalities, innocent victims and people who fought for truth and justice. It is also the story of a society: above all Milan, divided in two, full of passion, fervor, hatred . . . like Paris during the Dreyfus case, as described by Proust.

—*Corrado Stajano*[11]

If the truth is buried underground, it swells and grows and becomes so explosive that the day it bursts, it blows everything wide open along with it. Time will tell . . . let them dare to summon me before a court of law! Let the inquiry be held in broad daylight.

—*Emile Zola*[12]

Apart from the Stajano's brief observation cited above, no serious comparison has been made between the Dreyfus case, which divided France at the turn of the century, and the Pinelli and Valpreda cases. In fact, some of the similarities between the three "affairs" are striking. Both scandals went to the heart of state authority and the relationship between justice, truth, and the legal process. Both cases divided major cities—Paris and Milan—down the middle. Both Dreyfus and Valpreda were imprisoned unjustly for years. Libel cases were used to reopen the cases because of the corruption and conservatism of the legal systems involved. Counter-information was used to combat the official versions of the authorities. Trials were moved ostensibly for reasons of public order, but often for more direct political motives. In the Dreyfus case, Zola's second libel trial was moved to Versailles "so as to limit the risks to public order,"[13] Valpreda's trial was shifted to Catanzaro.

The Dreyfus case was also full of cover-ups, forgeries, documents, interminable trials, suicides and mysterious deaths, riots, and courtroom shouting matches. The process was extremely long and dragged out. The army only officially apologized to Dreyfus in 1995, a hundred years after his arrest. Families played a key part of the battle for justice: Dreyfus's wife Lucie, his tireless brother Mathieu, and Licia Pinelli. Honest individuals stood out against the general process of misinformation and cover up. Journalists played a key part in the whole affair, from Zola's *J'Accuse* to Cederna's *Pinelli*.[14] Useful comparisons can also be made with the investigations into the Kennedy assassination in the United States, or into numerous other more minor miscarriages of justice that have attracted public attention this century, from Sacco and Vanzetti to Enzo Tortora to the Birmingham six.

But of course, there were huge differences between the two (or three) affairs. The centrality of anti-Semitism in the Dreyfus case, the mass mobilization of the left in the Pinelli and Valpreda affairs, the historic context, the national question inspired by the spying charges in France. But perhaps the greatest difference was in the protagonists. Dreyfus was an army officer. The left was slow to take up his case, and he never inspired much sympathy among the working class. Pinelli was far more popular—a peaceful, working-class, family man. As some workers argued in France, "Dreyfus would have fired on us too."

The Pinelli case—which is now largely forgotten—played a key role in the politics and history of the 1970s. It was part of the general radicalization of the left after 1969 that led many to take up arms as terrorists. Pinelli also provided yet another example of divided memory, whereby a crucial event produced different sets of memories and different versions of what had happened. With the demise of the anarchist movement, the importance of Pinelli went into decline, and the main protagonists of the story gave up hope of either justice being done or the truth emerging. Finally, the Pinelli mystery produced an extraordinary series of texts—films, newspaper articles, books, plays, and art—which built on and lived off the case. None of this was able to procure something very simple from the Italian state: a credible version of what had actually happened to a forty-one-year-old anarchist railway worker, innocent of any crime, who entered the police station in Milan by the front door, and died three days later.

Notes

1. For Licia Pinelli see Piero Scaramucci, *Licia Pinelli. Una storia quasi soltanto mia* (Milan: Mondadori, 1982).
2. "Quella morte di Pinelli in questura," *L'Unità*, December 15,1979.
3. "Cosa è un quadro?," *Baj, un quadro* (Milan: 1972), 45.
4. The best account is Gabriele Huber, "Forza e aporia di un'immagine di denuncia," *Enrico Baj* (Milan: 1994), 417–29.
5. *Le commedie di Dario Fo*, vol. 7 (Turin: Einaudi, 1988), 82.
6. The evidence we have, however, indicates that these debates had little to do with the Pinelli case.
7. *Le commedie di Dario Fo*, 83.
8. For Cederna's description of the play, see Camilla Cederna, *Pinelli: una finestra sulla strage* (Milan: Feltrinelli, 1971), 102–4.
9. See, for the text, *Le commedie di Dario Fo* and *Dario Fo: Morte accidentale di un anarchico*, ed. Jennifer Lorch (Manchester: Manchester University Press, 1997).

10. *La strage di stato dal golpe di Borghese all'incriminazione di Calabresi, la nuova sinistra* (Rome: 1970), later republished as *La strage di stato. Controinchiesta* (Rome: Samonà e Savelli, 1971).
11. "Piazza Fontana, qualcuno indaga ancora," *Corriere della Sera*, April 2, 1993.
12. Emile Zola, *The Dreyfus Affair: 'J'accuse' and Other Writings*, ed. Alain Pagès, trans. Eleanor Levieux (New Haven CT: Yale University Press, 1996), 52–53.
13. Eric Cahm, *The Dreyfus Affair in French Society and Politics* (London: Longman, 1996), 115.
14. The most thorough account is Jean-Denis Bredin, *The Affair: the Case of Alfred Dreyfus* (New York: G. Braziller, 1986).

6

The Genoa G8 and the Death of Carlo Giuliani

Duncan McDonnell

Introduction: Photos and Lenses

The death of Carlo Giuliani during the 2001 G8 in Genoa is encapsulated for many by a photograph, taken by Dylan Martinez of Reuters, which featured prominently in the Italian and international media the day after his shooting (see Figure 6.1). In it, Giuliani appears to be less than a meter away from the trapped conscript *carabiniere* policeman, Mario Placanica, and closing in swiftly on him with a fire extinguisher that he is ready to turn on. However, like all those accounts of Giuliani's death that have been presented as "the truth of what happened," the photo in fact only offers us an interpretation, predicated on the position (be it physical or ideological) of its creator and the lens through which events in Piazza Alimonda on July 20, 2001, are viewed. The image that emerges is thus dependent on a series of prior conscious and unconscious choices. In Martinez's case, these relate to his location in the piazza, the angle, frame, and timing of the photo, and the lens used to take it: a set of choices that determine the eventual composition and form of the photographer's representation of the reality of the scene before him. As Martine Joly observes, we tend to believe that the photograph "is a perfect copy of reality, a perfect mimesis," yet Martinez's choices, and in particular his use of a 70/200 mm telescopic lens, compress and distort that reality.[1] For example, as we can see from another much less-published picture, taken by Marco D'Auria of RaiNet from a different angle and without a telescopic lens, Giuliani appears to be at least three meters away from Placanica at the moment of

Figure 6.1

Martinez's famous shot.[2] This raises another key element determining our interpretation of the photograph: its timing—"the decisive moment," as Henri Cartier-Bresson called it. Although presented by the media as a faithful representation of "the shooting of Giuliani," on which we can base our reading of the event, in fact neither this photo nor any of the others taken by Martinez in Piazza Alimonda that day show us Placanica's "decisive moment," i.e., when he actually fires his gun. As Roland Barthes says, the photograph is "the absolute particular, the sovereign Contingency."[3] Unlike film, it does not offer a sequence or a span of moving images—a temporal and spatial context in which we can locate and better understand each frame. Rather, it offers us a single, biased reading of a single moment in time, a highly subjective and confined representation of whom and what we see. Thus the readers or viewers presented with Martinez's photo may think they are looking at an image of the shooting of Giuliani, but in fact they are looking at a *representation* of a moment *before* the shooting.[4] Moreover, their reading of the photograph and its meaning are shaped not only by their own preset lenses but also by the caption beneath the photo and the text of the article or news feature in which it appears. Yet another set of angles and lenses. Yet another set of subjective choices, representations and interpretations.

This chapter discusses the death of Carlo Giuliani and its diverse interpretations and representations by journalists, politicians, his family, and the wider public. It argues that the only resolution to the Giuliani case appears to be that of its official "non-resolution," (i.e., its induction into the pantheon of the *Misteri Italiani* [Italian mysteries]), a set of famous cases about which, over years of investigations, trials, and public discussion, there emerge only multiple subjective "truths" and hence no consensus on the facts, much less their meaning. Contested images and interpretations run through the life of the Italian Republic from the photograph of the body of Salvatore Giuliano in Castelvetrano to that of Carlo Giuliani in Genoa. The "facts" of cases are selected, interpreted and represented according to the preset lenses through which they are seen. As with other Italian mysteries, such as the Piazza Fontana bomb or the Pier Paolo Pasolini murder, what David Moss refers to in relation to the Aldo Moro case as an "interpretive Babel" has also formed around the death of Giuliani as we are presented with a mass of conflicting information from different perspectives, resulting in an ever less-interpretive consensus.[5] Within this Babel, Giuliani is cast either as a) a brave idealist/activist, a victim of the systematic and planned police brutality that characterized the Genoa G8 and was tacitly supported by the right, or b) a violent outsider/anarchist, a symbol of the no-global movement's lawlessness, to which the left turned a blind eye. The idea that perhaps he was neither but was simply a local young man who found himself largely by chance in Piazza Alimonda at 5:27 on the afternoon of July 20, 2001, with tragic consequences, holds little sway. Bifocal lenses serve no purpose in the struggle for "the truth" in a polarized society.

Stage Design

The 2001 G8 was held a month after the Silvio Berlusconi-led center-right *Casa delle Libertà* government took office and thus presented a grand stage for the Prime Minister's first outing as an international statesman since returning to power. The attention of the international media would be focused on Genoa at a level unprecedented even for a summit of this type. This was due to a series of reasons, from it being George W. Bush's first G8 meeting, to the publicity surrounding issues such as debt relief, to the anticipated massive mobilization of a wide variety of civil society organizations, associations, and protest groups, clustered together under the umbrella term "the no-global movement."

In particular, the expected "invasion" of the no-global movement attracted a lot of attention, with many in the Italian media examining it using the same lenses through which they had long viewed the country's radical left-wing *centri sociali*, even though the groups planning to come to

Genoa ranged from the largely Catholic Lilliput network to the moderate environmentalists of Legambiente.[6] Right-wing newspapers such as *Libero* and *Il Giornale* delved even further back into public memory, adopting the lens applied by Pasolini to the *sessantottini*,[7] to condemn the no-global protestors as a new generation of "spoiled sons and daughters of the bourgeoisie," intent on attacking the poor, underpaid police.[8] Moreover, sections of the media promoted a climate of fear in which the public was told to expect a mixture of riots, bombs, balloons filled with infected blood, and even possible attacks from the air and sea.

For its part, the new government did little to assuage public anxiety. Fueling fears that Genoa would become a war zone, a *Zona Rossa* (Red Zone) was established around the *centro storico* (old city), where the summit was to be held. Huge gates and barricades were erected across the dozens of lanes and roads leading into it, and residents were only allowed to move in and out through a few heavily-manned checkpoints, where they had to display a special pass and their identity cards. The area was thus transformed into a perfect stage on which the leaders and their entourages could parade undisturbed through a fortress of picturesque deserted streets, with thousands of police between them and the protestors several kilometers away in the *Zona Gialla* (Yellow Zone). As Concita De Gregorio observes, "They made Genoa into a theatre. A giant empty theatre, ready for the mise-en-scene."[9] The city was thus ready for its media event and Berlusconi for his photo opportunity at the center of attention. However, as Daniel Dayan and Elihu Katz warn, media events are unpredictable, as something can always go wrong.[10] And on July 20, 2001, the first working day of the summit, something did go wrong, and the attention went elsewhere.

The Body

The *disobbedienti* (disobedient) cortege sets off from the Stadio Carlini (Carlini Stadium) just after 1:30 PM, on what is to be a peaceful march.[11] Between ten and twenty thousand people take part. When they arrive at the *Casa dello Studente* (Student Residence) at the top of the long Corso Gastaldi, they can see the smoke from the cars set alight around Brignole Station and Borgo Incrociati by several hundred so-called Black Block protestors who have rampaged, unchecked, through various parts of the *Zona Gialla* for much of the morning. The organizers decide to proceed slowly toward Piazza delle Americhe. They have prior permission to do this. Announcements are made saying, "This is a peaceful march, anyone who thinks differently should leave."[12] When the march arrives at Via Tolemaide near the bottom of Corso Gastaldi, the leaders of the cortege and several left-wing members of Parliament try to find someone from the police with whom they can consult about how to proceed. The march halts. The police lines move forward. Images released afterward show that nobody in the march throws anything or makes any aggressive advance. Suddenly, the police release an avalanche of tear gas canisters at head height and then charge. The marchers at the front are trapped between the police and the thousands of people, still stopped at the back. More and more violent charges follow. More tear gas is fired.[13] In the ensuing three hours, scores of people are injured and taken to a hospital. The police charge the marchers all the way back up to the *Casa dello Studente*. Many of those who fall are beaten up and arrested.[14]

Two police vans move back into Piazza Alimonda near Corso Gastaldi. At the same time, several dozen people escape from Via Montevideo into Piazza Alimonda. A photographer from Reuters starts taking pictures from the church steps. One of the police vans stalls. A number of those present attack the van. Two shots ring out. The time is 5:27. There is a body on the ground beside the police van. The van passes over the body twice and drives off. A nearby policeman shouts at the protestors: "You bastards, you've killed him with your stones."[15] A journalist, Giulietto Chiesa, arrives in Piazza Alimonda shortly afterward. He sees the body, the head of which is covered by a balaclava, and calls *La Stampa* and *Rai News 24*. The body lies on the ground for over an hour while a crowd of journalists, photographers, cameramen, police, and protestors looks on.[16] At 5:50, a doctor verifies the death of a male identified as: "Surname 'NN,' Name 'NN,' Born in 'NN,' Resident in Via 'NON RILEVABILE (UNKNOWN).'"[17] By 6:00 the images are on the Internet.

The Reconstruction

The anonymous man in Piazza Alimonda quickly acquired a set of identities in the hours and days after his death as media outlets plunged into an inflationary news spiral in which the race to be first with the news, or at least keep pace, prevailed over checking whether that news was reliable or not.[18] Similarly, there was a rush by journalists and politicians to put forward "the truth" of the event, based not on verifiable evidence (which was scarce), but on the default settings of the lenses with which they already viewed police, protesters, politics, and society in general. As Zygmunt Bauman says, the concept of "truth" forms part of the rhetoric in the battle to secure and maintain power, and the struggle between multiple "truths" can be seen in the different accounts presented of events at the Genoa G8.[19] As Giulio Anselmi wrote on the second anniversary of the shooting in

Piazza Alimonda: "we have had a television truth, a [no-global] movement truth, a government truth, and a regime truth: the first consisted solely of fire and flames, the second saw only the attacks of the police, the third shirked all responsibility, and the fourth, flying in the face of the evidence, defended 'our boys' in uniform."[20]

The processes described above swung rapidly into action following the news of a fatality in Genoa with rumor and supposition presented as fact in the competition to provide news first and establish "the truth." By 7:00 PM on July 20, websites and radio stations were referring to the death of a "Spanish" or "Basque" protestor. On the RAI 1 main evening news at 8:00, Antonio Caprarica presented "the terrible images of the dead young Spanish man, who belonged to the extremist wing of the no-global movement."[21] At 10:30, on the RAI 1 flagship current affairs show *Porta a Porta* (Door-to-Door), Bruno Vespa named the dead man as "Carlo Giuliani" and added that he was a young man with previous convictions who lived on the streets: "a *punkkabestia*."[22] Half an hour later, the police informed the Giuliani family. Vespa's information came from the Questura (police headquarters) in Genoa, which released a statement saying that the protestor who had been shot was "Carlo Giuliani, resident in Genoa" and that he had committed a series of previous offenses. Police told journalists informally, "We knew him well here at the police station. He used to beg on the streets. He was one of those, what do you call them? Punkkabestia: those guys who go around with their dogs and don"t wash. He was a dropout; he used to sleep in the lanes, in cardboard boxes. He was a bum."[23] During that evening's edition of *Porta a Porta*, the leader of the far-right *Alleanza Nazionale* and Vice Prime Minister, Gianfranco Fini, affirmed that the death of Carlo Giuliani was the result of an act of "legitimate self-defense" and, referring to the no-global movement in terms of "terrorism", added that Giuliani might have been launching "a gas bomb."[24]

The following morning, the main daily newspapers, like Fini the night before, reflected their normal political stances in their reports of what had happened in Piazza Alimonda. Thus, *Il Giornale* (owned by the Berlusconi family) led with "And so 'the people of Seattle' got their martyr," while the center-left *La Repubblica*'s title was "G8: tragedy in Genoa."[25] Newspapers also split along political lines in their use of the terms "morto" (dead) or "ucciso" (killed). Hence, *Il Tempo* opened with "Guerrilla warfare in Genoa: one dead," while *L'Unità* had "The worst possible outcome: a young man killed." Comment pieces in newspapers broadly of the center tended to follow their counterparts in RAI 1 in their version of "the truth" of how Giuliani was shot and who he was, despite the partial and unsubstantiated nature of the information at their disposal. Thus, the editor of *La Stampa*,

Marcello Sorgi, asserted that "the photos we have published document the fact that the Carabiniere fired in order to defend himself," while Costantino Muscau in the *Corriere della Sera* offered no background information on Giuliani other than the comment that "the police were already familiar with this young man: at seventeen he had been charged with resisting arrest and insulting a public official."[26]

It was not only much of the Italian media that offered a representation of Giuliani's life and death based on hearsay and biased information. Journalists from all over the world repeated a series of "facts" that emerged about Giuliani immediately after his death without checking them or at least acknowledging their potential unreliability. For example, Rory Carroll's account of the death in the British newspaper *The Observer* on July 22, 2001, entitled "The wild boy who became a martyr," begins with the line "A history student, petty criminal and outsider, Carlo Giuliani became an anarchist martyr on a street he knew well, sprinting through the cobbled lanes of his boyhood to challenge authority for the last time."[27] In addition to the bizarre statement that Giuliani was "sprinting through the cobbled lanes," which are nowhere near Piazza Alimonda nor where he grew up, Carroll faithfully reproduces the "truth" of Giuliani's life put forward by the police and the Italian right, casting him as a criminal "outsider," a repeated challenger of authority and an "anarchist martyr." Carroll then writes that "Carlo occasionally returned home to Via San Pantaleo to see his sister and father, Giuliano, whose marriage had broken up. He did so last Friday, only hours before his death." In fact, Giuliani's parents had not split up; they lived together in the family home in Genoa. Their daughter, however, lived in Milan, and their son did not return home on the day of his death.

This brings us to the Giuliani family's "truth" of what happened on July 20, 2001. In addition to providing a lot of useful biographical information about Carlo, it also shows us the extent to which it was *by chance* that he ended up in Corso Gastaldi on that day. However, in its account of what happened next, i.e., when he found himself in Piazza Alimonda beside the police jeep, picked up the fire extinguisher, and was then shot, this representation of Giuliani's death is also (understandably) heavily determined by the lenses through which his parents view the event.

There are two principal Giuliani family accounts of Carlo's death: the 2002 book *Un anno senza Carlo* (A Year Without Carlo), co-written by his parents with Antonella Marrone, and the Francesca Comencini film *Carlo Giuliani, Ragazzo* (Carlo Giuliani, A Young Man), presented at Cannes the same year, in which Haidi Giuliani acts as narrator. In addition, Concita De Gregorio's *Non lavate questo sangue* (Don't Wash This Blood), which deals more generally with the events of the G8, also includes substantial material based on interviews with the Giuliani family. From these we learn that, on the morning of his death, Carlo wakes up early in the apartment where he lives with a girl called Cristina and her young daughter. Later he and a friend talk on the phone about whether or not they will go to the G8 protests. A few days previously, he had told his father: "I don't know if I'm going to go [to the march]. I might go to the beach instead. We'll see." In the end, Giuliani says to his friend, "OK, let's go and have a look at what's going on. This is our city, after all."[28] Nonetheless, obviously still undecided about what to do, when he leaves the apartment at midday, he has his swimming trunks on under his trousers, just in case.[29]

Giuliani meets up with his friend and they set off to find out what is happening. At 2:00, they are in Corso Torino, where they can see the results of the "Black Block" vandalism. They go to Piazza Manin, where the mainly Catholic group *ManiTese* (Hands Outstretched) and the pacifists of *Manibianche* (White Hands) are protesting. While Giuliani is in Piazza Manin, his father calls him on his mobile phone and warns him to be careful. Giuliani tells him not to worry.[30] A Black Block group passes by unchallenged, following which the police charge at the pacifists sitting on the ground. People are injured, arrested, and taken to a hospital. Giuliani flees. He and his friend separate. He bumps into another friend and goes to his house. They have a snack at the "Genoano" bar in via Tommaso Pendola at around 4:30. At 5:00, his friend loses sight of Carlo in the crowds. Giuliani has decided to go toward Corso Gastaldi and link up with the march coming from the Stadio Carlini. Around twenty minutes later, he is in Piazza Alimonda.

It is at this point, in their interpretation and representation of how and why their son died, that the lenses of Giuliani's parents come into play, resulting in another subjective "truth" of what happened at 5:27. Haidi Giuliani says of Carlo's decision to pick up the fire extinguisher that "he could only have reacted in that way if he had found himself faced with a great injustice and that is probably what he was thinking in the moment when he found himself faced with a man pointing a gun in front of him."[31] Put simply: "Carlo lifts up the fire extinguisher because he sees the gun and wants to stop it [being used]."[32] This view of Giuliani's actions, which of course can be no more than supposition, has been repeated as "the truth" by many commentators on the left.[33] Interestingly, in a letter to *L'Unità* on January 4, 2002 about his son's death, after writing that "Carlo noticed the gun and wanted to disarm the Carabiniere," Giuliano Giuliani adds: "This is my truth, I don't demand it be that of others."[34] Some months later, he would ask, "Do we really want to make this into another of the many

'Italian mysteries'?"[35] Yet, by his acceptance and promotion of multiple and opposed subjective truths in his letter to *L'Unità* earlier that year, he had already (unwittingly) subscribed to the main premise for the creation of yet another "Italian mystery."

Mystery and Memory

In this mist of multiple truths, the only features to emerge with clarity are the familiar ones of the "Italian mystery." In the years since the shooting in Piazza Alimonda, the Giuliani case has presented the standard ingredients of such mysteries, and almost every element of the case has been the subject of contention and hypothesis, from how many *carabinieri* were in the police van, to the time of Placanica's arrival at the hospital, to the allegation that they changed vehicles on the way there, to how many shots were fired in Piazza Alimonda, to whose gun fired the bullet that killed Giuliani.[36] The conspiracy theorists have been helped by the way in which the authorities have handled the case. Take, for example, the autopsy: according to Alessandro Mantovani, the radiologist who did the CAT scan on Giuliani's brain noticed a "metal fragment" that could have been a piece of bullet, yet those who then performed the autopsy did not notice this, even though they apparently had the radiologist's report in front of them on the table.[37] To add to the mystery, according to Giuliano Pisapia, by 2002 the CAT scan could no longer be found, notwithstanding the legal obligation to keep such records for five years.[38] Moreover, the autopsy revealed no trace of fractures on Giuliani's body despite the police van having passed over him twice. As he was cremated, no further investigations can be conducted on the corpse, thus ensuring no resolution of the controversy.

Another cornerstone of the "Italian mystery" is the question of memory and commemoration. Like the anarchist Pino Pinelli, Giuliani has entered left iconography as the innocent victim of a corrupt, fascistic state, and his death now tends to be treated together with the other notorious episodes of the G8, such as the police abuses in the Diaz School and Bolzaneto Hospital. Giuliani has also become inextricably linked with the no-global movement despite the fact that he was not a member of any of the groups present and, as we have seen, was undecided whether even to go to the protests on July 20. For example, in their article about the movement, Donatella della Porta and Herbert Reiter refer to the "twenty-three-year-old Genovese activist, Carlo Giuliani."[39] Giuliani's image has been used on murals in Italy and around the world, and his name has been appropriated as a symbol of left-wing protest against oppression. Thus, a Veneto Resistance veteran at an April 25 commemoration in 2002 spoke of him as "a partisan,"[40] and when forty thousand people demonstrated against the Iraq war in Piazza De Ferrari in Genoa in March 2003, there was a round of applause "in memory of Carlo Giuliani."[41] In 2006, the far-left *Communist Refoundation* party even renamed their office in the Senate in his honor, provoking protests from the center-right.[42]

Haidi Giuliani, who herself became a *Communist Refoundation* Senator in 2006, has said, "Nobody wants my son to become a hero, a martyr, but he is already a symbol in this country and a lot of people identify with him."[43] As in the case of the protagonist of another famous "Italian mystery," Wilma Montesi, there has been a generational identification with Giuliani (among left-wing youth at least) and thousands of young people who did not know him personally were present at his funeral. Similarly, in the ensuing years, the anniversary of his death has been marked by events across Italy and abroad that have attracted large crowds. On the first anniversary, tens of thousands of people marched in Genoa. As part of the second anniversary commemorations, attended by over ten thousand people, a conference was held in the Genoa City Council Chamber by the "Committee of victims of the state" that dealt with cases such as the Bologna Station bombing, Ustica, and Pinelli, in addition to that of Giuliani—representing the "official" admission of his death into the exalted hall of the "Italian Mysteries."[44]

Conclusion: Trapped in a Photograph

Roland Barthes writes that "the age of photography corresponds precisely to the explosion of the private into the public, or rather into the creation of a new social value, which is the publicity of the private: the private is consumed as such, publicly."[45] Carlo Giuliani has been offered and consumed publicly by the various operators behind the lenses used to look at his death. Taking a photo of someone also means "embalming" them in a specific moment, and both Giuliani and Mario Placanica have been embalmed in a moment that occurred at Piazza Alimonda at 5:27 PM on July 20, 2001. Their public identities have become who they are (according to the lens of the viewer) in Martinez's photograph. It is a particularly ironic destiny for Giuliani, who, according to his sister, disliked being photographed and would turn away whenever she tried to take his picture.[46] Writing in the *Corriere della Sera* in August 2001, Marco Imarisio says that the *carabiniere* Placanica "will always be a dark, barely visible silhouette . . . as if time has remained forever stuck at the moment in which that photograph was taken."[47] The photograph has fossilized its two main protagonists and been used to make sense of what happened, with Giuliani put forward either as a symbol of idealism or violent protest and Placanica either as a symbol of repression or the defense of law and order. Little beside remains.

The day after Carlo Giuliani's death, a young man called Sirio went to the scene of the shooting and, obliterating out the name of the nineteenth-century Cardinal Gaetano Alimonda on the piazza sign, wrote *"Carlo Giuliani, ragazzo"* ("Carlo Giuliani, a young man"). When a foreign journalist questioned him about Giuliani, he replied, irritated, in faltering English: "He was not a punk, he was not a miserable person. He was just a guy."[48] Perhaps Sirio got closer to "the truth" about Carlo Giuliani than anyone else.

Notes

1. Martine Joly, *Introduzione all'analisi dell'immagine* (Turin: Lindau, 1999), 150. Originally published as *Introduction à l'analyse de l'image* (Paris: éditions Nathan, 1994).
2. See http://www.globalproject.info/IMG/jpg/05-6.jpg.
3. Roland Barthes, *Camera Lucida* (London: Vintage, 2000), 4. Originally published as *La Chambre Claire* (Paris: Editions du Seuil, 1980).
4. In fact, in their picture gallery, Reuters lists the image as "File photo of Carabiniere officer Placanica pointing a gun *before* shooting protester Giuliani" (emphasis added).
5. David Moss, "Il caso Moro 1978–2004: stregoneria, oracoli e magia," in *Working Papers del Dipartimento di studi sociali e politici* 12 (2004): 12–13, http://www.socio.uniml.it/ricerca_pubblicazioni.php (accessed May 10, 2005).
6. See Stefano Cristante, "Grandi eventi mediali: le novità di Genova per la communicazione di massa," in *Violenza Mediata: Il ruolo dell'informazione nel G8 di Genova*, ed. Stefano Cristante, 7–20 (Rome: Riuniti, 2003).
7. The term "sessantottino" refers to activists from the 1968 student movement, whom Pier Paolo Pasolini criticized in his famous poem "Il PCI ai giovani!"
8. See, for example, Mauro Bottarelli, "Quelli che ne prendono tante per 40 mila lire," *Libero*, July 17, 2001.
9. Concita De Gregorio, *Non lavate questo sangue: i giorni di Genova* (Rome-Bari: Laterza, 2002), 13.
10. Daniel Dayan and Elihu Katz, *Media Events: Live Broadcasting of History* (Cambridge, MA: Harvard University Press, 1994), 5.
11. This reconstruction is mainly based on the accounts of events in corso Gastaldi and piazza Alimonda by Laura Tartarini, "Il disegno della repressione," in *Il Caso Genova: da Piazza Alimonda alla Scuola Diaz*, ed. Simona Bonsignori, 79–97 (Rome: Manifestolibri, 2002); and Giulietto Chiesa, *G8/Genova* (Turin: Einaudi, 2001), 29–55.
12. Tartarini, "Il disegno della repressione," 80.
13. Ibid., 81–82.

14. Ibid., 83–84.

15. De Gregorio, *Non lavate questo sangue*, 45.

16. Chiesa, *G8/Genova*, 52.

17. "NN" stands for "unknown," "Non rilevabile" means "information not obtainable." See Giuliano Pisapia, "Dai misteri del caso Giuliani agli orrori di Bolzaneto," in Bonsignori, *Il caso Genoa*, 55.

18. See Pierre Bourdieu, *Sur La Télévision* (Paris: Liber-Raisons d'agir, 1996).

19. Zygmunt Bauman, *Il disagio della postmodernità* (Milan: Mondadori, 2002), 140.

20. Giulio Anselmi, "Una sola parola d'ordine: 'Non dimenticare Genova,'" *La Repubblica* (Genoa edition), July 20, 2003.

21. Cited in Cristante, *Violenza mediata*, 136.

22. Haidi Giuliani and Giuliano Giuliani (with Antonella Marrone), *Un anno senza Carlo*, (Milan: Baldini and Castoldi, 2002), 54.

23. De Gregorio, *Non lavate questo sangue*, 52.

24. Cristante, *Violenza mediata*, 139.

25. For a fuller account of how the Italian media handled the Giuliani killing, see "The hot game" in Cristante, *Violenza mediata*, 77–148.

26. Marcello Sorgi, "Brusco richiamo alla realtà," *La Stampa*, July 21, 2001; Costantino Muscau, "Guerriglia a Genova: un morto, centinaia di feriti," *Corriere della Sera*, July 21, 2001.

27. Rory Carroll, "The wild boy who became a martyr," *The Observer*, July 22, 2001.

28. De Gregorio, *Non lavate questo sangue*, 42.

29. Giuliani and Giuliani, *Un anno senza Carlo*, 35.

30. Ibid., 45.

31. Ibid., 17.

32. Ibid., 14.

33. See, for example, Piero Sansonetti, *Dal '68 ai No-Global: Trent'anni di movimento* (Milan: Baldini and Castoldi, 2002), 81.

34. Giuliano Giuliani, "La verità sulla morte di mio figlio, Carlo Giuliani," *L'Unità*, January 4, 2002.

35. Giovanni Mari, "è un altro dei misteri d'Italia," *Il Secolo XIX*, December 3, 2002.

36. See, for example, the accounts of the Giuliani death on websites such as http://www.sherwood.it/piazzalimonda/ and http://www.ilbarbieredellasera.com.

37. See Alessandro Mantovani, "Legittimo sparare a Giuliani," *Il manifesto*, May 6, 2003.

38. Pisapia, "Dai misteri del caso Giuliani agli orrori di Bolzaneto," 61.

39. Donatella della Porta and Herbert Reiter, "'You're the G8, We're the Six Billion': The Genoa Demonstrations,' in *Italian Politics*, vol. 17, ed. Paolo Bellucci and Martin Bell, 105–24 (New York: Berghahn, 2002), 106.

40. Giuliani and Giuliani, *Un anno senza Carlo*, 45.

41. "Senza titolo," *La Repubblica*, March 21, 2003, p. 16.

42. See Carmelo Lopapa, "Senato, rissa sulla sala Giuliani," *La Repubblica*, October 20, 2006, p. 32.

43. Giuliani and Giuliani, *Un anno senza Carlo*, 13.

44. See Giovanni Mari, "I no global dribblano la city," *Il Secolo XIX*, July 12, 2003.
45. Barthes, *Camera Lucida*, 98.
46. Giuliani and Giuliani, *Un anno senza Carlo*, 69.
47. Marco Imarisio, "Mi dispiace, sto male per la morte di Carlo," *Corriere della Sera*, August 19, 2001.
48. De Gregorio, *Non lavate questo sangue*, 53.

Part III

The Moro Affair

7

The Moro Affair: Interpretations and Consequences

Tobias Abse

The Indisputable Facts

Aldo Moro, the President of the Christian Democratic Party (DC) and a former Prime Minister, was kidnapped by an armed gang on March 16, 1978, on the very morning when he was due to attend the parliamentary installation of a new Christian Democrat government, to be led by Giulio Andreotti and supported by the Italian Communist Party (PCI), a government that had emerged out of prolonged negotiations in which Moro had played the leading role. His kidnappers captured him in Rome's Via Fani after a gun battle in which they killed all five of his bodyguards, two of whom were with him in his Fiat 130, while the other three were travelling in an Alfa Romeo immediately behind it. Four of his escorts were shot dead in less than a minute and the fifth man was mortally wounded, dying in a hospital within a few hours without regaining consciousness. Moro's captivity lasted fifty-four days, although most authors refer to this period slightly inaccurately as "the fifty-five days." Moro was shot dead on the morning of May 9, and his body was left in a red Renault in Via Caetani in central Rome, almost halfway between the headquarters of the Christian Democratic and Communist parties.

The Official Version

The official version of the story, sustained over the years by the two leading figures in the government of the time, Prime Minister Andreotti and

Interior Minister Francesco Cossiga, as well as by the Red Brigade (BR) members convicted of the crimes, attributes both the kidnapping and the killing of Moro to the Red Brigades acting alone, on their own initiative and without any external support or collusion from professional criminals or members of any security service, whether Italian or foreign. The success of the kidnapping and subsequent get-away are attributed to the BR's efficient preparation and Moro's own excessively regular routine. It is claimed that Moro was held throughout the fifty-four days in a single location in Via Montalcini in Rome and that he was killed there on May 9; his corpse was subsequently transported to Via Caetani. The embarrassing failure of the security forces to find Moro or his captors during the fifty-four days, despite a massive mobilization of the police, army, and *carabinieri*, is ascribed to incompetence, for which Cossiga took overall responsibility by resigning immediately after the discovery of Moro's body. These aspects of the official version are upheld by both the former government ministers and terrorist chiefs such as BR leader Mario Moretti. The remaining elements of the official version concerning the impracticality of negotiations and Moro's state of mind are more reliant on the word of Andreotti and Cossiga. The official version assumes that negotiation with the terrorists would have been both impractical and morally wrong and that the unwavering support of both Cossiga and Andreotti for such a hard line in the face of BR demands was the product of the same deeply-felt "sense of the state" avowed by the PCI, the other political force noted for its rigor throughout the affair, and rested on the assumption that the slightest concession would have put the institutions of parliamentary democracy at risk. Moro's own advocacy of negotiation between the state and the BR in numerous letters written during his captivity and delivered to his family, friends, and political associates by the BR, is said to reflect his loss of intellectual autonomy, even if it is now acknowledged that the *post-mortem* evidence does not sustain the original governmental claims that Moro was drugged or tortured; the assumption is nonetheless made that he adopted the viewpoint of his captors and can be treated as a mere example of an allegedly widespread psychological phenomenon amongst kidnap victims known as the Stockholm Syndrome.

Alternative Interpretations

The Moro affair has given rise to a vast literature over the last three decades. While the last few years have seen a new wave of books produced by people who had been members of, or consultants to, the parliamentary *Commissione Stragi* (Massacre Commission), which wound up in March

2001 after thirteen years of research, it seems more useful to classify the various genres of writing about the Moro case, rather than devoting this chapter exclusively to an examination of the works produced immediately before, on, or soon after the twenty-fifth anniversary. The proponents of the official version, principally the American historian Richard Drake and the Italian civil servant Vladimiro Satta, are inclined to divide the literature into two categories: on the one hand the official version, in large measure based on the exhaustive judicial investigations, represented essentially by their own published works[1] and the trial judges' sentences over the years, and on the other hand the conspiracy theorists. This binary division is too simplistic. On the one hand, Drake and Satta clearly do constitute a distinct category, which will be discussed later. On the other hand, to bracket all those who dissent from the official version as "conspiracy theorists" is ridiculous. There is a difference between those like Sicilian crime novelist Leonardo Sciascia, American journalist Robert Katz, and Moro's own magistrate brother, Alfredo Carlo Moro,[2] who in a broad sense side with the Moro family's version of the affair, believe that negotiations between either the Italian state or the Christian Democratic Party and the Red Brigades were possible, and suspect that Andreotti and Cossiga, in opposing negotiations, were motivated by factors other than their self-proclaimed "sense of the state," and those who espouse some variant of what would be regarded as conspiracy theories even by more open-minded readers without Drake and Satta's *a priori* commitment to the official version. Drake's total incapacity to see the difference between these two sorts of argument is best illustrated by his failure to acknowledge the shifts in Katz's position over time. Drake claimed in 1995 that Katz, "restating the argument he has been making for fifteen years . . . reasoned that Moretti's book lends further support to the conspiracy theory."[3] In actual fact, Katz's 1980 text *Days of Wrath* is not a conspiracy theory book, specifically rejecting "the CIA-plot-theory."[4] On the other hand, *Il Caso Moro*, the 1986 film on which Katz collaborated, is a conspiracy theory film, which contains a number of elements absent from Katz's book.

It seems reasonable, therefore, to subdivide the conspiracy theorists into two main categories. First, there are the exponents of what might be seen as the broadly plausible idea that the CIA and/or the Italian Secret Service made some use of the Red Brigades to block the ascent of the PCI toward governmental office in 1976–79, in a kind of continuation of the earlier "strategy of tension" involving collusion between these secret services and neo-Fascist terrorists. In short, whether former PCI senator and Moro Commission member Sergio Flamigni or Philip Willan, the Rome-based British journalist who provides the main English-language summary of what is quite a widespread interpretation of Italy's cold war history, are right or wrong, there is a rational kernel to their case about the alleged manipulation of the Red Brigades, however extravagant some of their specific claims may be at times.[5] Secondly, there are those who are on a par with the believers in flying saucers and cannot really be seen as contributing to historical or political debate, in however eccentric a fashion—it seems a matter of chance that they have chosen to focus on Moro's murder rather than, say, the death of Marilyn Monroe. Fasanella and Rocca, the writers of the latest work on Igor Markevitch, the composer and conductor who, they allege, acted as a mysterious intermediary in clandestine negotiations purportedly going on during the last days of Moro's life, clearly fall into this category—believers in the Rosicrucians, the Knights of Malta, and various associated orders engaged in world conspiracies have nothing to contribute to elucidating the Moro case.[6] Obviously, there is a spectrum of conspiracy theories, and it might be argued that those who invoke Mossad or the KGB as playing a significant role in Italian Red terrorism lie somewhere between those who play up the role of the CIA and those who believe in the occult. Whatever connection may have existed between more hard-line Secchian sections of the PCI and Czechoslovakia in the 1940s and 1950s, when former resistance fighters facing prosecution for wartime killings fled to Prague, the repeated failure to unearth any material about Italian 1970s terrorists in the archives of the former Eastern bloc in the years after 1989 would seem to suggest that there was no significant link between the BR and either Moscow or Prague. What was once a plausible theory, which appealed to Sciascia at the time he wrote his minority report for the Moro Commission[7] and led Amendola to seek a meeting with the Czech ambassador to Italy in the latter days of Moro's captivity—on May 4, 1978[8]—now seems to have become the preserve of hard-line right-wingers, some of whom use it as a cynical defensive counter to the Italian left's long-standing emphasis on the CIA's proven intervention in Italian politics, and others of whom genuinely see "reds under the bed" wherever they look. While Mossad's penchant for assassinating Palestinians is undeniable, and Moro's line on the Middle East certainly did not go down well in Tel Aviv, one's instinct, given the long history of the "world Jewish conspiracy" exemplified by the Protocols of the Elders of Zion, is that those who claim that Moro's last prison was in Rome's Jewish ghetto, not Via Montalcini, and infer, from this already debatable premise, that Mossad was involved in his kidnapping and murder,[9] are closer in spirit to the occultists than to those whose justified suspicions of the CIA's role in Italian politics during the cold war have become inflamed to an extent that borders on the paranoid.

The Academic Defense of the Official Version

As will have become apparent from the previous section, the majority of writers on the case, whether or not they have been genuine conspiracy theorists, have disputed the official version. However, the official line now has two advocates with more apparent political detachment and greater methodological rigor than the politicians and polemicists who previously dominated both sides of the debate, the American historian Richard Drake and the Italian Vladimiro Satta, to whom reference has already been made. Drake, who had already touched on the case in a chapter in his more general 1989 work *The Revolutionary Mystique and Terrorism in Contemporary Italy*, wrote a monograph entitled *The Aldo Moro Murder Case*, published in 1995, which seemed to have a far more solid evidential base, largely in legal records, than earlier Anglophone accounts. If Drake, as an established American academic without obvious links to Andreotti or Cossiga, gave the official version, blessed with the *imprimatur* of Harvard University Press, more credibility in the English-speaking world, Satta emerged as the intellectual victor in the Italian literary contest around the twenty-fifth anniversary. Satta's extremely well-documented and, for the most part, very closely argued work *Odissea nel Caso Moro* (Odyssey in the Moro Case) claims definitively to refute every variant of conspiracy theory surrounding the episode and defends the official version primarily based on the five trials of the terrorists involved in the case. Satta's own role in the Italian civil service as the *document specialist* to the *Commissione Stragi* gave him deeper knowledge of the commission's records than any of the politicians serving on it, including the President of the Commission, Giovanni Pellegrino, who had already published a book-length interview, *Segreto di Stato* (State Secret), half of which was devoted to the Moro case, in 2000.[10] Satta could not resist the temptation to use his superior knowledge to expose the inconsistencies in the various theories advanced by Pellegrino and other parliamentary commissioners over the years, which reinforced the impression that he was above the political fray.

The question will be asked whether, after three decades, during which all Moro's jailers and kidnappers have been arrested, tried, sentenced, and imprisoned, it is not time to accept the official version as Satta and Drake suggest. One has to respond by pointing out that the official version in its extreme form rests upon a number of dubious assumptions. These include the idea that Andreotti and Cossiga are reliable and truthful witnesses, dedicated servants of the Italian state and lifelong democrats; that Eleonora Moro was so distraught over her husband's murder that her recall of events between March 16 and May 9, 1978, was seriously flawed; and that the campaign of denigration against the captive Moro—the "opera-tion Moro isn't Moro" as Alessandro Silj dubbed it in his 1978 book on the Italian press during the kidnap[11]—carried out by the Italian government and media on March 30–31, 1978, was essentially justified. The official ver-sion also assumes that the former BR terrorists like Moretti or Morucci are now likely to be telling the whole truth and nothing but the truth, regard-less of the number of times they have changed their stories over the years.

Andreotti's Testimony

Andreotti, prime minister at the time of Moro's kidnapping and murder, was described by Moro in the memorial he wrote in captivity as "a cold, inscrutable operator, without doubts, without emotions, without a single ounce of human compassion. . . . Andreotti, of whose orders the others have all been obedient executors."[12] Proponents of the official version place a vast amount of reliance on judicial proceedings and verdicts, including evidence given by *pentiti* ("penitents," ex-mafiosi and ex-terrorists who turn state's evidence), which played far more of a role than successful detective work in the terrorists' eventual capture and conviction. They are now hoist by their own petard after Andreotti's Palermo and Perugia trials. While *the Court of Cassation* has recently overturned the Perugia verdict, holding Andreotti responsible for ordering the murder of Carmine Pecorelli, the final verdict both cast doubt on the credibility of *pentiti* in general—for if the most famous *pentito* of all, Tomasso Buscetta, is posthu-mously discredited, how much reliance can one place on any *pentito*?—and leaves the Pecorelli killing unsolved, since all plausible instigators and executors have now been acquitted. It had been widely alleged that the motivation for the Pecorelli murder was an attempt on the journalist's part to blackmail Andreotti; blackmail was an integral part of Pecorelli's strange brand of investigative journalism. While Andreotti was involved in a num-ber of financial scandals, some of which Pecorelli had publicized, it is gen-erally believed that Pecorelli, through his P2 and Intelligence Service contacts, knew something about the Moro case, about which he published a number of articles making coded challenges to the official version, and that this knowledge, rather than his customary allegations of financial and political corruption, proved fatal. Andreotti was delighted by his acquittal by the Palermo court investigating allegations about mafia links made by Buscetta and numerous other *pentiti*. However, the detailed judgment proved far more ambiguous: the court believed Andreotti had close links with mafiosi such as the Salvo cousins until 1980—in other words, for a period covered by the Statute of Limitations. In short, the acquittal rests on a technicality; it does not absolve Andreotti of mafia links, it merely absolves him of maintaining these links into a period covered by penal sanctions. Insofar as this assessment has any logic, it must be based on the notion of a linkage with the old, Palermo-dominated mafia, as opposed to the new, Corleone-dominated mafia. Be that as it may, it would suggest that in 1978, Andreotti was hardly the truthful man devoted to upholding the rule of law that Drake and Satta see him as. Why should we believe his word against that of Eleonora Moro on such matters as her claim that her husband had requested an armored car, a request which, if it had been granted in time, might have made the kidnap more difficult or even impossible? Why should a man who denied he had even met the Salvo cousins, despite photographic evidence to the contrary, not lie about a more easily contested issue?[13]

Cossiga's Testimony

Francesco Cossiga was the Minister of the Interior at the time of Moro's kidnapping and murder. Cossiga's defenders are eager to present him as a man of principle whose shining integrity led him to resign immediately after the discovery of Moro's body in the red Renault in Via Caetani, accepting full responsibility for the failure of the security forces to track down the kidnappers. However, they are not so eager to remind us that in September 1980 Cossiga had to resign as PM because of a leakage of confidential information to a terrorist who had committed at least one murder. The *pentito* Roberto Sandalo had told the authorities that his fellow *Prima Linea* terrorist Marco Donat Cattin had escaped to France in April 1980 after his father, the Deputy Secretary of the Christian Democratic Party, had received from Cossiga a warning of his imminent arrest.[14] The latter episode does not suggest we can take at face value his pompous pose as principled defender of the state against any deals with terrorists, even if the price was the death of his patron and erstwhile friend Aldo Moro.[15] One might also point out that Cossiga was Prime Minister at the time of the shooting down of an Italian civilian aircraft at Ustica in June 1980 and the Bologna railway station bombing of August 1980, and his accounts of both those events have been far from full or frank. Given such a record of duplicity and obfuscation, should we accept his word against that of Eleonora Moro, who alleged that he denied the existence of a Via Gradoli anywhere in Rome during a visit he made to the Moro household in the immediate aftermath of the fruitless search of the village of Gradoli, identified as the place of Moro's captivity at the famous séance of April 2? It is worth noting that Eleanora's version was confirmed by her son, Giovanni

Moro, while Andreotti was unaccountably eager to back up Cossiga's denial at a hearing of the *Commissione Stragi* in 1997, though he had not been present at the meeting between Cossiga and the Moro family.

This dispute about whether Cossiga denied the existence of a Via Gradoli is no trivial matter. If the police had discovered Moretti's hideout at Via Gradoli 96 before April 18, it might well have enabled the authorities to capture Moretti, the leading figure in the kidnap operation, or to track down a living Moro. Furthermore, why should we believe that Cossiga's infamous Plan Victor—according to which a living Moro, rescued from the Red Brigades, would have been sequestered in a psychiatric clinic for an indefinite period—was motivated by sincere concern for Moro's welfare, a desire to protect him from any inclination toward suicide or self-harm, as Satta claims? It seems very doubtful that Cossiga really believed that Moro had gone mad—for, as Sciascia pointed out in his minority report to the Moro commission, Cossiga finally admitted that Moro's letters from the Red Brigade prison proved that "Moro, with his lucidity, intelligence and logic, had understood what those who were bargaining with him really wanted."[16] If Cossiga had such confidence in Moro's lucidity, then Plan Victor can only be seen as reminiscent of the systematic abuse of psychiatry against political dissidents in Brezhnev's Soviet Union. In short, the argument advanced in varying degrees by Robert Katz, Leonardo Sciascia, Robin Erika Wagner-Pacifici,[17] and even, in a more nuanced way, by Alison Jamieson—namely that Moro's colleagues, principally Andreotti and Cossiga, did not want to save Moro's life after his kidnapping by any form of negotiation—is a valid one. As Giovanni Moro has recently reiterated, "It is a fact that—in that case and only in that case—the Italian state decided neither to negotiate with the terrorists nor to seriously attempt to free the prisoner."[18]

P2 and the Secret Services

The Moro family and their supporters have long claimed that Moro's advocacy of negotiations was a rational and practical option and that his former colleagues Andreotti and Cossiga vilified him through the "Operation Moro isn't Moro" to an extent that suggests they had little interest in getting him back alive, given their own unwillingness to negotiate and the apparent inability of the security services to track down his hiding place in the "People's Prison." Though these claims seem justified, it is hard to construct an alternative to the Satta/Drake official version on a firm basis of documentary evidence. By and large, all one can do is pose awkward questions. The heads of the domestic and military intelligence services, SISDE and SISMI, as well as the head of the Finance Police at the time of the Moro Affair, were P2 members, and the committees advising Cossiga during the crisis were riddled with P2 members. This would suggest that the manifold failures in police work during the fifty-four days were not accidental, given P2's adamant opposition to the Historic Compromise with the PCI which Moro had brought about, but this is very unlikely to be proved to the satisfaction of supporters of the official version precisely because of the secretive methods employed by P2 throughout its existence. The deviant role of the secret services (or at the very least sections of them) in earlier and later episodes of Italian terrorism is generally acknowledged, so the argument advanced by Satta in favor of their good, or at worst totally incompetent, conduct in 1978 seems to rely very heavily on the extent of the services' disorganization as a result of the 1977 reform and on personal rivalries between the heads of the newly created SISMI and SISDE—in other words, on the notion that they would have been incapable of playing a wrecking role, rather than a belief in some sort of genuine transformation of their moral code that turned them into loyal servants of parliamentary democracy.

State Infiltration of the BR?

The question of state infiltration of the BR at the time of the Moro affair—a theory put forward by Flamigni and Willan in particular—has not been fully resolved in a negative sense by Satta, despite all his claims to have done so. While allegations have been made against various BR members, the most significant doubts concern Mario Moretti and Giovanni Senzani, who successively led the organization after the arrest of its founding leader, Renato Curcio; nobody has questioned their sincerity. Only some of the case made out against Moretti and Senzani by Flamigni has been addressed, let alone refuted. Even Satta is too aware of the oddities of the Florentine criminologist turned terrorist chief—who started off as a trusted member of the establishment and did not drift toward terrorism from the student or worker radicalization of the late 1960s—to advance a cast-iron case against his being a double agent; his main concern is to try and claim that Senzani only played a major role in the BR after 1978 and therefore could not have played any role in deciding Moro's fate. While part of the case against Moretti is circumstantial—he seemed to have a remarkable capacity to escape arrest when the original leadership group of the BR was being rounded up in 1974–76 and indeed subsequently until April 1981—the most telling accusations against him have come from the BR veteran Alberto Franceschini.[19] It should be pointed out that Franceschini has gained nothing in material terms from casting doubt on Moretti's good faith; instead, he has been subjected to much harsher punishment in terms of the length and intensity of his imprisonment than the man who played the leading role in Moro's kidnap and murder, so supporters of the official version, for whom Moretti's integrity is as crucial as that of Andreotti or Cossiga, have been reduced to casting doubt on Franceschini's sanity, suggesting that prolonged imprisonment had weakened his hold on reality and left him prey to paranoid delusions.

The False Communiqué

The one episode where the official version makes no sense at all, as opposed to just being open to doubt, is that of the false BR Communiqué No. 7 on April 18, which claimed Moro was dead and led to the prolonged and pointless search for his body in the frozen Lake Duchessa. Nobody now disputes that the communiqué was forged by Antonio Chicchiarelli, a professional criminal with no connection to the BR, who was murdered in mysterious circumstances on September 26, 1984. While Satta limits himself to assuming Chicchiarelli was not acting on his own initiative, Jamieson, who "has done international security work with special reference to political security," as the publishers of her book rather coyly point out, is among the authors who link him to the Italian intelligence services. This should convince those skeptical about Willan's more elaborate argument to the same effect. Eleonora Moro's opinion, expressed in 1980 to the Moro Commission, that the Communiqué was a "dress rehearsal to see how public opinion and the people would react to a fact of this kind" seems far more convincing than Satta's pious claim that "either the apocryphal text was aiming to arouse a popular movement of indignation against the BR and favorable to the situation of the hostage or it was born with the primary aim of creating internal difficulties amongst the terrorists and inducing them to come out into the open."[20]

Conclusion

It seems best to end this by no means exhaustive discussion of the weaknesses in the official version by reminding people that Eleonora Moro resorted to subterfuge to keep her husband's body out of the hands of the state, having him buried in a private ceremony in the village of Torrita Tiburna. She also refused to attend the state memorial service in the Church of San Giovanni in Laterano, which was attended by Andreotti and other "men of power" and at which the Pope said Mass. Giovanni Moro has refused to sit next to Andreotti and Cossiga at any of the official commemorations over the years. Unlike his sister, Maria Fida, he has no wish to meet any of the BR members involved in his father's kidnapping, let alone forgive them. Nor does he believe they have told the whole truth. Those who believe the official version are welcome to do so; there is no reason to assume we will learn any more about the affair from Andreotti, Cossiga or Moretti; Pecorelli, General Dalla Chiesa, and Chicchiarelli, all of whom may have known rather more than what is now in the public domain, met with violent deaths within a few years of Moro's own tragic end.

Notes

1. Richard Drake has written a monograph on the case, *The Aldo Moro Murder Case* (Cambridge, MA: Harvard University Press, 1995), but his earlier, more general work, *The Revolutionary Mystique and Terrorism in Contemporary Italy* (Bloomington: Indiana University Press, 1989), esp. chap. 4, "Aldo Moro and Italy's difficult democracy," also contains some relevant material. Drake seems to have adopted a harder line in 1995 than in 1989, particularly in characterizing Katz's views. Vladimiro Satta's major published work is *Odissea nel Caso Moro: Viaggio controcorrente attraverso la documentazione della Commissione Stragi* (Rome: EDUP, 2003). He has also published some articles on the case in *Nuova Storia Contemporanea*, and another monograph, *Caso Moro senza Misteri*, is in preparation.

2. Leonardo Sciascia, *L'Affaire Moro* (Palermo: Sellerio, 1978); and *The Moro Affair* (extended edition), trans. Sacha Rabinovitch (London: Granta, 2002); Robert Katz, *Days of Wrath: the Public Agony of Aldo Moro* (London: Granata, 1980); and Alfredo Carlo Moro, *Storia di un delitto annunciato* (Rome: Editori Riuniti, 1998).

3. Drake, *The Aldo Moro Murder Case*, 301.

4. Katz, *Days of Wrath*, 298

5. Sergio Flamigni, *La tela del ragno: il delitto Moro* (Milan: Kaos, 1993); *Convergenze parallele: le Brigate rosse, i servizi segreti e il delitto Moro* (Milan: Kaos, 1998); and Flamigni, *Il covo di Stato: Via Gradoli, 96 e il delitto Moro* (Milan: Kaos, 1999); Philip Willan, *Puppet-masters: The Political Uses of Terrorism in Italy* (London: Constable, 1991). In 2002, Willan's book was re-issued by a minor American publisher, Authors' Choice Press, San José. Apart from a sentence about 9/11 on the back cover, there does not appear to have been any attempt to update the Constable edition, which seems strange for a living author who remains an active practicing journalist reporting on Italian politics. The original edition was ahead of its time, before the Tangentopoli scandals of 1992–93, which might have allowed it to gain a more sympathetic reception in the British broadsheet press.

6. Giovanni Fasanella and Giuseppe Rocca, *Il misterioso intermediario: Igor Markevic e il caso Moro* (Turin: Einaudi, 2002).

7. Leonardo Sciascia, *The Moro Affair*, 117–19. This 1982 report, as should be obvious, was not in the original version of *L'Affaire Moro*.

8. Satta, *Odissea*, 35.

9. See, for example, Silvio Bonfigli and Giacopo Sce, *Il delitto infinito: ultime notizie sul sequestro Moro* (Milan: Kaos, 2002), 157–210. These authors are probably less obsessed with this theory than some other commentators, as their book also discusses the possible roles of the CIA and the Italian Secret Services, as well as the ambiguities in the career of Mario Moretti.

10. Giovanni Fasanella and Claudio Sestrieri with Giovanni Pellegrino, *Segreto di Stato: La verità da Gladio al Caso Moro* (Turin: Einaudi, 2000). See pp. 125–240 for Pellegrino's views on the Moro case.

11. Alessandro Silj, *Brigate Rosse—Stato* (Florence: Vallecchi, 1978).

12. Translation taken from Alison Jamieson, *The Heart Attacked: Terrorism and Conflict in the Italian State* (London: Boyars, 1989), 175.

13. The American ambassador to Italy during the fifty-four days, who defends Andreotti from "the accusation that he and other DC leaders deliberately failed to rescue Aldo Moro . . . a charge I consider totally unfounded," nevertheless remarked in another context that, "I was once again mystified by Andreotti's habit of saying things that could so easily be disproved." Richard M. Gardner, *Mission Italy: On the Front Lines of the Cold War* (Lanham, MD: Rowman and Littlefield, 2005), 312, 295.

14. Alison Jamieson, *The Heart Attacked*, 180.

15. Cossiga was well aware that the "line of firmness" meant Moro's death "unless he had been liberated militarily"—Cossiga's statement to Commissione Stragi, November 6, 1997, quoted in Agostino Giovagnoli, *Il Caso Moro: una tragedia repubblicana* (Bologna: Il Mulino, 2005), 347.

16. Sciascia, *The Moro Affair*, 114–15.

17. Robin Erika Wagner-Pacifici, *The Moro Morality Play: Terrorism as Social Drama* (Chicago: University of Chicago Press, 1986).

18. *La Repubblica*, September 5, 2003.

19. The most coherent exposition of Franceschini's views can be found in Giovanni Fasanella and Alberto Franceschini, *Che cosa sono le BR* (Milan: Rizzoli, 2004).

20. Satta, *Odissea*, 288–89.

8

From History to Mystery: The Parliamentary Inquiries into the Kidnapping and Murder of Aldo Moro, 1979–2001

David Moss

On March 16, 1978, Aldo Moro was kidnapped by the Red Brigades, who held him captive in a "people's prison" in Via Montalcino for fifty-four days and murdered him on May 9. Three decades later, this apparently straightforward description of the tragedy had become remarkably controversial. Many key details were now disputed: who had planned and participated in the kidnapping, where Moro had been held captive, whether anyone apart from the kidnappers had had contact with him, whether any of the possibly compromising documents he might have written in the "people's prison" had been removed and destroyed, who had made the final decision to murder rather than release him. Radical doubts were not voiced only by irreducible conspiracy theorists. In 1998 the Italian President, Scalfaro, declared his belief that the real organizers of the kidnapping had yet to be identified, and in 1999 Moro's son Giovanni claimed that two decades of investigation had served only to reinforce the view that the truth lay further away than ever.[1] For events pored over by police, judges and lawyers, politicians, academics, and journalists for a quarter of a century—during which most of the protagonists have retired or died; their political parties, along with the Red Brigades themselves, have vanished;

and the awareness of the event among younger Italians has become minimal—the escalation rather than abatement of controversy about even the facts of his fate seems deeply paradoxical.

Much of the blame for this failure to turn the tragedy from mystery into history has been leveled at the work of the parliamentary committees of inquiry, which between 1979 and 2001 attempted without success to resolve the controversies. This chapter is therefore devoted to the analysis of that failure, tracking the evolution of the key features of the inquiries and assessing their contributions to the outcome. My primary concern is to examine the instruments of interpretation and the relations among their users, rather than to propose yet another explanation of the event.[2] I suggest that such an analysis enables us to catch at least one of Italy's many post-war political mysteries in the process of its manufacture.

Obstacles to an Authoritative Version

The kidnapping was an unprecedented confrontation between antagonists who had little knowledge of one another's political languages, decision-making processes, and organizational constraints. It took place against the background of an equally unprecedented form of political collaboration between Italy's two major parties, the DC and the PCI. In those circumstances, actions and reactions based on guesswork, misunderstanding, and suspicion on every side were inevitable. What was strategy, improvisation, bungling, or coincidence would be hard to disentangle later, especially as the passage of time between the event and its investigation lengthened. But three specific obstacles to any parliamentary achievement of a consensual version of the tragedy by the parliamentary committees of inquiry presented themselves from the outset. First, doubts about the identities and intentions of the protagonists predated the kidnapping and were bound to create great interpretive uncertainties and conflicts. Were the Red Brigades really "red"? What was Moro's genuine political vision? How far was it shared by his party, the DC? How far could the police and security services, in the middle of reorganization, be trusted? The events of the previous ten years left all these questions open. Second, much of the key information out of which any acceptable account could be composed was distributed among a small group of people who had managed the kidnapping but had become estranged as a result of the failure either to rescue Moro or to find a way of negotiating his release. Moro himself was dead and could not clarify what he intended by the deeply paradoxical writings of his final days. The DC strategy was handled by no more than ten senior politicians, although regular informal consultations with other party leaders were held: the formal decision-making bodies of the government and party were simply recipients of periodic briefings. Even the fifteen members of the Red Brigades involved in some aspect of the kidnapping each had only partial knowledge of the overall event. Just one member (Moretti) knew what was happening in the "people's prison" and in the "Executive Committee" of the BR responsible for deciding Moro's fate. Finally, the initiatives taken by Moro's family were exclusively determined by his wife, Eleonora, who did not share details of her information or actions either with their four adult children or with Moro's brother, or with her husband's close political associates.[3] The tragic outcome of the kidnapping converted the distrust among these protagonists into entrenched hostility, each set showing little inclination to believe that the others' statements of what they had or had not done to rescue Moro were the truth, the whole truth, and nothing but the truth. So the Parliamentary committees of inquiry were therefore required to compose a coherent, plausible narrative out of fragments colored by anger, guilt, and remorse and embedded in overall views that could never be dispassionate or disinterested.

The third obstacle to a single consensual political account of the tragedy lies in the nature of Italian parliamentary committees as investigative instruments. Since 1948, forty-six committees of inquiry have been held, covering general issues of public concern (e.g., poverty, unemployment, mafia) and specific cases of political or economic malfeasance (e.g., SIFAR, Sindona, the Federconsorzi). Each committee is established under Article 82 of the Constitution, which requires that its membership reflect the distribution of seats among the Parliamentary parties and provides it with the same powers as the judiciary to gather evidence, consult documents, and call witnesses. However, the judicial rules for gathering and processing evidence do not apply: most testimony to parliamentary inquiries is not sworn, witnesses are not permitted legal representation, and the committee has no direct powers to deal with refusal to appear or with obvious reticence or clearly false testimony. The combination of a membership drawn from a wide range of political parties and virtually untrammeled freedom to gather and interpret evidence guarantees that proceedings will be marked by deep disagreements among committee members, who will evaluate evidence differently and reach different conclusions. Not surprisingly, therefore, very few Parliamentary inquiries into events involving political parties or their personnel are free of controversy and produce a consensual outcome: the Sindona inquiry generated two reports, the SIFAR case four, and the P2 investigations five. Moreover, the limits on the kind and number of reports submitted are further relaxed by the absence of any obligation for Parliament to discuss them, still less to take action on their recommendations. In practice, very few reports have been debated, questions tabled or motions proposed.[4]

Given the framework governing Parliamentary inquiries and the track record of its predecessors, expectations that the committee examining the Moro tragedy could indeed serve as its "authoritative institutional interpreter for the national community," as the first committee of inquiry defined its role, or as "the ideal institutional site for laying the foundations of national collective memory," as senior members of the last committee rephrased the objective, should not have been high.[5] But the difficulties were greatly exacerbated by the specific features of the inquiries.

Changes in Agenda and Members

Calls for the establishment of a Parliamentary committee were made by members of Moro's party faction within a few days of his murder but were initially resisted by the major parties on the grounds that the outcome of the judicial inquiries might be compromised by a parallel political investigation.[6] The resistance was overcome, and in November 1979 a bicameral committee (*Commissione parlamentare d'inchiesta sulla strage di Via Fani, sul sequestro e l'assassinio di Aldo Moro e sul terrorismo in Italia*; hereafter CPM) was established. Its task was to clarify the details of the kidnapping, assess the reasons for the state's failure to protect and recover Moro, and determine whether the BR had enjoyed any crucial active or passive support from outsiders. The CPM was also required to produce a broader report on the objectives, organization, funding, and linkages of all terrorist groups, accompanied by an assessment of the results of the state's overall response to violence and the adequacy of the resources at its disposal. The Committee concluded its investigations of the Moro case in 1983 but, given the constraints of time and resources, did not even attempt to address the wider issues.

Proposals were therefore immediately made to renew the inquiry. After a short-lived single-chamber committee in 1986–87, a fresh bicameral inquiry, the *Commissione parlamentare d'inchiesta sul terrorismo in Italia e sulle cause della mancata individuazione dei responsabili delle stragi* (CPS) was launched in 1988. It was given three tasks: further scrutiny of the Moro affair in the light of new evidence, an overall evaluation of the state's repression of terrorism, and an investigation of why the major right-wing massacres since 1969 had remained unpunished. Its remit was soon expanded to cover the Ustica tragedy of 1980 and the revelations that Andreotti had made in 1990 about the existence of Gladio. To deal with the Gladio issue, the retrospective time limit of 1969 was removed so that all instances of political violence and subversive organization throughout the entire postwar period became available for the committee's scrutiny. At its point of maximum activity, therefore, the committee was investigating simultaneously no fewer than thirty-two separate episodes of political violence. Unsurprisingly, the initial time-frame of eighteen months for the investigations proved wildly unrealistic. Apart from regular prorogations, the committee had to be reconstituted after the 1992, 1994, and 1996 elections before finally being wound up on the eve of the national elections of 2001.

That brief institutional history of the inquiries suggests something of the changing interpretive context for the Moro investigations. The CPM's narrowly-focused task had been to place the attack in the evolution, organization, and ambitions of its material executors, the BR. The terms of reference for the CPS after 1988, however, assimilated it to the category of "unpunished massacres," notably the neo-Fascist bomb massacres of 1969–84. The first chairman of the CPS, Libero Gualtieri, interpreted the new terms of reference as an invitation not to conduct quasi-judicial investigations into any of the specific events but rather to unify in a single interpretative scheme the elements that had emerged in the judicial investigations already concluded.[7] Putting the Moro inquiry into this framework meant switching attention away from the facts already established on specific issues and toward the search for a wider explanation of the common features that remained mysterious and the responsibilities hitherto concealed. The full force of this interpretive re-contextualization was initially restrained by the assignment of work on the Moro case to a small subgroup of the committee. But from 1996 onward the Moro inquiry became just one of the issues addressed by the entire committee and could therefore no longer be insulated from the speculations that characterized many of the other, very different, cases under consideration.

The duration of the inquiry—across twenty-two years, three separate committees, and six legislatures—had direct consequences for the continuity of personnel, preservation of focus, and formation of institutional memory. Just two members of the original CPM were appointed to the CPS in 1988, and no member of the original CPS was still a member by 2001. The normal rotation of committee personnel for political and party reasons—which ensured that one-quarter of the CPM's membership had been replaced by 1983 and that up to one-half of the CPS membership was replaced in each of the four legislatures between 1988 and 2001—was further exaggerated by the abnormally large turnover in parliamentarians in the three elections of 1992, 1994, and 1996. Upheavals on that scale meant a decline in levels of parliamentary experience of any kind among investigators. Of the CPS committee of 1994, for example, only two members—neither of them the new chairman, Pellegrino—had been parliamentarians before 1990, and no member had had any experience of work on a parliamentary inquiry. A total of some 270 parliamentarians took at least some part in the inquiry for periods that varied between a few weeks and seven years.

Along with the lengthening list of sometime participants came the accumulation of testimonies, memoranda, submissions, judicial proceedings, and almost any political, administrative, or scholarly document that at least one member thought might possibly be useful. By 2001 the archives of the CPS contained 1.5 million pages of documents, in addition to the *circa* fifty-one thousand documents gathered by the CPM. The opportunities for novice, often short-term, committee members to master their contents and reach interpretive agreement were therefore not great, especially since they received no dispensation from other political duties.[8] In consequence, increasing weight fell not only on the direction of the work by the chairs of the successive committees (Gualtieri, 1988–94; Pellegrino, 1994–2001) but also on the guidance offered after 1994 by a growing number of committee consultants with increasingly diverse expertise. Those shifts in agendas and memberships help to account for the division of the committees' interpretive trajectory into two distinct phases.

The Tragedy as History, 1979–94

Between 1979 and 1994 the committees of inquiry transmitted to Parliament eight reports on aspects of the Moro case. In 1983 the CPM produced a total of six separate reports: a majority report (endorsed by the DC, PCI, PSDI, and PRI, plus "observations" by the *Gruppo misto* and the PDUP) and five minority reports, the most significant authored by the Socialist Party. Its successor committee, the CPS, approved without significant dissent two further reports in 1992 and 1994, examining new information, which turned out to be the last interpretation of the events to be officially endorsed.

As this sequence of its outcomes indicates, the committee had moved by 1994 to a broad consensual view on the events of March–May 1978. The initial disagreements, central to the debates in the CPM, concerned what could or should have been done to save Moro—a prolongation of the dispute during the later stages of the kidnapping itself between supporters of hard-line (*fermezza*) and flexible (*trattativa*) responses by the government toward the Red Brigades' demands. That clash—exaggerated, speculative, and irrelevant to establishing the facts—made a central issue of the interpretation of Moro's letters from the "people's prison"—the most credible piece of evidence that negotiations for his release might even be possible. But it lost much of its force in the light of the political rapprochement between the two men who symbolized the two approaches, Andreotti and Craxi respectively. Craxi's appointment as Prime Minister in 1983 and Andreotti's appointment as his Foreign Minister inaugurated an alliance that was to last until the political and personal disgrace of both men in the early 1990s. The reports reiterated that there was no serious evidence for help given directly or indirectly to the BR by outsiders hostile to Moro but acknowledged that some minor issues remained to be resolved. Interpretive consistency was built around the narrow focus on the nature of the relationships of Moro himself to his captors and to the addressees of his letters, alongside the authorial continuity of the reports. For the principal author of both the 1992 and 1994 reports was Luigi Granelli, a longstanding Christian Democrat ally of Moro and his close ministerial colleague between 1973 and 1976, assisted in both reports by the only CPM member to be appointed to the CPS, Francesco Macis (of the PCI/Pds). In effect the 1994 report brought to a close the responsibilities of Moro's peers for producing a public account of his death.

The authority of this account was reinforced in two ways. First, the other major institutional interpreter, the judiciary, sealed its own interpretation in 1993 when the Court of Cassation definitively endorsed the last of the six verdicts by courts in Rome, all of which had assigned full responsibility to the core BR members involved. No doubt this consistency was helped by an interpretive continuity analogous to that of the Parliamentary inquiries: the major judicial investigations had been directed by a single magistrate (Priore), and the principal trials were handled by the same experienced judge (Santiapichi). The potentially problematic relations between parliamentary committee and judiciary scrutinizing the same events turned out instead to be harmonious, reinforced by the use of magistrates, including Priore himself, and police investigators as the principal group of committee consultants between 1988 and 1994.

No credible alternatives to the Parliamentary interpretation came from the two groups best placed and most motivated to contest it: Moro's captors and his family. The BR had not provided their promised account of the event or disseminated the materials from Moro's alleged "confessions." The details provided by members with partial knowledge of the events, notably Morucci and Faranda, only confirmed the sole responsibilities of the BR. Moro's family and personal staff, although convinced that the political elite had not done what it could and should have done to save Moro, were not at this stage concerned to promote a rival interpretation of what had taken place. Rather, they were concerned to offer evidence to the inquiries, dispel suspicions that they were concealing information about contact with Moro during the kidnapping, and rebuild his reputation after the damage caused by the contents of his final letters.[9] A partial reconciliation with Moro's party colleagues was signaled by Maria Fida Moro's becoming a Christian Democrat senator in 1987, which acted as a check against any deliberate public undermining of her party's interpretations of events. By 1994, therefore, whatever reservations might be expressed privately, the basic ingredients of the tragedy—the responsibilities, motives, and objectives of the different sets of protagonists—appeared to be beyond serious public contestation. After 1994, however, this somewhat artificial consensus fell apart.

The Tragedy as Mystery 1994–2001

In the early 1990s two new kinds of evidence for the CPS to work on came to light. First, documents unequivocally attributable to Moro were discovered in a former BR base in Milan in 1990. They contained a copy of a handwritten "memoir" (*memoriale*), part of which had been found in typescript in 1978 but disregarded by the Parliamentary inquirers. In contrast to his letters, his memoir dealt principally with national and international aspects of his career. The second type of fresh evidence came in the confessions offered from 1993 onward by Moro's kidnappers, which provided essential details of their actions and intentions. The two kinds of evidence pushed interpretations in opposite directions, given the simultaneous relaxation of the previous interpretive constraints and the changes to the interpretive community itself.

The relaxation came in various forms. The virtual elimination of political violence by the 1990s removed any remaining pressure on political parties to preserve consensus in interpreting violence. Moreover, the all-but-complete change in membership in 1994 released the CPS from any identification with its predecessor's versions of events. None of its new members had known Moro, participated in the responses to the kidnapping, or even belonged to the DC, so no position taken in the past needed defending. New speculations could be entertained, and new personnel were recruited to help provide them, in the form of committee consultants. In contrast to the CPM, which had not used consultants, the CPS made extensive use of them. Between 1988 and 1994 it engaged twenty-five magistrates and police officers who had themselves been involved in the investigations of the violence under consideration, a collaboration that reinforced the concordance between parliamentary and judicial conclusions. But from the mid-1990s onward the further twenty-four consultants appointed were mainly drawn from among academic social scientists, historians, and journalists.[10] In a departure from the previous practice of nomination by the chairman, these consultants were recruited by the different political groupings on the committee, injecting the political divisions between these groups directly into the work of interpretation.[11]

The combination of committee members' inexperience, the chairman's conviction that the persistence of a few puzzling features demanded a completely fresh explanatory framework, and the new type of consultant expertise introduced a new interpretive dynamic. First, the academics and journalists who served as consultants after 1994 were more at home than their judicial and police predecessors with composing accounts for public consumption that were both comprehensive and unconstrained by the limitations of having to rely on evidence admissible in court. Their professional expertise inclined them to set the analysis of specific events in overarching politico-historical frameworks. Second, the chairman's insistence that outsiders sympathetic to Western interests had intervened in the kidnapping to obtain any compromising documents Moro might have produced and to cut short further collaboration with the Communist Party tied the events to the recurrent illegal involvement of security services in post-war Italian politics.[12] Such a view, for which neither evidence nor an explanation why Moro should not simply have been murdered in Via Fani was offered, certainly met the requirement on the committee to identify the so-far unpunished architects of violence. But it could hardly avoid provoking the retaliatory insistence by the parties of the center-right that, true to their name, the BR had simply been the pawns of Soviet bloc interests. Third, the abandonment of the division of labor within the committee, which had previously kept the inquiries into different acts of violence under the control of different subgroups, removed the insulation between the treatments of quite distinct events and guaranteed interpretive confrontations, especially since the consultants largely responsible for them were associated with different political groupings. Moreover, as academic or news professionals, they were also keen to publish interpretations of materials to which they had been given privileged access, generating a flow of books by both committee members and by consultants at the same time as the committee was engaged in its hearings.[13] Such public disagreements eliminated any chance of a consensual final report by a committee that had come to serve less as a national institutional interpreter than as an amplifier for any speculative identification of hitherto unidentified responsibilities. The CPS was therefore wound up without producing a final report, despite dedicating most of the last three years of its inquiries to the Moro case.

The CPS's receptiveness to the idea of international involvement was strongly supported by Moro's family and staff.[14] The discovery in 1990 of further letters written by Moro to family members in 1978 was a stimulus to reassert their loyalty to his memory, especially since the dissolution of his party in 1994 removed the main institutional vehicle for his reputation. Moreover, the new focus on Moro's now authenticated memoir, with its reflections on the major national and international events in which he had been a protagonist, drew attention away from identification of its author solely with his letters from the "people's prison" and their humiliating reminder of the impotence of his final days. The family's conviction that not enough had been done by Moro's party colleagues to protect him or obtain his release was thus converted into the view that the BR had been the mere executors of a much larger political plot: Moro had been murdered for strategic, not symbolic, reasons. This view was promoted both in Maria Fida Moro's summary of the allegedly still inexplicable aspects of the kidnapping and in a detailed public exposition by Moro's brother of all the reasons not to consider the event as closed.[15]

This view was directly at odds with the belated but increasingly full descriptions vouchsafed by Moro's captors. Until 1993 only limited insider evidence, often unconfirmed or based on hearsay, had been available. But, in the wake of the general recognition of the failure of "armed struggle" and the determination to reconstruct their identities by public acknowledgement of their crimes, from late 1993 onward Moro's "jailers"—who alone knew the pressures exerted on Moro and perhaps also the intentions behind his more perplexing letters—provided accounts they insisted were both accurate and complete.[16] All repeated that Moro had been selected because he was the least protected of the senior DC leaders; and they denied receiving outside help at any stage. Although cultivation of that suspicion would have reinforced the view that they themselves had been unwittingly manipulated, perhaps even by duplicitous fellow BR members, and would have deflected some of the blame attaching to them, none took this line. The evidence from insiders thus unequivocally endorsed the verdict of sole BR responsibility reached by the first parliamentary committee and by the courts. Inevitably, however, the more closely the multiplying BR testimonies were scrutinized, the more opportunities they offered to skeptics to identify discrepancies and inconsistencies and thus to claim that their authors were concealing the true responsibilities for the kidnapping.[17] The hospitality offered by the CPS to such claims caused many BR members to refuse to testify to it, denying the committee direct exposure to key insider evidence, throwing suspicion over every detail assumed to have been firmly established, and making it impossible to find any accommodation between rival versions of the tragedy.

Conclusion

What the prolonged course of the parliamentary inquiry illustrates is the diversity of the factors that shaped the efforts to establish public memory. Some were internal to the workings of the inquiry: the changing terms of reference, the turnover of members and use of consultants, the dispersal of vital information among mutually hostile protagonists, and the belated emergence of new evidence. Others governed the nature and supply of ingredients on which the committees relied: the defeat of "armed struggle" and the attempts by its protagonists to reconstruct their identities, the determination of Moro's family to prevent his posthumous reputation resting solely on his conduct in the kidnapping, and the transformation of party-political relationships in the 1990s. The interplay of these factors, both social and political, ensured that an inquiry that had earlier approached its original goal of establishing a definitive history turned into the institutional instrument for the manufacture of a mystery.

Notes

1. Oscar Luigi Scalfaro, *Le assemblee elettive nella evoluzione della democrazia italiana (1978–1998)* (Rome: Camera dei Deputati, 1998); Giovanni Moro, testimony to the Parliamentary Committee of Inquiry on March 9, 1999 http://www.parlamento.it/parlam/bicam/terror/stenografici/steno48.htm.

2. For a thorough account of the kidnapping, see Agostino Giovagnoli, *Il caso Moro. Una tragedia repubblicana* (Bologna: Il Mulino, 2005). The most detailed and plausible dissolution of its alleged mysteries is Vladimiro Satta, *Odissea nel caso Moro* (Rome: EDUP, 2003). Satta was the archivist of the second parliamentary committee of inquiry.

3. Moro's wife also instructed one of his political confidants (Ancora) and a close contact in the PCI (Barca) not to intervene (testimony of Luciano Barca to the CPS, meeting no. 47, February 17, 1999, transcript at http://www.parlamento.it/parlam/bicam/terror/stenografici/steno47.htm.

   The reasons for her determination to try to manage initiatives on her own are not clear: perhaps, since from the outset she was convinced that the kidnapping had been orchestrated by Moro's political enemies, she wanted to restrict knowledge of her own actions to those entirely trustworthy members of her husband's immediate staff.

4. B. Caravita di Torrito, "L'inchiesta parlamentare," in *Il Parlamento, Storia d'Italia, Annali 17*, ed. Luciano Violante, 727–41 (Turin: Einaudi, 2001).

5. For these ambitions, see respectively, the *Commissione Parlamentare d'inchiesta sulla strage di Via Fani, sul sequestro e l'assassinio di Aldo Moro e sul terrorismo in Italia* (CPM), vols. 1–11 (Rome: Senato della Repubblica, 1983–84), 1; and Fabrizio Cicchitto, Gianluigi Da Rold, and Francesco Gironda, *La disinformazione in Commissione Stragi* (Milan: Bietti, 2002), 162.

6. Vittorio Cervone, *Ho fatto di tutto per salvare Moro* (Turin: Marietti, 1980).

7. See Gualtieri's statement to the Senate on March 17, 1988, supporting the establishment of the CPS, quoted by his successor as CPS chair, Pellegrino, at his committee's meeting on February 17, 1999.

8. More than half the meetings had to begin after 8 PM and, according to the CPS chair, were frequently inquorate. In only six percent of those meetings did more than ten members (i.e., at least one-quarter of the total membership) ask a question or make a comment.

9. Maria Fida Moro, *La casa dei cento natali* (Milan: Rizzoli, 1982); and Maria Fida Moro, *In viaggio con il mio papà* (Milan: Rizzoli, 1985).

10. For details, see A. D'Agnelli, "Conoscenza storica e giudizio politico: Il ruolo degli storici nelle Commissioni parlamentari d'inchiesta sul terrorismo." Report to the SISSCO convention "Uso pubblico: lo storico come consulente," Lecce, September 25–27, 2003. The consultants included the editor of the first commercial edition of Moro's memoir, Biscione.

11. See the interview with the vice-president of the CPS in Vincenzo R. Manca, *I segreti di San Macuto* (Milan: Edizioni Bietti, 2001), 282.

12. See Giovanni Pellegrino, *Luci sulle stragi* (Milan: Lupetti, 1996); Giovanni Fasanella, Claudio Sestieri, Giovanni Pellegrino, *Segreto di Stato: La verità da Gladio al caso Moro* (Turin: Einaudi, 2000).

13. For accounts by consultants, see Silvio Bonfigli and Jacopo Scé, *Il delitto infinito* (Milan: Kaos, 2002); Francesco Biscione, *Il delitto Moro: Strategia di un assassinio politico* (Rome: Editori Riuniti, 1998). For other intepretations based on committee documents, see Fabrizio Cicchitto et al., *La disinformazione in Commissione Stragi*, and Satta, *Odissea*.

14. The CPS chair gave particular weight to the claims of international involvement made to the committee in 1995 by one of Moro's closest staff members, Corrado Guerzoni, allowing the examination of the truth of Guerzoni's claims to dominate the committee's subsequent investigations (Satta, *Odissea*, 15)

15. Maria Fida Moro, ed., *La nebulosa del caso Moro* (Milan: Selene Edizioni, 2004); Alfredo Carlo Moro, *Storia di un delitto annunciato: Le ombre del caso Moro* (Rome: Editori Riuniti, 1998).

16. Anna Laura Braghetti (with Paola Tavella), *Il prigioniero* (Milan: Mondadori, 1998); Mario Moretti, *Brigate rosse. Una storia italiana* (Milan: Anabasi, 1994). A third captor, Maccari, identified in 1993, confessed in 1996. He was the only one of Moro's four "jailers" to testify to the CPS.

17. A further source of discrepancies between interpretations of the event lay in the direction in which the CPS gathered new evidence. Between 1996 and 2001 it heard from thirty-one witnesses specifically on the Moro case, twenty-four of whom had not appeared in front of the earlier committee.

Part IV

Mafia Murders

9

The Murder of Emanuele Notarbartolo and the Origins of the Mystique of the Mafia

Salvatore Coluccello

The influence of the mafia in economic life, in financial institutions, and in the banks, emerged clearly with the Notarbartolo affair and shocked the entire nation. Emanuele Notarbartolo was the mafia's first "excellent cadaver" drawn from Sicily's social elite. His assassination in 1893, and the sensational series of trials that resulted over the following decade, John Dickie observes, "split Sicilian society in two and astonished public opinion across Italy by exposing the mafia's relationship with politicians, legal officials, and police."[1] The main characters in the affair were two completely different people. Marquis Emanuele Notarbartolo was a descendant of one of the most important aristocratic families in Palermo, admired and highly regarded by all for the moral rectitude and administrative capacity that he had demonstrated as Mayor of Palermo (1873–76) and director general of the *Banco di Sicilia* (1876–90). Notarbartolo was part of the right-wing grouping that supported elitist policies but remained faithful to certain moral principles that opposed political interference in administration. He had in fact stood against the mafioso clientele class that was emerging at the time.

In complete contrast, Raffaele Palizzolo was a member of parliament, elected in 1882, and had considerable powers of patronage. Suspected of being the head mafioso of Caccamo and protector of certain bandits in that area, he had been elected governor of the *Banco di Sicilia* (Bank of Sicily). He was part of the new class of *homines novi* who, unlike Notarbartolo, used politics as a source not only of prestige but also wealth. He was well known for his unscrupulous use of characters on the fringes of legality, henchmen who were an integral part of the local criminal world. During the trial for the murder of Notarbartolo, the famous jurist Gaetano Mosca eloquently described Palizzolo's qualities:

> A man who, without education or special merits, without any ability in producing wealth or in the liberal professions, without possessing a great fortune, without being enrolled in a political party, took his chances in public life and thanks to his activity, audacity, and, it must be said, his effrontery, made his fortune.[2]

Mosca went on to emphasize Palizzolo's capacity to attract the goodwill of the electorate. He had been elected in the town and provincial councils of Palermo to protect a vast network of clients among the lower classes and small dealers:

> He did a great number of favors of all sorts, great and small, legal and illegal. In a single day, he would obtain a gun license for a ruffian [or] an illicit gratification for a council employee, find a charitable institution for an orphan, and push through an affair that the usual bureaucratic delays would have taken six months to complete. He was incredibly popular, if popularity can be described as being easily available for people of all classes, all groups and morality. His house was open indiscriminately to gentlemen and knaves. He welcomed everyone, promised everything, shook everyone's hand, chattered tirelessly with everyone, made everyone understand ... with subtle allusions, how many powerful connections he had, [and] what his relationships with ministers and presidents of the council were, and he even hinted at the particular goodwill which his majesty the King bore towards him.[3]

Palizzolo had managed to accumulate various, diverse positions for himself. Member of Parliament from 1882 to 1898, he was a member of the town and provincial council of Palermo, present in the administrative councils of various organizations such as charitable congregations and groups dedicated to good works. In these various capacities he represented some fifty economic and politico-cultural associations. He had managed to become an administrative council member of the *Banco di Sicilia*, despite opposition from Notarbartolo, who suspected him of having organized his kidnapping in 1882. The authors of that crime, reveals Barone, "discovered by the police on an estate next to property that belonged to Palizzolo, ... turned out to be mafiosi from Caccamo and Villabate, clients of the MP from Palermo."[4]

Up until then, the mafia had limited its influence to the council and judicial offices, but now it tried to move in on the banks. One of the most important was the *Banco di Sicilia*, which, with its agrarian credit, had long attracted the attention of the mafiosi. From 1889, mafioso penetration of the Bank was openly talked about; particularly influential and aggressive politicians were denounced as puppets of the mafia; even Prime Minister Francesco Crispi was accused of involvement. Notarbartolo had been director of the *Banco di Sicilia* for fourteen years. He had attempted to sort out the irregular administration of the bank, but, under pressure from important players in Sicilian politics, he had been removed from this post. Too many people enjoyed benefits and privileges under the traditional administration, both in the form of personal *storni* (transfers), and above all, preferential financial help.[5]

Of these names, the one of Francesco Crispi stuck out. When the illicit relationship between Crispi and some banks in Rome came to light, it was common belief in Palermo that Antonio Di Rudinì—an influential Sicilian politician—would have succeeded in having Notarbartolo re-elected as director of the *Banco*, and that consequently other serious irregularities would have been denounced. Giolitti, then prime minister had also just announced a cleanup operation for the *Banco di Sicilia* because the ex-director, the Duke della Verdura, had speculated on the stock market with the bank's money. Here, too, Notarbartolo, suspected of passing information to the government, was the man to eliminate. On the evening of February 1, 1893, in a first-class railway carriage between Termini Imerese and Palermo, Notarbartolo was assassinated. The first scandal surrounding the Notarbartolo murder, Dickie argues, is that "it took nearly seven years for the case to come to court."[6]

Despite the numerous clues, the judicial inquiry for the crime remained fairly low-key, limiting its attention to the presumed executors of the crime. Its principal aim was to let the presumed instigator of the murder off the hook, and the accused were freed after the investigation because of lack of evidence and objective confirmation. Palizzolo in fact could count on protection from certain areas of the police headquarters and the judiciary, from numerous friendships, and from his considerable political influence. The case thus seemed closed, but thanks to the old friendship with Di Rudinì and his successor, General Pelloux, Notarbartolo's family managed to have the case reopened in 1896. Notarbartolo's son, Leopoldo, raised the problem of presumed partiality. The trial was therefore taken from the magistrates of Palermo and moved to the Court of Assizes in Milan.

The initial attempt to shelve the trial failed, and the examination of two hitherto unknown railway men provided evidence, not only against Palizzolo, but more generally against the mafia. For the first, Notarbartolo's son could denounce Palizzolo publicly as the instigator of the crime, and two members of the *cosca* (gang) of Villabate, Matteo Filippello and Giuseppe Fontana, as the perpetrators. One of the striking aspects of Notarbartolo's son's testimony, maintains Dickie, was that "he was not a witness for the prosecution. In Italy victims can pursue actions for damages during criminal trials, and they can even play a role in arguing the case for the prosecution. He was one such civil complainant."[7] The first testimonies collected by the magistrates at Palermo had accused Fontana and the railway men Carollo and Garulfi as the hit men.

The trial in Milan therefore became a denunciation of the criminal grouping, but it was above all an indictment of the methods used in politics by the Sicilian ruling class. The witnesses for the prosecution revealed the corrupt political environment of the city. Desperate attempts were made to annul the results of the Milanese trial: the chief prosecutor in Palermo, Vincenzo Cosenza, tried to have the formal investigation into Palizzolo's involvement assigned to him,[8] but the state bodies and national public opinion opposed this attempt. For the first time, the national press, including *Corriere della Sera* and other important daily newspapers, paid great attention to the problem of the mafia. There was great interest in the case, and the question of the mafia began to fascinate all the Italians.

In an attempt to explain the origins and reasons for the survival of the phenomenon, scholars of all political colors and experts in the problems of the South began to debate the question. The trial unleashed a series of polemical arguments that were predominantly political. The basic theories that emerged were of two sorts. The first sort was proposed mainly by observers and writers from the South who, while not necessarily *in odore di mafia* (reeking of mafia) themselves, were sometimes acting in bad faith. This theory was defensive and decisively refuted the analogy of mafia crime, considering it a chauvinistic invention of the North to discredit Sicily. This was a position taken up by Pitrè: mafia and being mafioso were two words that belonged to the Sicilian soul and were therefore misunderstood outside Sicily. According to Pitrè, the two words mafia and mafioso belonged to the Sicilian soul and were therefore completely misunderstood outside Sicily. One of the foremost supporters of this theory was Vincenzo Morello, a journalist of Calabrese origins, who signed editorials and articles in the *Tribuna di Roma* with the *nom de plume* "Rastignac." In his opinion, the mafia was above all "a state of mind, . . . a sort of second-rate knightly order, and knights were a sort of first-rate mafia."[9] The second theory was supported by socialist thinkers and held that the mafia had originally been a good institution but that, over time, it had festered and had become a real social cancer. The main supporter of this theory was

Napoleone Colajanni, but other authoritative people from the worlds of culture and politics echoed his thoughts.

Some articles and reports about life on the island were shocking in their crudity. An article about the collusion between mafia and politics in Palermo that appeared in *Il Giorno* of Milan, described Sicily in offensive terms as being "a paradise inhabited by demons, which turns out to be a cancer in the foot of Italy, a province where neither civil traditions nor laws are possible."[10] Napoleone Colajanni, who can certainly not be accused of being a Sicilian sympathizer, reacted by returning the insult: "[Those] ... born and raised on the far side of the Tronto, have been splashing around happily in the sewers and they have brought lurid and pestilential material here."[11]

Italy at the end of the century was shaken by police repression, and the Notarbartolo affair came to symbolize those democratic forces that fought the connivance between the political class, state machinery, and the mafia. Barone observes that "the trial at Milan was considered the first against the national connections of the mafia, a back-to-front "Dreyfus affair" where hidden forces had impeded the prosecution of the guilty for seven years."[12]

On December 1, 1900, in a speech to parliament about the affair, Giuffridda De Felice declared to the country that "the organization is divided into three levels: the first formed by true criminals: the second includes middle class elements and some from the police: and the third contains the high-handed bourgeoisie and the lords of the mafia with their yellow gloves."[13]

In the end, the case had dramatic effects on the Sicilian government, which was forced to seek permission to proceed with the trial of Palizzolo (denied several times previously), and he was arrested after the trial in Milan. The trial in the Lombard capital in fact did not charge Palizzolo with instigating the crime, nor did it state that Notarbartolo had really been killed by the mafia, but it did reveal the nature of the environment around Palizzolo, the secrecy that he exploited, and the violence that characterized his public and administrative life. The debate that had brought Palizzolo to trial had taken place in a fraught atmosphere where the old conflicts (still unresolved) between North and South had emerged. When the trial in Milan was suspended and a new examination began in Palermo, Palizzolo and his accomplices took the opportunity to pull strings and attempted to manipulate the course of justice. To this end, Palizzolo's men decided to play on Sicilian sensibility: they bribed the journalists of the *Fracassa*[14] "to bring all the Sicilian stereotypes out of the attic, and to polish up the image of the island that had been dishonored by the racist preconceptions of the judges at Milan."[15]

The reactions of the people of Palermo were, however, contradictory. So as not to leave the game in the hands of socialists and radicals, the Prince of Camporeale organized a popular meeting where thirty thousand people attended the unveiling of the bust of Notarbartolo. On January 10, 1900, the trial was interrupted on grounds of presumed partiality, and another was held in Bologna.

After some two hundred sessions in Bologna (from September 9, 1900 to July 31, 1902), Palizzolo and Fontana were convicted and sentenced to thirty years in prison. The most important figures in Sicilian and national public life were called to the bench to bear witness:

> Among these, ministers, generals, questors, police officials, politicians, people from the world of economy and finance, including Ignazio Florio; the web of connivance and *omertà* from which Palizzolo had benefited emerged clearly, as did the problem of the mafia which was printed all over the front pages of the national press.[16]

Once again, as in Milan, the trial's central theme was the mafia. All the witnesses called to give evidence for or against the accused were asked "What is the mafia?" Since it was widely believed that the mafia existed only in Sicily, the debate concentrated on Sicily, and the trial in Bologna turned into a trial against Sicilians. Mosca's judgment on the debate in Bologna is partly a synthesis of the sentiment shared by many Sicilians of the period, but it also helps us to understand the events better. Mosca was not a subversive Sicilianist, yet he wrote:

> Little or nothing could be proved against the man accused of the murders of Notarbartolo and Miceli, but he appeared in the worst possible light; if not a delinquent himself then at least he was the protector of delinquents, suspected even of relations with brigands [while] all of Sicily was put in the stocks, all its defects, problems and weaknesses in public and private life were pitilessly displayed, analyzed, sometimes passionately exaggerated, other times unwisely denied; and during those long years of passion, Palizzolo always appeared as the man who embodied and personified what was least good of the region which had spawned him; in part justly, in part unjustly, his name became the symbol of all those moral problems which troubled the noble island.[17]

For the friends who defended him, Palizzolo was the innocent victim of an abuse of power toward Sicily, so his defense almost became a Sicilianist insurrection. Even Pitrè was called to the court in Bologna to give evidence on behalf of Palizzolo. The ethnologist affirmed that Palizzolo was an "upright and honest person, . . . the victim of a series of unfortunate errors made by others."[18] Palizzolo was portrayed as a hero, a symbol of Sicilian protest and the mafia. Instead of being condemned as a criminal phenomenon, his role was justified, and he was portrayed as a bearer of values that were sometimes exaggerated but always worthy of respect:

> If we want to talk about the classic meaning of the word mafia, I can say that mafia is that superior, excellent, not ordinary quality of things, applied to people and things. The official meaning given to the word these days is the awareness, sometimes exaggerated, of one's own personality, superiority, dignity or someone who won't accept oppression; in people inclined to bad deeds, and in general in the slums, these qualities can lead to delinquency. Thus a word which for centuries [was] used for fine things and people ended up meaning a bad thing, because of the evolution of the language.[19]

Pitrè went on to say that only from 1863 did "the word mafia begin to mean something bad" and concluded that *I mafiusi della Vicaria* (The Mafiosi of Vicaria) by Rizzotto planted "the new meaning in the conscience of the public."[20]

At the same time, another mafia trial being held in Palermo came to its conclusion, but all the accused were set free. The sentence given in Bologna that convicted Palizzolo and Fontana therefore seemed to go against expectations. Their convictions were followed by an explosion of protest that became a real political problem. Palizzolo's supporters were neither mafiosi nor violent ruffians; the protest was guided mainly by members of the ruling classes who were not at all concerned about appearing to defend the mafia. On August 3, about thirty people, including Pitrè, met and decided to promote a committee *Pro Sicilia*, a political movement, as the historian Giuseppe Barone rightly observes, "which apart from defending Palizzolo as the victim of a judicial error, played on separatist regionalism, in order to force the state to concede public works and special laws."[21]

Defined by Colajanni as "the revenge of the mafia," the *Pro Sicilia* committee cannot really be given this title, because among its supporters there were also adversaries of Palizzolo. The movement also cut across the Socialist Party and important members of the island's ruling class, "six deputies, . . . jurists, . . . members of the landowning nobility, . . . industrialists and prelates."[22] The daily paper *L'Ora*, owned by the Florio family, became the reference point for *Pro Sicilia*.

The manifesto of the *Pro Sicilia* committee was drawn up by Pitrè, who carried out his job most thoroughly. On August 7, in the *Giornale di Sicilia*, he complained that for a while the Italian press has been talking about the island, sometimes to note its physical attractions, sometimes to emphasize its moral defects. . . . Now one cannot talk about Sicily without talking about the mafia, and mafia and Sicily has become one and the same thing. The mafia is an indigenous plant of Sicily and its deadly flower decorates the breast of every Sicilian. The recent trial at Bologna has crowned the ill-omened process, begun unconsciously, continued thoughtlessly and concluded unhappily. In Sicily, all moral sense has got lost; delinquency in its worst form, in its most criminal manifestations reigns in Sicily with its citadel at Palermo. Here the most atrocious wicked deeds are organized by a shadowy sect who has its leaders in the highest spheres and its roots in the lowest slums. . . . All this is terrible and the soul of every good Sicilian bursts with indignation![23]

Pitrè, one of the most committed fomenters of a tough Sicilianist reaction, defended with much indignation Sicily's honor around which "the sinister and malevolent legend" of the mafia had been created:

And now to the damage caused by the bad reputation, the load of auguries for the future is added, and they say we should expect a healthy regenerative purification, now that the country is saved from the mafia (with the condemnation of Palizzolo) and talk about the new horizons to which we will have the right to aspire.[24]

The Sicilian question then became the Southern question in some articles:

Sicily has until now been forgotten by all except for the taxman; it has no roads, no railways, no redevelopment, while many of the improvements found in other regions are paid with Sicilian money. Sicily doesn't want reimbursements; it only wants to retain its honor. This is right and I always support those in the right.[25]

With the Palizzolo case, the paradigm of the mafia crystallized into a cultural phenomenon, as other authoritative representatives of the island's intelligentsia, such as Gaspare Mosca, who had maintained prudent tones at the beginning of the trial, took up Pitrè's theories:

The spirit of the mafia can be seen as a way of feeling which means not turning to official justice and avenging one's self (not specifically Sicilian although it is more developed there) or as the antisocial sentiment of small organized minorities, . . . exclusive to the rising classes, the gabellotti [strong men].[26]

Sicilianism, which became an ideological-cultural movement during the Notarbartolo trial, was not in itself a mafioso ideology, but it soon came to be used in this way. The links between mafioso ideology and Sicilianism occurred where the traditional values of the Sicilian people were indiscriminately defended (one of the slogans of Sicilianism had been in fact the affirmation that the mafia did not exist, at least not as a specific criminal reality). This aspect of Sicilianism was exploited by the mafia in order to gain followers from the Sicilian cultural milieu, and, thanks to the historical context and the generally low levels of education, the mystification was confirmed of the problem, something that certainly could never have occurred in an earlier period. This episode enabled the mafioso culture to spread its tentacles among the people. As Dalla Chiesa rightly observes:

> nor could the successive inclusion of elements of popular or democratic origins in the cultural-intellectual elite bring the necessary de-mystification, as the propaganda of mafioso origin had sunk too deep for too long. This original error dangerously discredited Sicilian culture and politics up until our times, and polluted (in a different way) even the conscience of the most progressive forces consequently.[27]

Sicilianism has assisted the mafia much more than systematic violence has ever done.

The political function of Sicilianism has often been fulfilled in a certain way manipulating and channeling a gamut of "sentimental attitudes." Before becoming a political ideology based on the autonomy and independence of the island, Sicilianism was primarily a confused sense of solidarity among Sicilians and against governments, occupations, and interventions from the outside, a vague and complex feeling that even ends up containing some elements of the mafia spirit. As the historian Giuseppe Carlo Marino has clearly demonstrated, Sicilianism is a complex mechanism of varying states of mind, such as an exaggerated sense of *campanilismo* (local pride), which swings from "a frustrated superiority complex to an unacknowledged inferiority complex."[28] This sense of local pride reacts to stimuli from the outside (such as the often unfair accusation that Sicily equals mafia) and often unites Sicilians. The Sicilian ruling classes have often cleverly manipulated this unity to refute accusations of corruption and bad government, thereby "helping to consolidate the sentiment of a special Sicilian condition that is almost an essential saving or damning quality."[29]

The mobilization of the *Pro Sicilia* committee was so effective that the Supreme Court of Appeal overturned the sentence because of a procedural flaw, and a retrial was held in Florence on September 5, 1903. Many years had passed since the crime and the scandal had shocked Milan; the great public interest that had marked the first two trials was now fading. The evidence "collapsed piece by piece like stones in a disassembled mosaic, and the tragic atmosphere that had animated the trial in Bologna were missing."[30] The only witness to break the law of *omertà* (conspiracy of silence) was found hanging in a room in Florence a few days before the trial, having apparently committed suicide.

The Notarbartolo case was closed on July 23, 1904, with a general acquittal for lack of evidence, typical for mafia trials. After the acquittal, Palizzolo returned to Palermo by boat where he received a hero's welcome.[31] Yet, as Dickie rightly argues, "the jubilation did not last long."[32] In the November parliamentary elections he was not elected. "Despite his triumph, he was now too compromised and his powerful friends abandoned him."[33]

In 1900 the police delegate Antonino Cutrera published a book called *La mafia e i mafiosi* (The Mafia and the Mafiosi) at Palermo; it became a classic for research on the mafia. Cutrera knew all about the compromises that the government had made with the Sicilian *notables*, having had firsthand experience during his years of service; he knew that the key to the question was the continual agreements made in exchange for governmental majorities at the moment of the elections. Referring to the great impression that the Notarbartolo murder had made and the emotion that the trial had provoked in the public, Cutrera wrote that an external observer would have thought that the mafia was a recent phenomenon.[34] In other words, how could one reconcile the heartfelt indignation of the people with the persistence of the phenomenon? The reply identified precisely the cause of the errors and failures that inevitably occurred when the fight against the mafia dealt only with the emotional aspect.

In fact, the acquittal of Palizzolo marked the end of a decade that had seen the mafia at the center of political struggle and cultural debate. The interest in Sicily and the rest of the country was much more widespread and deeply felt than before, and the most important national newspapers—and, just as importantly, many scholars—were drawn into the debate. Obviously, the image of the mafia was altered by these events. The phenomenon had been seen as a national problem, principally, as Renda explains, "to be exploited as a reason for considering Sicilians unsuitable for a role in the national government of the country equal to that of the regions of the Center and North."[35] With the failure of the governments of Crispi and Di Rudinì and the end-of-century crisis, the problem of the mafia no longer had national importance and became a local fact, cultivated by Sicilian scholars such as Alongi, Cutrera, Mosca, Colajanni, and Pitrè. On the scene of mafia culture though, only Pitrè had the same sort of weight as the inquiries of Franchetti and Bonfadini had had. Pitrè was not a "mafiologist" but he was the real victor of the political and cultural debate of the years 1899–1902. It was not the appearance of the volumes *Usi e Costumi dei Siciliani* (Customs and Manners of the Sicilians), published a decade earlier, in which only a few pages were dedicated to the mafia, that gave Pitrè the title of ideological defender of the mafia, but rather his evidence during the trial of Bologna in defense of Palizzolo, and his article published in the *Giornale di Sicilia* in 1902 in which the mafia was justified as bearer of Sicilian values, sometimes exaggerated but worthy of respect, rather than being condemned as a criminal. We can certainly conclude that if the inquiry by Franchetti and Sonnino was attacked for being anti-Sicilian, Pitrè characterized and defined the cultural aspect of the debate about the mafia in the Sicilianist sense.

Notes

1. John Dickie, *Cosa Nostra* (London: Hodder and Stoughton, 2004), 128.
2. Gaetano Mosca, *Uomini e cose di Sicilia* (Palermo: Sellerio, 1980), 52.
3. Ibid., 52.
4. Giuseppe Barone, "Mafia e finanza: il delitto Notarbartolo", in *Storia d'Italia, le regioni, la Sicilia* (Torino: Einaudi, 1987), 310.
5. Dickie argues that the Bank's money was being used to protect the share price of NGI, the Florio's shipping company, during delicate contract negotiations with the government. Dickie, *Cosa Nostra*, 134.
6. Ibid., 138.
7. Ibid.
8. Dickie writes that "he would later do his best to undermine Sangiorgi's prosecution of the mafia of the Conca d'Oro" ibid.
9. Enzo Magrì, *L'onorevole padrino* (Milano: Rizzoli, 1992), 53.
10. *Il giorno*, January 8, 1900.
11. Francesco Renda, *Storia della mafia* (Palermo: Sigma, 1997), 156.
12. Barone, "Mafia e finanza: il delitto Notarbartolo," 313
13. Magrì, *L'onorevole padrino*, 64.
14. A newspaper was founded by the committee that supported Palizzolo's innocence; Amalia Crisantino, *Capire la mafia* (Palermo: La Luna, 1994), 44.
15. Barone, "Mafia e finanza: il delitto Notarbartolo," 314.
16. Francesco Renda, *Storia della Sicilia*, vol. 2 (Palermo: Sellerio, 1985), 245.
17. Mosca, *Uomini e cose di Sicilia*, 158.
18. Giuseppe Bonomo, *Pitrè, la Sicilia e i siciliani* (Palermo: Sellerio, 1989), 343.
19. Ibid.
20. Ibid.
21. Barone, "Mafia e finanza: il delitto Notarbartolo," 318.
22. Ibid.
23. Bonomo, *Pitrè, la Sicilia e i siciliani*, 346.
24. Ibid.

25. Nando Dalla Chiesa, *Il potere mafioso* (Milano: Mazzotta, 1976), 175.

26. Mosca, *Uomini e cose di Sicilia*, 175.

27. Dalla Chiesa, *Il potere mafioso*, 179.

28. Giuseppe Carlo Marino, *L'opposizione mafiosa* (Palermo: Flaccovio, 1996), 12.

29. Ibid.

30. Leopolodo Notarbartolo, *Memorie di mio padre* (Pistoia: Seppia, 1949), 394.

31. The Florios' newspaper *L'Ora*, observes Dickie, said the city had been liberated from a nightmare by the Florentine jury. Palizzolo supporters had pictures of him on their lapels. The Festival of the Madonna del Carmine had been postponed to allow the returning hero to take part. Dickie, *Cosa Nostra*, 150.

32. Ibid.

33. Ibid., 151.

34. Antonino Cutrera, *La mafia ed i mafiosi. Saggio di sociologia criminale* (Palermo: Reber, 1900).

35. Renda, *Storia della mafia*, 164.

10

Mafia and Antimafia: Sciascia and Borsellino in Vincenzo Consolo's *Lo spasimo di Palermo*

Daragh O'Connell

In this study, the figure of Paolo Borsellino and his assassination are analyzed in a literary context in relation to Vincenzo Consolo's 1998 novel
Lo spasimo di Palermo (The Agony of Palermo). This narrative constitutes
a break within the Sicilian literary tradition and is one of the first examples
in Sicilian literature in which a judicial figure is accorded positive values
and heroic status. Consolo's *Giudice* (Judge) figure is the unnamed, though
thinly veiled Paolo Borsellino, whose assassination at the end of the novel
represents the death of the Italian state and articulates Consolo's own dis-
avowal of the novel form. Conversely, positive values accorded to an institutional figure such as a judge are notably lacking in the writings of
Consolo's mentor Leonardo Sciascia: the figure of the judge, who ought to
embody and be an agent of justice, is more often portrayed as an unjust,
negative element corrupted by and partaker in the shadowy power structures of Italian life.[1] Consolo's text establishes a dialogue with Sciascia's
polemical pronouncements on the *professionisti dell'antimafia* (antimafia
professionals) and attempts to reconcile the literary and judicial antimafia
traditions of the island.

The assassinations of Giovanni Falcone and Paolo Borsellino in May
and July of 1992 sent shock waves throughout Europe. The ramifications of
these acts, neatly classified as the *strategia stragista* (strategy of massacre),

were manifold: for Cosa Nostra it signaled a change in direction and political affiliation and would lead to the eventual capture and incarceration of Totò Riina and many other top level mafiosi; initially for the Italian state it marked a re-evaluation of legislation in tackling organized crime, with the introduction of laws envisaged by Falcone; and perhaps more resonantly, there seemed to be a move away from the culture of silence and tacit acceptance on the part of Sicilians, to which the scenes at the funerals and the later marches and cultural initiatives attest.

More than a decade after these horrific events, however, an unclear picture emerges from Sicily: various *pentiti* (literally "penitents"; used of ex-mafiosi who turn state's evidence) have sketched an uneven picture of those two days in May and July. The most recent boss of bosses, Bernardo Provenzano, was captured on April 11, 2006, just outside the town of Corleone, and it is still unclear which direction the mafia will favor next. The recent testimonies of the antimafia magistrates Gian Carlo Caselli and Antonio Ingroia, have thrown great light on the issues affecting the fight against Cosa Nostra today. The *strategia stragista* of Riina was quickly replaced by what they term the *strategia del silenzio* (strategy of silence) favored by Provenzano, or more technically, the *cono d'ombra* (cone of darkness)—a strategy to render Cosa Nostra invisible.[2] Recent studies into the contemporary situation have actually intimated a new term to replace that of Cosa Nostra: *Cosa Nuova* (New Thing).[3] Added to this is the irrevocable change in the makeup of the Italian party political system. Despite some stunning initial victories, the actual fight against the mafia was halted by the Berlusconi government with legislation deliberately intended to question the value of *pentiti* as a tool against the mafia, and reforms of the judiciary to curb the power of investigative magistrates, because of their supposedly intractable anti-Berlusconi stance, have greatly hindered progress.

While all of these issues are of great importance and are currently undergoing a process of transition, another aspect of the legacy of Falcone and Borsellino that tends to be overlooked is the cultural legacy, and in particular, the sometimes thorny issue of the relationship between Sicilian writers and the mafia. What today we call Sicilian literature is, in effect, a literature wrought with uneasy and sometimes obfuscating pronouncements on the subject of the mafia. More noteworthy still is the representation of the Italian state and its institutions when viewed through the lens of the Sicilian writer. No other literature in Italy is as pessimistic or as critical of state intentions as the Sicilian.

Paradoxically, it was not until the postwar period and the concomitant return to power of the mafia in those years that Sicilian writers began to voice their disquiet about the rampant abuses and increasing encroachment of the mafia. Prior to this period, literary luminaries such as Giovanni Verga, Luigi Capuana, Federico De Roberto, and Luigi Pirandello had all either denied its existence or ignored the phenomenon in their works. The great ethnologist Giuseppe Pitrè even went so far as to completely deny its existence through a tortuously convoluted etymological, though ultimately revealing, explanation of the terms *mafia* and *omertà* (code of silence).[4] It was not until the emergence of a new generation of writers that the voices of dissent were heard and the opening of this island wound could begin. Foremost among these voices was Leonardo Sciascia, who quite rightly became the figurehead for the new writing. His own consternation with his fellow islanders of the past is best expressed in an essay on the subject "Literature and Mafia" in the collection *Cruciverba* (1983):

> I would only like to consider the paradoxical situation in which a literature committed to not betraying the truth, to communicating reality, with regard to the mafia has observed a sort of *omertà* or has given a representation of it more characterized by abstract philological and etymological meanings of it.[5]

Today the situation is quite different, and writing about the mafia has become de rigueur, though not always with an understanding of the competing discourses within such a contentious subject. What is of interest, however, is how Sicilian intellectuals responded to the assassinations of Falcone and Borsellino in 1992—how, in the absence of Sciascia, they confronted these events either through public statements or creative acts.[6]

The cultural discourse on the mafia is one that is largely informed by literary expression; antimafia judges past and present, from Falcone and Borsellino to their successors like Caselli and Ingroia, have all at one stage or another cited their debt to Sciascia for unveiling the mafia culture pervading western and central Sicily. They cite above all, Sciascia's *giallo* (detective novel), or rather, 'anti-giallo' *Il giorno della civetta* (The Day of the Owl, 1961) as the text on which they grounded their antimafia stance. But the role assigned to Sciascia by the media and others as the cultural spokesperson for the Sicilian antimafia movement was one with which he was very uneasy. To fully appreciate the newness and various operations conducted by Consolo in *Lo spasimo*, it is necessary to reexamine the context from which they emerge, and understand Sciascia's role in it.

In the last decade of his life, Sciascia became embroiled in a series of controversies that have cast a shadow over his reputation. After the assassination of Carlo Alberto Dalla Chiesa in 1982, his son Nando attacked Italian intellectuals, and Sciascia in particular, for contributing to a *pax mafiosa* due to their silence on the death of his father.[7] He even went so far as to accuse Sciascia of "playing the mafia's game." Sciascia's responses were scathing and set the tone for many of his pronouncements on antimafia subjects of later years collected in *A futura memoria* (To Future Memory, 1989).[8] Peter and Jane Schneider have written that it is difficult for Sicilians "to sustain a thorough and consistent antimafia stance without turning their backs on, or appearing to reject their own roots," and that this polemic demonstrates the complexities inherent in seeking emancipation from the mafia without "embracing the almost racialized categorization of Sicilians that permeates the national discourse on the South."[9] The later polemics came under the title *I professionisti dell'antimafia* (The Professionals of Anti-Mafia), which the Schneiders are wrong in attributing to Sciascia himself; the Sicilian writer made it clear that it was an editorial decision.[10] Furthermore, their study argues that Sciascia was out of step with the new culture of the *Coordinamento antimafia* (Antimafia Network), ostensibly because of a generational gap, and that the nature and power of the mafia had changed irrevocably from Sciascia's conception of it as a rural phenomenon. They based their findings almost exclusively on his 1961 essay *Pirandello e la Sicilia* (Pirandello and Sicily) and the 1979 interview book *La Sicilia come metafora* (Sicily as a Metaphor). A more encompassing approach to Sciascia's position, however, can be achieved by also reading his middle and later works, especially with regard to their isolation of the themes of justice and power, and not limiting Sciascia to his early, mafia-focused works.

However, what is unquestionably true of Sciascia's pieces that made up his attack on the antimafia movement is that they had a dire effect on two men, Giovanni Falcone and Paolo Borsellino. In the latter half of the 1980s, during the so-called *Primavera palermitana* (Palermo Spring), a period of marked renewal and optimism due largely to the astonishing successes of the antimafia pool during the maxi-trials, Sciascia astounded everybody by openly criticizing the umbrella organization of the *Coordinamento antimafia*. His particular target was Palermo's mayor Leoluca Orlando, but he also used as an example of the dangerous power of this new movement the selection of Paolo Borsellino over more senior figures to the procurator's office of Marsala. Somebody had furnished Sciascia with the minutes of the 1986 decision of the CSM's (*Consiglio Superiore della Magistratura*—the governing body of Italy's independent judicial branch). In later pieces he designed to distance himself from the furor that ensued, Sciascia stated that he did not know Borsellino personally and had only used the example to highlight how antimafia magistrates won advancement while others did not. It was hardly a tenable position, but Sciascia was unwilling to retract his statements. Both Lucentini and Collura, Borsellino and Sciascia's biographers, respectively, recount that Borsellino and Sciascia later met on two occasions and clarified their positions. Sciascia is also said to have apologized personally to Borsellino for having named him.[11]

The true victim in all of this, however, was Falcone. He understood that a chorus of opportunists was waiting in the wings to join the dissent, attack the work of the antimafia pool by co-opting Sciascia, and thus dismantle the credibility of the maxi-trials and their procedures; this, indeed, did happen. According to his biographer La Licata, Falcone, is reported to have said when he later broke with Leoluca Orlando, "Sciascia was perfectly right: I'm not referring to the concrete examples he used, but more in general."[12] Moreover, Falcone was later surreptitiously passed over for the role of Palermo's chief prosecutor, due in part to the machinations of colleague Vincenzo Geraci in the CSM and in part to the skilful manipulation of some of the arguments Sciascia had used against Borsellino's promotion.[13]

But what exactly was Sciascia attacking in these articles? From the very outset of his career, Sciascia's works displayed a deep mistrust of the power structures of the state, especially that of the judiciary. Moreover, he issued a warning about the dangers of certain unchecked measures against the mafia when he stated that he was the first to have given "a non-apologetic representation of the phenomenon, but always with the worry that one would finish up defeating it utilizing the same means that fascism had used to defeat it (one mafia against another)."[14] The articles in *A futura memoria* highlight his deep commitment to democratic means and belief in the pure principles of law, coupled with the fear that the judicial system can arrogate to itself special powers that go beyond democracy, and recall instead the Sicilian memory of the Inquisition and fascism:

> But democracy is not impotent in combating the mafia. Or rather: there is nothing within its system, its principles, which would necessarily bring it to not being able to combat the mafia. . . . Rather, it has within its hands the instrument which tyranny does not: the law, everyone equal under the law, the scales of justice. If one were to substitute the symbol of the scales with that of handcuffs—as some fanatics of the antimafia network desire deep down—we would be irredeemably lost, in a way that not even fascism managed.[15]

What Sciascia called for was "a return to the rules, to the law, to the constitution," instead of the "handcuff culture."[16] According to Farrell, Sciascia's "trust in justice allied with a distrust of judges and judgment provided an uncomfortably paradoxical position for a writer motivated by a visceral hatred for the rule of mere strength."[17] Sciascia's position has something akin to Walter Benjamin's notion of the workings of institutional law as a "tendency to retribution,"[18] though he believed there to be a pure concept of law outside of reality. Di Grado writes that Sciascia "hesitated between the cult of law and the thirst for justice, between the guarantees of his enlightened-liberal formation and the avenging nature of Friar Diego La Matina."[19] There is a curious binary in Sciascia's works between the judge figure and that of the Inquisitor, as in *Todo modo*, when Don Gaetano says of the procurator Scalambri, "He does not forget he is an inquisitor and judge as I don't forget I am a priest."[20]

Save for the "piccolo giudice" ("little judge") of *Porte aperte* (Open Doors), all of Sciascia's judicial figures are cast in a shadowy and threatening light, as is evident in *La strega e il capitano* (The Witch and the Captain) where he states, "The administration of justice has always been terrifying wherever it is practiced. Especially when faiths, beliefs, superstitions, reasons of State or reasons of faction dominate it and insinuate themselves in it."[21] Sciascia's judges are almost all villains, the most recognizable being the judge Riches in *Il contesto* (The Context, 1971) and his infamous anti-enlightenment speech, or perhaps more tellingly, the smug and disturbingly idiotic Procurator in *Una storia semplice* (A Simple Story, 1989). Sciascia's attacks on the antimafia movement were in effect warnings about where such a movement could arrive if its powers were not checked.

This, then, is the cultural and social background from which *Lo spasimo di Palermo* finds articulation. Throughout Consolo's career he has demonstrated a strong sense of moral outrage with regard to the mafia and wedded this to a literary poetics, which at every turn strives to speak out against injustice. More often than not, critical appraisals of Consolo's narratives tend to focus on their linguistic, stylistic, and hyperliterary aspects, the "specifically Consolian poetic procedures of grafting intertexts on to his own, selecting and placing side-by-side diverse, and often jarring languages and dialects, vacillating between high and low registers, and fusing metrical forms into his narrative prose."[22] What can be overlooked is the almost Sciascian civic humanism with which his work is imbued and an *impegno* (engagement) against all abuse of power. But above all, Consolo's stance is directed at those who hold the keys to the power structures of Italy: not solely its elected representatives but also its legislators, codifiers, lawmakers, media tycoons, advertising executives, presidents and directors of public and private corporations, print and television editors, and cultural spokespersons and writers.

Lo spasimo di Palermo, however, is much more than another chronicle of the Sicilian mafia. Consolo's protagonist, Gioacchino Martinez, is an autobiographical construct: a writer who has lost all faith in the genre of the novel, he is a victim of the culture industry, but more importantly, an internal exile who was forced to leave Sicily in the 1950s and go to Milan because of the ever-encroaching power of the mafia. At the novel's outset the protagonist arrives in Paris to visit his son—another exile, forced to be so because of his affiliation to far-left political groupings during the so-called *anni di piombo* (Years of Lead). In the lobby of his hotel Gioacchino is confronted with the image of a silent-screen hero of his youth on a poster: *Judex*.[23] The shock of this image reawakens memories in him, causing him to relive the traumas of his life—the joys and pains, and the involuntary and conscious guilt of his past. At the Gaumont during a private screening, Gioacchino finally views the end of the episode from his youth, and this leads to considerations on the serial form that will have further implications as the narrative progresses:

> In the end destiny punishes and reconciles, placates every contrast. . . . Thus the *feuilleton* always concludes outside of the law, the courts, the pre-civil vendetta dissolves into sentiment, the order of power and money is recomposed. The dark shadow lengthens, the devouring sect cowers, the black silhouette of the avenger triumphs.[24]

The figure of the *giustiziere*, or avenger, takes on increasing importance as the narrative proceeds and leads the protagonist to consider Sicilian examples of those who seek justice or vengeance without availing themselves of the law, in particular the secret sect of the "Beati Paoli" who held their secret tribunals and administered justice in the underground passageways of the Palermo of lore.[25] In the second half of the novel, Gioacchino returns to Palermo after many years and takes up residence in Via D'Astorga, the name Consolo gives to his imagined Via D'Amelio. Not long after his return Gioacchino encounters an investigative judge, the son of an elderly lady who lives across the street. The judge recognizes Gioacchino and offers to accompany him home with his escort:

> In the car the judge softened a little his rigid expression, with a faint smile under his graying moustache.
> "I've read your books . . . difficult, they say. In one of them some lines about Palermo have remained with me", he half-closed his eyes and recited: "Palermo is fetid, infected. This fervid July it exhales the sweetish smell of blood and jasmine . . . "
> "A number of years have passed since then . . . " Gioacchino said.
> "But nothing has changed, believe me. You'll see, next July will be the same . . . or maybe worse."[26]

Despite the premonitory and ominous undertones, the Borsellino figure is actually quoting verbatim from Consolo's 1988 collection of short stories

Le pietre di Pantalica (The Stones of Pantalica), rendering the intertextuality of the passage a curious form of self-plagiarism:

> Palermo is fetid, infected. This fervid July it exhales the sweetish smell of blood and jasmine, the pungent odor of disinfectant and frying oil. . . . The murdered, tied hand and foot like kids, throats cut, beheaded, gutted closed in black refuse bags, in car booths, since the beginning of the year are over seventy.[27]

With the identities of Consolo and Borsellino thus established from these literary constructs, the reader is left in no doubt as to the direction the narrative will take. The inevitability of the outcome makes its articulation all the more interesting, as Consolo endeavors to reconcile the chasm between the cultural and judicial strands of the antimafia stance through recourse to Sciascia and renewal of those traditions. Di Grado states that the meeting between the two "has the feel of a much-needed and liberating reconciliation, after the *professionisti dell'antimafia* polemics."[28]

Who then assassinates the Borsellino figure in Consolo's novel? The narrative remains deeply ambiguous on this point, an ambiguity that is redolent of some of Sciascia's fiction, but one that also implicates the state, or rather, certain bodies within the state that act outside of the law in open collusion with the mafia. The "glabrous man" who spies on Gioacchino in Paris is a member of the secret services; he turns up again in Milan and once more in Palermo. Initially, Gioacchino believes he is being followed because of his son's past activities, but the sight of the "glabro" in the *Grand Hôtel des Palmes* in Palermo quashes that naïve belief.[29] Gioacchino's journey to Palermo is accompanied by the presence of a talkative *baffuto* (mustachioed man) with a concealed weapon. This is a clear allusion to the "With Moustache" and "Without Moustache" figures of Elio Vittorini's *Conversazione in Sicilia* and therefore another component of the state's police. Why such figures should be monitoring Gioacchino is only made clear with the realization that the husband of his caretaker's daughter is in fact a mafioso. The knowing nod between the *baffuto* and this mafioso underlines the connection between Cosa Nostra and some darker element within the state. Nothing is explicit in the novel, and Consolo is keen to open out the web of culpability and extend it beyond the actual executors of the massacre. The final pages before the huge bomb explosion that kills the Borsellino figure and his escort are in the form of a confessional letter to his son Mauro. This letter constitutes the moral and artistic nexus of the novel and offers the reader a lucid and taut description of personal and collective responsibility in Italy in its metaphorical center: Palermo. The various symbolic threads of the narrative come together before the all-too-inevitable climax: "You know that this city has become a battlefield, a daily bloodbath. They shoot guns, explode bombs, they tear apart human lives, carbonize bodies, squashed body parts on trees and asphalt—oh, the infernal crater on the airport road!—It is a bestial fury, an extermination."[30]

He states that their principal target is the judges, and for the first time in the Sicilian tradition these judges are called "judges of a new culture, firm ethics and complete commitment," different from the judges before them or those still active. They are forced to fight on two fronts, the first of which is the war within their institutions, within the judicial branch, and in remarkably Sciascian terms he names this arm of the judiciary as "enthralled by power or nostalgic for the hangman":

> I met a judge, an Assistant Procurator, who used to work with the murdered one. . . . I see him from the window sometimes arrive with his escort in Astorga Street to visit his ageing mother. . . . I see him ever more pallid, tense, the eternal cigarette between his fingers. I feel sorry for him, believe me, and every one of them involved in this war.[31]

Consolo continues the theme of these new ethical judges, who work within the law, and makes the connection between Borsellino and the Judex of his youth. This in turn will lead to further considerations on the nature of justice and law and how the two may compliment each other:

> When he gets out of his car, crosses the street, places himself in the doorway, it's then that I see on the back of my Assistant Procurator, the black cape of Judex, the hero of the interrupted film of my childhood long ago. . . . The black cape is a paradox that is transformed into the robe of the one who investigates and judges using the force of the law. And it is for me also literary. What I mean is: as well as in England, in the France of State and Rights there grew the figure of the avenger who judges and sentences outside of the law. Balzac, Dumas and Sue are its fathers, with vast filiations, up to *Judex*'s Bernède and Feuillade and to our own Natoli, whose *Beati Paoli* has been the gospel for mafiosi.[32]

Borsellino then, represents something wholly new, yet paradoxically something much older than the historical and modern cultural models and configurations of a *justicier*. Consolo seems to be alluding to one of the original meanings for the term, and thus reunites it to its original referent. In the Mortillaro Sicilian-Italian dictionary we read: "*Giustizièri*—Originally was a term signifying Magistrate maintainer of justice."[33] If Sciascia considers Diego La Matina, Cres, Rogas, and the painter in *Todo modo* as models for the *giustiziere*, in that they hold a vision of personal justice that transcends and works outside institutional law, conversely, Consolo's figure of justice also represents justice as it is expressed in law, and it is through him that the application of law justice is rendered. In short, he is the complete *Giustiziere*.

However, this is short lived, and the Borsellino figure is unsustainable. No matter who the true instigators are of the murder that is about to unfold, Consolo implicates an entire nation, including himself, as well as a way of life, for the coming end:

> In this country, conversely, in this rabble of families, this maternal confessional of absolution, where the state is occupied by mafia or secret sects of Dévorants, by shadowy and all-powerful Ferraguses or Cagliostros, where all of us, governors and citizens alike, work hard at eluding and breaking the law, the judge who applies the law seems to us like a Judex, an intolerable avenger, to be excluded, removed. Or killed.[34]

The end of this passage shares a remarkable kinship with and step forward from Sciascia's most complete statement on the figure of the judge from *Porte aperte*:

> And here one must say that the judge, the man who chooses the occupation of judging his peers, for southern Mediterranean people, for every south, is a comprehensible figure if corrupt; if he is unreadable in his feelings and intentions, as if disjoined from human and common opinion, he is then incomprehensible, if neither by goods or friendship or compassion he allows himself to be corrupted.[35]

Consolo's Judge figure extends Southern incomprehension to national distrust and distaste. In the aftermath of Borsellino's murder Sciascia's "incomprehensible" judge is transformed by Consolo into the new judge, a Sicilian Judex, working for justice inside the boundaries of law, but therefore "intolerable." As is already known, he will be assassinated, yet what has never been commented on is the fact that Consolo has his protagonist, the pessimistic writer of difficult novels, rush from his apartment to warn the judge only to be himself blown up by same the bomb that kills the judge and his escort. The deaths of the judge and writer figures coincide with Consolo's own abandonment of narrative. This is a strange case indeed of "Death of the Author," but one that perhaps alludes to a final reconciliation between the two most important strands of the antimafia tradition in Sicily. In Consolo's text the killing of Borsellino becomes a site for the reconciliation of these traditions. The novel then, is a critical and creative experiencing of the antimafia discourse, mediated and articulated through a conscious engagement with Sciascia's polemical pronouncements and a redefinition of the role of the judiciary in the fight against the mafia in Sicilian life and culture.

Notes

1. I am using the term *giudice* loosely throughout, following the Italian model, though the very real distinction between the judges who sit in judgment and investigative judges/magistrates (Falcone and Borsellino) should be borne in mind. Consolo does not highlight the distinction.
2. Gian Carlo Caselli and Antonio Ingroia, *L'eredità scomoda. Da Falcone ad Andreotti. Sette anni a Palermo* (Milan: Feltrinelli, 2001), 87.
3. Ernesto Oliva and Salvo Palazzolo, *L'altra mafia: biografia di Bernardo Provenzano* (Catanzaro: Rubbettino, 2001), 7.
4. Giuseppe Pitrè, *Usi e costumi, credenze e pregiudizi del popolo siciliano* (Catania: Clio, 1993), 287–301. First published, 1891.
5. Leonardo Sciascia, *Opere 1971–1983* (Milan: Bompiani, 1989), 1108.
6. The site for the assassination of Borsellino was Palermo's Via D'Amelio where his mother lived. It is a common practice of the Italian media to mark such national atrocities through the naming of the location, hence Falcone's assassination two months previously was given the appellation *strage di Capaci*.
7. Nando Dalla Chiesa, *Delitto imperfetto: Il generale, la mafia, la società italiana* (Rome: Editori Riuniti, 2003), 260–64.
8. Sciascia had also chosen the moment of General Dalla Chiesa's death to reveal that Dalla Chiesa was not, as had hitherto been presumed, the model for his Captain Bellodi character in *Il giorno della civetta*. The timing was very odd and enraged Dalla Chiesa's son.
9. Peter Schneider and Jane Schneider, "Il Caso Sciascia: Dilemmas of the Antimafia Movement in Sicily," in *Italy's 'Southern Question': Orientalism in One Country*, ed. Jane Schneider (Oxford: Berg, 1998), 245.
10. Sciascia, *Opere 1971–1983*, 878.
11. Umberto Lucentini, *Paolo Borsellino* (Milan: San Paolo, 2003), 131–45; Matteo Collura, *Il maestro di Regalpetra. Vita di Leonardo Sciascia* (Milan: Longanesi, 1996), 343–44.
12. Francesco La Licata, *Storia di Giovanni Falcone* (Milan: Feltrinelli, 2003), 118.
13. For an excellent reading of this whole period and the weakening of Falcone's position, see Alexander Stille, *Excellent Cadavers. The Mafia and the Death of the First Italian Republic* (London: Vintage, 1995), 212–59.
14. Sciascia, *Opere 1971–1983*, 769.
15. Ibid., 877.
16. Ibid., 875.
17. Joseph Farrell, *Leonardo Sciascia* (Edinburgh: Edinburgh University Press, 1995), 31.

18. Walter Benjamin, "The Meaning of Time in the Moral Universe," in *Selected Writings, 1913–1926* by Walter Benjamin (Cambridge MA: Belknap Press, 1996), 286.

19. Antonio Di Grado, '*Quale in lui stesso alfine l'eternità lo muta . . .* ' *Per Sciascia dieci anni dopo* (Caltanisetta-Rome: S. Sciascia, 1999), 77. Diego La Matina was a historical figure who murdered the Lord Inquisitor Giovanni Lopez de Cisneros and was the inspiration for Sciascia's 1964 *Morte dell'Inquisitore*.

20. Sciascia, *Opere 1971–1983*, 175.

21. Leonardo Sciascia, *Opere: 1984–1989* (Milan: Bompiani, 1991), 216.

22. Daragh O'Connell, "Consolo's 'trista conca': Dantean anagnorisis and echo in *Il sorriso dell'ignoto marinaio*," in *Echi danteschi/Dantean Echoes*, ed. R. Bertoni (Turin: Trauben, 2003), 100.

23. *Judex* was created and directed by Louis Feuillade (1873–1925) and written by Arthur Bernède (1871–1937). This screen serial ran to 24 episodes between 1916 and 1918. The Judex of the title is a black-caped crusader and mysterious avenger drawn from the French tradition of the *justicier*. Gioacchino's fascination with this character stems from the fact that as a child his viewing of one of the episodes was interrupted by allied bombing. His desire to see how the episode ended leads him to view a restored version at the Gaumont in Paris.

24. Vincenzo Consolo, *Lo spasimo di Palermo* (Milan: Mondadori, 1998), 47.

25. The legend of the secret avenging sect of the "Beati Paoli" was made popular in Sicily by Luigi Natoli's serialized novel *I Beati Paoli* (originally published in 239 episodes for the *Giornale di Sicilia*; later published in book form, it went on to become the most popular book in Sicily after the Bible).

26. Consolo, *Lo spasimo di Palermo*, 115.

27. Vincenzo Consolo, *Le pietre di Pantalica* (Milan: Mondadori, 1988), 166.

28. Di Grado, *Per Sciascia*, 123.

29. This is no innocent choice of hotel, for it is said to be the site where the American mafia met with their Sicilian counterparts in the 1950s to introduce structure and cohesion into the organization.

30. Consolo, *Lo Spasimo di Palermo*, 128.

31. Ibid., 128–29.

32. Ibid., 129.

33. Vincenzo Mortillaro, *Nuovo Dizionario Siciliano-Italiano* (Palermo: Stabilimento tipografico Lao, 1876).

34. Consolo, *Lo spasimo di Palermo*, 129–30.

35. Sciascia, *Opere: 1984–1989*, 376.

Part V

True Crime

11

Chi l'ha vista? Reflections on the Montesi Case

Karen Pinkus

Narrative Logics of Justice

The Montesi scandal, sometimes called "the first modern mediatic case," centers on the disappearance and death of a young Roman woman from the *ceti medi* (middle classes), a woman of no particular importance, a *ragazza qualunque* (Any-girl). In my book on the scandal, I have argued that the case cannot be known outside of the cinema of the period, and in the following brief essay I develop more precisely my thinking on the relationship of filmic narrative to questions of disappearance, (true) crime, justice, and closure.[1] Justice for the "forgotten," as Giorgio Agamben describes in *The Idea of Prose* is a tradition, a voice, rather than a form of revenge or a definitive endpoint. Such an idea of justice goes toward accounting for the explosion of narratives and films, especially in Italian culture, that attempt to rewrite (or re-cinematize) unresolved (and ultimately unresolvable) cases and mysteries from the past.[2] In real life, families seek "closure," even if in ending a narrative, or in punishing a criminal, the overall good of society—the Law—is not well served. This is why, for example, a family may bring a civil suit against a defendant in a democracy, outside the horizon of the Law. In fact, the Montesi family did, reluctantly, bring a civil suit that was quickly retracted for complex and contradictory reasons. In the end, the family received neither closure nor justice in the traditional narrative sense.[3]

With this minimal groundwork, I will begin by attempting to narrate, in the most neutral manner possible, the facts of the death of Wilma Montesi as they were accepted prior to the scandal that was set off by her death, prior to any discourse that, in a juridical context, might count as hearsay.[4] On April 9, 1953, Wilma Montesi, the twenty-one-year old daughter of a carpenter, helped clean up after a modest lunch. Her mother and sister decided to see a film, but Wilma preferred to stay at home. In the evening, when Wilma's mother and sister returned to their apartment on Via Tagliamento, along with Wilma's father and younger brother, Wilma was gone. Family members searched for her around Rome. A telegram was dispatched to her fiancé, a police officer stationed in Potenza. Two days later her body was discovered in the shallow water on a private beach at Tor Vaianica, dressed in skirt and sweater, but without stockings or garter belt. The beach was approximately 20 kilometers from Ostia, the nearest public beach, accessible by public transportation. Wilma was buried shortly afterward in her nearly-finished wedding gown at the Verano cemetery.

These are the bare facts that were never disputed by any of the parties involved; the only facts that can be comfortably recounted in the voice of certainty, neutrality, and common sense; they are "above and beyond any interpretation," like the bare facts of a person's civil status that are recounted to police prior to any investigation or to an analyst prior to any analysis, as if any narration of facts *could* exist outside of or prior to interpretation. And admittedly, it is possible that I may have already inflected these bare facts with my knowledge of what was to come, or contaminated them in some way with posterior information. The only way to expand our discussion on this case is to have recourse to the statements of those who witnessed, not the event of her death, the moment of her absence, but her presence before and after the event.

Medical examiners put forth three plausible hypotheses: suicide, accidental drowning, and a *disgrazia* or misfortune. The case of Wilma Montesi was closed—or, to translate the Italian term literally, "archived"—with a verdict of "accidental death." In any case, the cause of death was clearly drowning. The Law declared an end to the narrative.

But about six months later, a Roman scandal sheet ran an article implicating "highly placed individuals" in Montesi's death. Tabloid journalist Silvano Muto wrote of drugs and orgies at a hunting preserve outside of Rome, managed by an ambitious former member of Mussolini's secret police and frequented by the son of the powerful politician. The individuals were not named, and when he was questioned, Muto told police he made up the story to gain publicity for his newspaper. He was given a slap on the wrist and sent away, but another witness, a vivacious aspiring actress named Anna Maria Caglio, came forward, with the prodding of certain Jesuit priests, to say that she recognized the figures in Muto's article as Ugo Montagna, her former lover, and Piero Piccioni, son of the powerful foreign minister, Christian Democrat Attilio Piccioni, a presumed successor to the aging De Gasperi. Nearly a year after Wilma Montesi's death, tabloidist Silvano Muto was tried. The charge against him, "tendentious reporting," was another remnant of Fascism, an atavistic law still on the books and meant to squelch communist propaganda. But the charge was dropped and the trial suspended at the moment that the prosecutor felt there was sufficient evidence to open a formal judicial inquiry into the possible involvement of Piccioni, Montagna, and police chief Sergio Polito in Wilma's death. Finally, after many years, Piccioni and Montagna were acquitted in a trial held in Venice. In essence, the court had determined that the excessive "media attention" in Rome would detract from the operations of the judicial process. The acquittal of Ugo Montagna, along with that of Sergio Polito, the chief of police accused of being an accessory, suggested that the fate of these defendants hung on that of Piccioni. He was acquitted of the crime, a phrasing that not only absolved him of any involvement and allowed him (not to mention the Christian Democrat leadership) to return to "normalcy" but also virtually assures that a crime was indeed committed by some other, as yet unnamed, party. Piero Piccioni went on to become a creative and prolific composer of film scores. The Venice court's *motivazione*, far from providing closure for the case or "justice for Wilma," put into effect a logical concatenation in which the family's hypothesis that she died accidentally while bathing her feet was de facto dismissed, even ridiculed, along with their claims that Wilma was a "good girl" who never went out alone and certainly could not have been involved with "people in high places."

In its *motivazione* (given reasons), the Venice tribunal essentially opened up three lines of logic: First, the Montesi family suffered from a willful lack of knowledge about the girl's life as she had indeed left the house, alone, and perhaps on more than one occasion; it was entirely possible that she led a double life. Second, someone, somehow, had sought to indict one or more members of the ruling class; that is, some person or persons had exploited the girl's death for the purpose of bringing down the right wing of the Christian Democrat party—the name of Fanfani was circulated at various moments. Finally, as some crime had indeed been committed (albeit not by Piccioni and *compagnia bella*), another defendant had to be sought. The target was Wilma's uncle Giuseppe, who was jailed for an extraordinarily long time on trumped up charges of libeling his former colleagues at a Roman printing plant. Just as Piero Piccioni had seemed, to some, a placeholder to fill a preexisting slot or a drive for scandal, Giuseppe was, in some sense, an easy substitution for Piccioni. Giuseppe received phone calls from women at work. He had boasted to colleagues that he rented a bachelor flat in Ostia, nearby to where Wilma's body was discovered. He had a child out of wedlock with the sister of his "official fiancée," and his finances were questionable. Eventually, though, the state failed to find evidence against the uncle in the death of his niece. The lack of evidence is the fault of the state, an indictment of the justice system, but one that also allows for the public to simultaneously and privately condemn Giuseppe. In the end, when we view the Montesi case retrospectively, by the time all of the various trials and investigations were finished—that is to say, nearly a decade after the girl's death—we find that the culture at large, which was so fervently engaged with the scandal between Wilma's disappearance in 1953 and the end of the Venice trial in 1957, was divided between those who persisted in condemning the ruling class and those who excused the ruling class and instead condemned the womanizing bachelor uncle. In the course of the intervening years, a number of related trials had taken place primarily on questions of libel and perjury, which is to say that the culture at large was working through broad questions of the freedom of the press in the post-fascist age and the nature of testimony in a democratic judicial system. The constitution went into effect in 1948, but by the time of the Montesi trials, the organization of the judiciary was still in flux.[5]

In a wonderful essay on the case, sociologist Hans Enzensberger notes that while the judicial codes of all western democracies are more or less the same—and in this sense, the relative freshness of the Italian constitution does not necessarily disqualify it from certain general observations—those of Germany and Italy are remarkably different. In Germany the public views the criminal as absolute Other;[6] he is estranged from daily life and thrust into the hands of experts, specialists who take care of him and mete out proper punishment in accordance with a penal code that is strictly technical. In Italy, by contrast, the public identifies absolutely with the criminal, who could be any of them. The Italian system is more populist (*popolare*) and spontaneous, hence the Montesi case became an opportunity for obsessive national self-examination. Neutrality was not an option, and participation was a form of mass spectacle. But whatever conclusion was reached by the public, and whatever the degree of identification with the criminal(s) and witnesses, one thing only remains clear: Wilma Montesi disappeared.

Initially, then, my instincts told me that Wilma had not been well served by the legal system, and it was my duty to employ a critical methodology that allowed for and even embraced contradiction, to bring her back to center stage, and *to do right by her*.[7] Few would deny that the judiciary, in the early 1950s, was a closed system, still very much linked with the Fascist Party, vehemently anti-communist, and highly conservative, and it did not begin to undergo any substantive reforms until later in the decade, when the Montesi trials were over. Had the magistrates—not a particularly well-compensated class of men—let their professionalism lapse? Had they been complicit—even unwittingly—in a cover-up in order to protect political allies? Had Wilma, then, as a marginal subject, been wronged in this systemic corruption? I found that I had little sympathy for the "character" of Wilma Montesi as she emerged from my research: a girl whose major contribution to Italian culture seems to have been the adolescent postcards she sent her fiancé, which she also dutifully copied into a notebook. Wilma Montesi was only one of numerous girls who ended up on the page four of the newspapers, as part of the *cronaca* (routine news).

Similarly, in an interview, the Bologna writers' collective Wu Ming (formerly Luther Blissett) explained that they had an idea of writing a novel about the Montesi case, which they believed might represent the Italian equivalent of the Kennedy assassination, a case that indelibly imprinted itself on the national conscience. While undertaking their research, though, the authors became overwhelmed by the richness of the year itself, 1954, the eventual protagonist of the book.

> So a banal *fatto di cronaca* was used to mount various scandals, caught up in a battle to the death of various factions of the Christian Democrats. We learned everything there was to know about the scandal, but we were convinced that Piero Piccioni wasn't the assassin. We followed false leads and red herrings in the papers. But in the course of our research we found ourselves fascinated by the thousands of other stories that demanded our attention. And we have told a few of them.[8]

For the collective, the Montesi case was interesting in that the left had been able to exploit scandal to denigrate the right, a strategy, incidentally, that was very much encouraged by no less a figure than Communist Party leader Palmiro Togliatti. But ultimately Wu Ming saw the affair as one of internal struggle within the DC and so of diminished importance. Specifically, the members of the collective saw the case as an example of power eluding the best-laid plans of the powerful. In this sense, the Montesi case provides an optimistic message for the left. Even in the novel of Wu Ming, eventually titled *54*, Wilma Montesi disappears.[9] The authors frame the case as part of a general discussion among men in a bar, but they do not speculate on whether or not a crime was committed.

For me, the injustice, the lack of a resolution to her case did not present itself as something done to a female figure by a patriarchy that sought to limit her potential or mobility, but rather as a problem of narrative, intimately bound up with the cinematic. In a sense, then, I had constructed my own form of (en)closure: the cinematic and the everyday. Ennio Flaiano, Fellini's collaborator on *La dolce vita* and many other projects, wrote: "Is another reality at all necessary? Is this rosy Roman reality not sufficient? Certainly, it is hard to live and be judged in a city where the one industry is cinema. One ends up believing that life is a function of the cinema, one becomes the photographic eye, one sees reality as a reflection of what lives and palpitates on the screen."[10] Flaiano's journal entry seems axiomatic for the Montesi case. End of story?

Chi l'ha vista?

My own title, "Chi l'ha vista?" refers to a popular television program on RaiTre. It is based on *America's Most Wanted*, and both are interactive programs where viewers help solve crimes. In Italy's version, reporters often file pre-taped reports from small towns where local characters (the equivalent of what one of the lawyers in the Montesi trial called "tropical vegetation") speak in dialects, or refer to regional institutions. Meanwhile, the host, Daniela Poggi, sits in an ultramodern studio in Rome, waiting to receive calls. It is a spectacle that emphasizes the peculiar geography of Italy, and this is a large part of its appeal, I would argue. On the American program, a host presents unsolved crimes and asks for help capturing the criminals. The Italian program, even as its title suggests, shifts the emphasis away from the criminal to the victim. Not all of the cases presented are even prosecutable crimes. Many of the most significant episodes on *Chi l'ha visto?* involve people who have, simply, disappeared. But in a modern democracy, in a society of surveillance, is it even possible to disappear? And could disappearance then return as a positive form of evasion or resistance?

The "mystery" of Wilma Montesi bears many structural and morphological similarities to the fictional account of Poe's "The Mystery of Marie Roget," and also to the actual case of drowning in nineteenth-century New York upon which Poe's story was based.[11] The body of Mary Rogers (translated into a French context and analyzed by Poe's fictional detective, Dupin) was found on the banks of the Hudson River after she went missing from her mother's middle-class home. Marie Roget, a particularly attractive young girl who accepts a "public" position as a cigar girl (in Poe's tale she is a perfume counter girl) garners a certain reputation among a restricted circle of gentlemen customers, suitors, and admirers. She takes on the burden of a form of "public" knowledge so that when her body is found, a male discourse, generated and disseminated by the press, both "knows" the solution to the mystery and seeks to preserve her chastity at any cost. In the real case, police eventually determined that the girl died of a botched abortion—a banal death, filled with pathos—but Poe/Dupin was himself duped by this solution. As in the Montesi case, though, the case of Marie Roget was for a period suspended between a missing person's case and the discovery of body, without any proof of a crime. In the slippages between the newspaper account of Mary Rogers, the public attempts to legitimate the victim, Poe's tale, and its critical reception, this case is also suffused with a general anxiety about women who leave behind the home and go out into the world.

The specter of female mobility in the city haunts the Montesi case. Termini is the terminal point for optimistic Italian girls coming to Rome; and then leaving Rome when they are spent. It is the point where Italian subjects become accountable for their provincial origins, or can be located by a democratic form of state surveillance. It is also a civic space where beggars congregate, where unsavory characters are escorted by police and put on trains to other places with writs of obligatory deportation. It is, in fact, characteristic of the period of the Montesi case that the police exploit various atavistic forms of control, remnants of the not-so-distant Fascist past. As the disappearance of Wilma occurred in Rome, the *de facto* mutual dependency of the national police force and the civic police (*quaestor*) in the city is of paramount significance. Both forces, staffed by men of ex-privilege who continue to operate along embedded lines of conduct while invoking a new rhetoric of democracy, are under the aegis of the Ministry of the Interior. Like the members of the Ministry of Justice, many are former Fascists. From their centrifugal, *terminal* point of power they enjoy the right to exile citizens to the provincial towns and peripheral cities of an Italy that is still overwhelmingly rural. Citizenship in the new democracy cannot be revoked, but *residency* in the capital is provisional.[12]

Disappearing on Film

If cinema is the privileged means for reading the case of Wilma Montesi, various cinematic examples might help us think about the nature of disappearance. For example, in Fellini's *The White Sheik* (released in 1952, one year before Wilma's death), the new bride Wanda is swept up into a caravan of photo-romance actors as they travel to Fregene for a shoot. For the viewer, there is never any doubt about her location. She doesn't actually disappear, in essence. Scenes of her neurotic fiancé and his upright family are intercut with scenes of Wanda and the Sheik, a cinematic style that is extremely mundane and familiar from any number of screwball comedies. Once Wanda comes back to Rome, she is immediately re-integrated into the seamless narrative of the newlywed couple. As Catherine Clément writes of the syncope or cutting off, in her book of the same title, once the woman returns, no one asks her where she has been. All is forgiven, or at least covered up.[13]

Ten years later, perhaps the most brilliant example of the ambiguity associated with female disappearance comes from Antonioni's *L'avventura*. A group of wealthy friends on a cruise stops at a tiny volcanic island within the group of the Aeolian Islands, northeast of Sicily. The cast and crew actually had their base at nearby Panarea, itself a tiny island with few comforts. In an early scene, Anna (Lea Massari) and Sandro (Gabriele Ferzetti) engage in one of their usual discussions about the ambiguous direction of their relationship. The camera frames them against the rock in various static poses, as Anna confesses her lack of feeling. Through an in-camera edit, the director moves from this couple to another one, Giulia and Corrado, as they engage in a banal spat about the changing weather conditions. Anna will never reappear. Of course, without recourse to devices of science fiction, it is impossible to represent disappearance, and this is precisely what Antonioni thematizes by not exploiting any advanced filmic techniques. The second couple, a mirror of Anna and Sandro, if they were to continue on together, is literally exposed over the fade out. It seems important to emphasize that Anna's disappearance could have been achieved without recourse to an editing facility, without physically cutting the film. When we view *L'avventura* for the first time, we are unaware that Anna's final appearance is somehow significant. On the contrary, the moment is particularly insignificant, wearisome, as Antonioni's critics have not failed to point out. When Anna is referenced in various clues and images that appear later on, the linearity of the film is constructed in such a way that there is no return to an earlier point, no homecoming or *nostos*. Anna's presence is not substituted by a reified absence, but by nothingness. What I mean by this is that she is subject to a slow ebbing away, rather than a violent excision. To remove her from the film, the producers had to physically take her away, to Panarea, and then back to Rome, we might assume. But the filming goes on, for an agonizingly long time. The viewer loses any sense of the conventions of filming—that Lea Massari's final scene may have been filmed prior to her early appearances on camera; that she may have remained to provide support as part of the ensemble. Instead, she disappears absolutely.

In various interviews, Antonioni has said that *L'avventura* is a broad observation about modern life. "Today we live in a period of extreme instability—political instability, moral instability, social instability, and even physical instability. . . . These characters find themselves on an island, in a rather dramatic situation; a girl in the party is lost. They start to look for her. The man who loves her should be worried, upset, anxious. And, really, at the beginning, he is. But then, slowly, his feelings grow weaker, because they have no strength." He is attracted by other feelings, by other "adventures," by other experiences just as unsteady and unstable.[14] Instability may be the general effect, but the core concept giving rise to the film was not a meditation on politics, but a quasi-aesthetic apperception of an actual female disappearance. "I remember very well how the idea of *L'avventura* came to me," Antonioni noted. "I was on a yacht with some friends.... One morning I found myself thinking of a girl who, years before, had disappeared, and nothing more was ever heard of her. We had looked for her everywhere for days and days, but to no avail. The yacht was sailing toward Ponza, by then nearby. And I thought, 'What if she were there? That's it!'"[15]

The film offers several hypotheses about the mystery. Someone thinks they may have heard a boat pass by the island. The camera lingers on the crashing waves, opening up the possibility that Anna may have drowned. Naturally, this is the most logical explanation, but the film embarrasses the viewer for succumbing to the obvious conclusion. In fact, there was a scene in the film that was eventually cut—Antonioni can't recall the reason, so we should not grant its elision undue significance—in which the protagonists speculate about Anna's whereabouts. "After a moment of silence, one says: 'Maybe she simply drowned.' Claudia suddenly turns to him: '"Simply"?' They all look at each other, dismayed. This is it. The dismay is the meaning of the film."[16] This deleted scene opens up the possibility that the dynamic of the group desires an unfathomable and inarticulable mystery, a mystery in the religious sense, a ritualized or initiatory experience, a revelation made to an elite group. A mystery would raise this rather unsympathetic group of bored and idle rich to a higher plane, to transcend everyday life. The group, the culture, pushes for such a mystery. The idea of a "simple drowning," as in the Montesi case, the "product" of an earlier and more innocent cinematic era, is quite simply, too quotidian for anyone to bear.

Notes

1. Karen Pinkus, *The Montesi Scandal: The Death of Wilma Montesi and the Birth of the Paparazzi in Fellini's Rome* (Chicago: University of Chicago Press, 2003).
2. See Sergia Adamo, "Narrating Justice: Literature and Law in Italian Culture," in *Between Literature and Law: On Voice and Voicelessness*, ed. Sergia Adamo and C. Bertoni, special issue of *Compar(a)ison* (forthcoming).
3. Corruption is not merely rampant, but is virtually guaranteed by the state form, just as Rights are guaranteed to its citizens. So it is essential to distinguish the Law from Justice, and perhaps more importantly, to note that while the political

parties may have argued that their opponents used the Montesi case to create a scandal, the entire legal system in Italy clearly supports bourgeois, patriarchal interests. The rhetoric of distrust in the legal system only masks this fundamental fact. Far from being misled by an idealized and reified bureaucracy, the parties on all sides in the Montesi case were doing exactly what was in their best interests. Because the Italian system is one of equilibrium based on a fragmentation of control and constant crisis, when the Christian Democrats tried to seize excess power with the so-called *legge truffa* in 1953, the system was thrown into tilt. In this sense, the Montesi case is a reflection of this rupture in the model of cyclical crisis.

4. The telegraphic narration I propose here is quite different from the way the case unfolds in my book, where affect (especially as intertwined with cinema and photography, with the aesthetic, in other words) is allowed to run wild.

5. Piero Calamandrei writes that in the present system of Italy, "there is thus a conflict between two principles. . . . It is true that in the act of passing sentence the judge is performing a sovereign function and takes orders from no superior, but it is also true that the judge is a public official employed by the state and bound to it in a master-servant relationship, . . . two qualities that appear incompatible are thus united in the same person—the constitutional independence of the function and the administrative dependence of the functionary" (40). See *Procedure and Democracy*, trans. John Clarke Adams and Helen Adams (New York: New York University Press, 1956). Though the constitution declares that judges may not be removed, there are many ways of squashing a career. Moreover, many lawyers become members of parliament. The new Italian constitution sought to separate the judiciary and executive branches, and there was even debate about abolishing the post of Minister of Justice. This did not happen, but the Superior Judicial Council, headed by the President of the Republic, and judges elected, mainly by other Council members, was established. This meant the complete divestment of power from the Minister of Justice.

6. Hans Magnus Enzensberger, "Wilma Montesi: Una vita dopo la morte" ["Wilma Montesi: Ein Leben nach dem Tode" (1969)] in *Politica e gangsterismo* (Rome: Savelli, 1979).

7. Enrica Capussotti writes about the contradictions between an antiquated and highly patriarchal judicial system and new modes of feminine mobility in her *Gioventù perduta. Gli anni Cinquanta dei giovani e del cinema in Italia* (Florence: Giunti, 2004).

8. Massimiliano Boschi, "'54,' quando i complotti non sono ciò che sembrano," *Sabata Sera* (Imola), Anno XLI, 18 (May 4, 2002).

9. I am not implying here that the collective perpetuates a form of ideological violence against Wilma or femininity in general. On their website (http://www.wumingfoundation.com) the collective has often defended themselves as feminists and have engaged in serious debates about sexual politics. The "disappearance" I note is not, then, a form of excision of femininity from history, but rather a collective choice about how to evoke a period in Italian culture. See Wu Ming, *54* (Turin: Einaudi, 2002).

10. Flaiano, a key witness to the Roman Dolce Vita and the imbrications of cinema and everyday, is quoted from his diaries, published as *The Via Veneto Papers (La solitudine del satiro)*, trans. John Satriano (Vermont: Marlboro Press, 1992), 22.

11. Two important works on the subject are *The Poetics of Murder: Detective Fiction and Literary Theory*, ed. Glenn W. Most and William W. Stowe (San Diego, CA: Harcourt Brace Jovanovich, 1983); and John Walsh, *Poe the Detective: The Curious Circumstances behind the Mystery of Marie Roget* (New Bruswick, NJ: Rutgers University Press, 1968).

12. As one journalist of the period noted, "The Italian State, with its laws, its decrees, its decree-laws, with its peculiar form of state-control, and its centralization, is organized precisely in such a way as to facilitate corrupt actions and deceit. We would be shocked if such actions did *not* go on. The Italian State is corrupt in its very structure, not in its men. . . . We cannot blame the Romans, just as we cannot blame the true and proper Rome, but that 'artificial' Rome, the capital of thieves who are, for the most part, not actually Romans, but the Huns of bribes and illicit activities." See Edilio Rusconi, "Processo al ladro ignoto" *Oggi*, March 25, 1957, p. 3. These huns to whom the journalist refers, it should be noted, are the Southern Italian functionaries who began to populate the city in significant numbers during the Fascist era. In the Montesi case we begin to see a tension between those Romans who view themselves as rightfully occupying the urban center *(Romani-di-Roma)* and those who come from the provinces, and especially from the South, and who often unwittingly betray their peripheral origins. I want to be clear that I am not suggesting a centrifugal geography akin to that of France, but I do wish to point out that the mechanisms of power that develop in the postwar period in Italy do bear some relationship to questions, not only of North and South, as many scholars have explored, but also center and margin, proper urbanity and improper regionalism.

13. Catherine Clément, *Syncope. The Philosophy of Rapture*, trans. Sally O'Driscoll and Deidre M. Mahoney (Minneapolis: University of Minnesota Press, 1994).

14. Michelangelo Antonioni, *The Architecture of Vision*, ed. Carlo Di Carlo and Giorgio Tinazzi (New York: Marsilio, 1996), 19.

15. Ibid., 58.

16. Ibid., 81.

12

Pasolini's Murder: Interpretation, Event Narratives, and Postmodern *Impegno*

Robert S. C. Gordon

Introduction

Pier Paolo Pasolini was murdered on the night of November 1–2, 1975, in a dirt field by Via dell'Idroscalo, near Ostia, outside Rome. He was beaten with a wooden plank and then run over by his own car, his heart crushed.[1] Vivid and disturbing photographs of his maimed body appeared in newspapers and magazines in the following days.[2] A Roman youth called Giuseppe or "Pino" Pelosi, "La Rana" (The Frog), who was below the age of criminal majority, was stopped by police later that night while driving Pasolini's car. In a drawn-out legal process, he was later be tried and convicted of Pasolini's murder. One level of court judged that he had not—as he claimed—acted alone in his assault, but rather in the company of "persons unknown."[3]

The murder—like so many events, actions and works within Pasolini's life—was immediately interpreted as a highly symbolic event, read and reread in a symptomatically excessive and overdetermined manner. The reasons for this are related both to Pasolini's own career and *oeuvre*, as well as the particular, complex position he held within the field of postwar Italian society and its culture, and also to broader processes of response to public death and personal and political violence that characterized the so-called *anni di piombo* ("years of lead") in Italy. More broadly still, Pasolini's murder and the history of representations of it also need to be inserted into a longer history of interpretations of public "death-events," their iconography and mediatization—from Mussolini to Moro, from JFK to Princess Diana[4]—and the ways these reflect deeper lay lines of a given cultural landscape.

This essay seeks to outline some of the contours of that landscape in the case of Pasolini's murder, to examine the field of interpretations and representations of his death as it developed in the 30 years after the event (and, some would say, proleptically, even prophetically, before his death also).[5] After briefly looking at immediate responses to the murder and at the key lines of interpretation established at that moment, it draws attention to a renewed wave of representations of his death from the mid-1990s onward. Coming as it did after a period of relative decline in Pasolini's literary and intellectual reputation[6] (a decline which broadly coincided with the wider fading of postwar cultural and political norms after 1989), this late re-flowering of interest in and obsessive reworking of his death paradoxically made of Pasolini—through the memory and representation of his death; through an amalgam of event, body, narrative, and ethics—a crucial player in the striking rise of a certain engaged postmodernist culture in Italy at the end of the century.

November 1975: Mimesis and Myth

Pasolini's death was met with a massive print and audio-visual media response in the shape of reportage, obituaries, tributes and more. Coverage was dominated by the cultural-intellectual elite of the day, many of them Rome-based and well acquainted with, if not all easy comrades of, Pasolini himself.[7] They offered instant reflection on the death of Pasolini, and through his death on his tricky position within the humanistic tradition of the Italian intellectual, and in particular the Marxist inflection of that tradition so characteristic of the postwar decades. Two threads stand out in the spread of commentary, both typical of public responses to deaths of prominent figures (and indeed to processes of mourning in general), but both pushed to a mannered extreme in the case of Pasolini. First, there was a form of *post mortem* mimetic ventriloquism on display: that is, the tendency to explain and tally the death using characteristics of the "life and work" and even the voice of the victim himself. One example of a great many was *Corriere della sera*'s headline on November 3, 1975, "Pasolini killed where he would have shot the film of his own death." Elsewhere, Pelosi was compared to Pasolini's *ragazzi di vita*, the low-life boys who populated his 1950s novels; the Ostia location to the quintessential Pasolinian *locus*, the "subproletarian" Roman *borgata* (slum); the encounter with Pelosi to the homosexual, pedophiliac prostitution, charged with violence and lucre, by which many of his fictional *ragazzi* lived.[8] This rhetoric of "the death fitting the life and work" cut in two distinct directions: on the one hand, Pasolini was being reduced to a caricature of himself, and responsibility for his death was being, in a sense, imputed to him and his own (scandalous) lifestyle: Pasolini as the "author" of his death. On the other hand, it tallied with his own highly self-conscious and uncomfortable blurring of boundaries between his scandalous work and his sense of self throughout his work in many different media and forms, filtered through a rhetoric dense with the primacy, authenticity and sheer physical and metaphysical "presence" of the body in both literature and life.[9] It also tallied with an extraordinary and complex obsession with death itself in his work, at both narrative and conceptual levels, including repeated treatments of his own violent murder.[10] This elaborate self-construction and its echoes in the responses to his death suggest, at the very least, the compelling rhetorical power of his work and public image, their capacity to infiltrate and shape the voices of others posthumously.

Complementing and contributing to all this was the second thread on display in the media coverage of his death: an incipient (or, rather, ongoing) process of mythicization. The dominant "myth" of Pasolini construed him as the damned and now dead poet, who was (and probably died because he was) solitary, marginal, and "different" (for which read "homosexual"), a prophetic vessel of essential truths and a timeless totality of knowledge. He was, in other words, being inserted into a late Romantic (Byronic) literary tradition; and, once again, in ways wholly in keeping with Pasolini's sustained and complex strategies of self-construction within his *oeuvre*, including his self-construction as "poet."

Again, we can pick out representative examples from the print media following November 2, 1975, to illustrate the point. His prophetic powers, following in the wake of his doom-laden journalistic critique of contemporary mores during the years 1973–5, are evident in his final interview, with Furio Colombo, published in *La stampa* on November 8, 1975, under the apocalyptic title "We are all in danger." And the sheer range of models and famous names thrown out to capture the essence of the man gives us the flavor of myth of the poet or prophet *maudit* under construction here: these included Ariel, St. Augustine, Christ, Céline, Don Quixote, Genet, Lorca, Midas, Mishima, Narcissus, Rimbaud, Savonarola, Socrates, Villon, and Winckelmann.

Much was missing, however, or at least underplayed, in the flood of mythicizing and mimetic comment from the days following his death. Little space was given to a narrative of Pasolini's death as a banal product of a deeply violent homophobic culture, rather than an event of profound metaphysical significance.[11] And relatively little prominence was given to the contextualization of Pasolini's death within the contemporary political (and criminal) violence of the "years of lead," despite allusions to or unspoken assumptions of neo-Fascist or criminal involvement.[12] Indeed, while cultural, literary, and myth-imbued discourse held sway, another form of coverage—event-driven journalistic investigation into the murder, the police investigations, and the judicial processes—was relatively muted.

In the ensuing decades, as the significance and profile of Pasolini as a cultural figure altered (whether diminished or embalmed in volumes of complete works and retrospectives),[13] as perspectives of both history and collective memory came to focus on the 1970s and its forms of violence (political, criminal, terroristic, state-sponsored, or a mix of these) as a crucial moment in recent Italian history, and as the 1968 generation grew older, so the nature and significance of representations of Pasolini's death came to shift also. There was a move away from the literary myth of the dead poet toward an analysis of the event, indeed the very scene of his death, as somehow encapsulating that wider generational history and collective memory. This move was especially marked in a series of diverse, but interestingly related, works from the mid-1990s onward.

1994–2004: The Murder Scene

Beginning around the twentieth anniversary of Pasolini's murder in 1995, and flowing on into the first years of the new century, a minor corpus of works appeared in different forms, media, and genre (fiction films, shorts, prose narrative, graphic novels, television programs, reflections, and memoirs), each of which returned to Pasolini, and in particular to the scene and event of his death. By briefly describing nine key texts from that corpus, we can begin to analyze the characteristic features of this microfield and its significance for the broader contemporary cultural field.

Caro Diario (Dear Diary; dir. Nanni Moretti, 1994)

Moretti's hugely successful film is divided into three whimsical, autobiographical episodes, typical of his signature film style.[14] Key images from the first episode helped establish Moretti for the first time as a major, exportable European *auteur*: most notably, the image of him on his moped, white helmet on his head, buzzing around the architectural maze of Rome's residential quarters. The episode is a characteristically postmodern, meandering encounter with the comic inconsequentialities of the city and its spaces; but it takes a striking turn toward melancholy and intense affective (and, implicitly, intellectual) engagement in its last five minutes. Against the backdrop of Nicola Pivani's Nymanesque piano score, Moretti flicks through those very newspapers and magazines of the days following November 2, 1975, and then takes his scooter and his camera on a long tracking journey toward Ostia and the dirt field, the site of Pasolini's murder. The camera offers closeups of the modest, somewhat ruined concrete memorial (by Mario Rosati) and of the old goalposts in the field. These two images seem to connote, respectively, memory and mourning (for ethics, ideology, and older forms of engagement) and innocence (the childhood of football and play). Both elements recur with some frequency in the corpus of material under scrutiny here, but it is perhaps the sheer affective power of Moretti's digressive journey to Ostia (and Moretti's own increasing significance as a cultural figure) which establishes this sequence (along with *Pasolini: un delitto italiano*, below) as the key origin of the recuperation of Pasolini, through his death, in these years.

Pasolini: un delitto italiano (Pasolini: An Italian
Crime; dir. Marco Tullio Giordana, 1995)

Giordana's film, and accompanying book of documents and investigations,[15] is a crucial text both for Pasolini's posthumous history and for the generational return to the 1970s within 1990s Italian culture. It is important for at least four reasons: first, for its direct and relentless focus on Pasolini's death as a means to understanding the man and the time; second, for the *giallo* (detective story) genre used by Giordana, a genre and paradigm of historical interpretation that will emerge over the following decade as extraordinarily dominant within the Italian cultural scene (see *Romanzo criminale* [Crime Story] and "Il caso Pier Paolo Pasolini" [The Case of Pier Paolo Pasolini] below); third, for its narrative style, blending archive documentation, *verité*, and enquiry with fictional narrative, in a (postmodern, but also historically rooted) mix; and finally, for its consequences as a cultural product with the power to intervene in judicial processes—the Pasolini murder case was reopened in its wake. Through Pasolini, then, Giordana began a process of questioning his generation's and Italy's history and identity in the broadest sense, so powerfully so that the phrase *un delitto italiano* has since entered Italian vocabulary as a way of evoking all the deep fractures and illicit power mechanisms at work beneath the surface of Italy's modern history.

Giordana's first film, *Maledetti vi amerò* (To Love the Damned, 1980), had already made allusions to the Pasolini and Moro cases and the fading of the extra-parliamentary, terrorist generation. Since *Pasolini: un delitto italiano*, he has continued in a highly Pasolinian vein of committed film-making (although his work is more conventionally narrative-driven than Pasolini's), including the anti-mafia film *I cento passi* (The Hundred Steps, 2000) and, above all, *La meglio gioventù* (The Best of Youth, 2003, the title taken from Pasolini's 1954 dialect poetry collection; although its epic narrative makes it more akin to Bernardo Bertolucci's *Novecento*, [1900], 1976).

Dario Bellezza, Il poeta assassinato *(Venice: Marsilio, 1996)*

Bellezza was a poet, greatly influenced and aided by Pasolini in his early career. He had published a reflection on Pasolini's death already in 1981;[16] and his last book, *Il poeta assassinato* (*The Assassinated Poet*), was published as he was dying of AIDS. For these reasons, this death-centered, reflective memoir is heavily loaded with the aura of poetry and death that surrounded earlier phases of memories of Pasolini. It is certainly power-fully evocative of Pasolini's Roman cultural circles, of Alberto Moravia, Elsa Morante, and others. Nevertheless, beneath the auratic and at time confessional prose, the pattern of the text overlaps with the patterns we see elsewhere in our corpus. Bellezza uses trial papers and archives, as well as memory and anecdote, to investigate the circumstances of the death as a criminal event, combining this with a broadening critique of the society that allowed it and even encouraged it to happen. He is, in reality, writing the book against himself, against his own *Morte di Pasolini*, and against the aestheticizing assumptions of those earlier years, that Pasolini's death could be somehow read through his poetry.[17] In this sense, it contains in miniature the trajectory we are tracing more broadly in the afterlife of Pasolini's murder; the shift from a phase of mourning and metaphysics to a phase of investigation and historical analysis.

Nerolio *(dir. Aurelio Grimaldi, 1996)*

Grimaldi's somewhat mannered black-and-white film *Nerolio* also com-bines fact and fiction, although the emphasis here is very much on the lat-ter. Its three episodes focus on Pasolini's sexuality and on his writings on the body and morality, drawing heavily on the author's massive posthumously published novel-fragment, *Petrolio* (1993). Pasolini planned for *Petrolio* an elaborate historical-ideological core, besides its sexual and experimental elements—he described it as the "*summa* of all my experiences, all my memories"[18]—and in this, and because of its publication in 1993, it should, in a sense, be included as part of the corpus of texts we are examining here. Grimaldi picks up on this, interspersing sexually explicit encounters from the novel-fragment with recitations of Pasolini's lapidary critique of contemporary mores and hypocrisies. The final episode offers us yet another reconstruction of the murder, this time following Pelosi's account of a one-on-one sexual encounter gone wrong. Like Moretti's visit to Ostia, the film takes us on a slow, tracking journey (with haunting accompanying music) across the dirt field, dwelling on the sordid physical reality of the site itself as somehow containing and connoting the meanings of the murder.

Pasolini oggi, *2000*

For the twenty-fifth anniversary of Pasolini's death, the television company Telepiù commissioned six short films on his legacy by young alternative filmmakers (Bruno Bigoni, Guido Chiesa, Daniel Ciprì and Franco Maresco, Davide Ferrario, Gianluigi Toccafondo, Daniele Vicari). The films were later shown at Turin and Berlin film festivals in 2001 under the title *Pasolini oggi* (*Pasolini Today*). Their approaches and styles were widely varying, but all were attempts to revisit Pasolini's work, through reprise (Toccafondo's animation synthesized Pasolini's Totò films of the mid-1960s), updating (Ferrario and Bigoni made new versions of Pasolini's "film-investigations" *La rabbia*, 1963, and *Comizi d'amore*, 1965); testimonies and reconstructions (Vicari interviewed Mario Cipriani, the protagonist of *La ricotta*, 1963; Guido Chiesa reconstructed the screen-tests for *Salò*; Ciprì and Maresco followed in Pasolini's footsteps in a trip he made to Palermo). All were attempts to create a "Pasolinian" mode for a new generation, while rejecting the myth of Pasolini.

Davide Toffolo, Intervista a Pasolini *(Pordenone: Biblioteca dell'immagine, 2002)*

Toffolo is a rock musician (part of the group *Tre Allegri Ragazzi Morti*, Three Merry Dead Boys) and graphic artist. In his graphic novel *Intervista a Pasolini*, we find a multi-media collage (a characteristically postmodern technique) of extracts of texts on and by Pasolini, graphic and photo-derived images, some drawn from Pasolini's own graphic work. Toffolo imagines meeting an enigmatic, ghostly Pasolini and filming in different locations a long interview with him. Contact is made by email (from pier-paolo_pasolini@libero.it). The core message of the book—another reprise of Pasolini's sociological writing, reclaimed for a 1990s generation—and its most intense imagery is to be found in a sequence in which Davide meets Pier Paolo in Ostia, once again revisiting the site of his murder.[19] The iconography overlaps with Moretti and others—the scooter, the sculpture, the wire fencing, the sea—and Toffolo adds two evocative images of his own—barking dogs and a cutting wind. In the (apocalyptic) wind, Pasolini recites his most devastating critique of contemporary Italy: his death-scene merges with and underscores his sociological message in a conflation which is something of a throwback to the Pasolini myths encountered earlier.

Giancarlo de Cataldo, Romanzo criminale *(Turin: Einaudi, 2002)*

Although its narrative begins in 1978, at the birth of the infamous Roman Magliana criminal gang, judge-turned-writer de Cataldo's important novel *Romanzo criminale* is worth including here for at least three reasons. First, it marks a further stage in the wave of *noir* writing in Italy, which uses genre to interrogate Italy's recent, violent past. Indeed, Giordana was to have directed the film of the book until production problems intervened. (The film, directed by Michele Placido, appeared in 2005.) Furthermore, it is essentially Pasolinian in its unmediated portrayal of the Roman under-world and its slums, with its dialect inflections and brutally direct narra-tive. Finally, it chronicles the same cluster of features of Roman life—criminals, mafia, neo-Fascists, corrupt elements of the state—circu-lating beneath the surface of Pasolini's analysis of modernity in Italy, which, for many, determined the hidden histories of so much of 1970s Italian history, Pasolini's murder included.

Carlo Lucarelli, "Il caso Pier Paolo Pasolini," Blu notte, *RaiTre, January 26, 2003*

Lucarelli, more than anyone else, has made it his concerted political and cultural project to solder the link between the new Italian *giallo* and an inter-rogation of recent Italian history and its unsolved crimes, mysteries and meanings, through television programs (entitled variously *Mistero in blu, Blu notte,* and *Misteri d'Italia*) and accompanying books. He investigated the

Pasolini murder in a January 2003 transmission, "Il caso Pier Paolo Pasolini," and in the follow-up book of 2004, *Nuovi misteri d'Italia*.[20] The role of genre as an interpretative historiographical instrument of a particular kind—one of *the* defining features of the field we are mapping—is at its most self-conscious and open here.

Alberto Garlini, Fútbol bailado *(Milan: Sironi, 2004)*

The most recent text in the corpus, Garlini's novel *Fútbol bailado* is an attempt at a narrative of epic sweep, interweaving the life stories of three principal (fictional) protagonists, with Pasolini as a fourth overseeing presence. The narrative spirals out from its core period between 1975 and 1982, and from a handful of microcosmic moments and intersections. In particular, the book is framed by two key "true-life," local events: first, the soccer match that took place on March 16, 1975, in Parma between the crew working on Pasolini's *Salò* and the crew working on of Bertolucci's *Novecento*; and second, Pasolini's murder.[21] Between these two core scenes (among others in the novel), Garlini interweaves his brilliant young soccer player, Francesco (whose "dancing" Brazilian skills give him the title of the book), the neo-Fascist Vincenzo, and the solitary Alberto. The narrative thread—which imagines Pasolini commissioning and setting up the date and place of his own death through Vincenzo, in a reprise of the myth of him as a prophet of his own demise seen above—throws up a cluster of features that we have seen at work before (almost a *summa* of the features in the nine texts we have considered): the fact-fiction hybrid; the use of real-scene detail, of imagined micro-history as a means to tapping into generational macrohistories; the role of play, childhood, and soccer, for Pasolini and for a certain generation that regrets its lost innocence and its lost ideological certainties (Francesco's story also stumbles into the soccer scandals of the 1980s); Pasolini as the source of a particular vision of Fascism and modernity, here (and perhaps in Giordana also) in contrast with the vision of Bertolucci's *Novecento*; and the Roman criminal underworld, and a particular way of writing about it, pitched somewhere between Pasolini's Roman narrative and de Cataldo.

Postmodern "*Impegno*"

Pasolini's death was posited above as one in a genealogy of modern, mediatized public deaths—from Mussolini to Moro, from JFK to Diana—each overlayed with and in the long run defined by a complex web of texts and images, of more or less arcane or paranoid narratives built on the silences and lacunae of public history and power. The corpus of texts set out in above would seem to confirm that Pasolini's murder has come to fit foursquare within this "paranoid" and quintessentially postmodern tradition, in which textual webs smother any rooted sense of truth, history, and ethical or ideological responsibility. Qualification of this standard postmodern line is needed, however, both in the specific case of representations of Pasolini's death and in the broader nature of the assimilation of postmodern forms and thoughts in Italian culture.[22] Whereas many of the formal moves and strategies in the representations of his death look postmodernist in hue—for example, games and tricksiness of form, hybridity, truth blended with fiction, and the dissolution of history and event into textuality (or hypertextuality)—several others suggest that the artists engaged in this fascination with his death are in fact using postmodern modes to shape out new forms of politically committed writing, of what the postwar era called *impegno*.[23] In fact, as was hinted at above, Pasolini himself seemed to be feeling his way toward a similar hybrid with his last work, *Petrolio*: postmodern formal play—notes, hypertexts, commentary, gaps, and numerical structures—subtending and somehow reinforcing a deadly serious substance—a totalizing and devastating critique of modernity. There are other parallel trajectories in late 1960s and 1970s Italy as well: both Leonardo Sciascia and Carlo Ginzburg, for example, were establishing in this period forms of historical writing, with a subtle contemporary and political undertow, which were acutely sensitive to the interplay of history and discourse, narrative, archive, and textuality. Indeed, perhaps the key bridging text from the 1970s to the hybrid works of the 1990s, in form, content, and purpose, was Sciascia's *L'affaire Moro*.[24]

Whatever the precedents in the 1970s, however, specific generational elements come into play in the 1990s: the texts described here use Pasolini's death as an emblem around which to organize a form of elusive collective memory, a shared narrative of the post-1968 generations and the meaning of their apparently futile political struggles. Of course, Pasolini had been infamously hostile to the 1968 students, explaining in his lengthy poetic excoriation "Il PCI ai giovani!!" why he sided with police who beat the students: they at least were genuinely sons of the poor. But the uses to which his death has been put show that that and later generations rewrote him as a bridging figure, a ghostly presence from a lost era of ideological clarity but also a potential token of a new, if oblique way of interrogating history.

Postscript: Pelosi's Confession

For decades, Pino Pelosi insisted he acted alone in killing Pasolini. He even wrote a book after leaving prison repeating his version of events.[25] But in May 2005, he dramatically changed his tune.[26] He appeared on television to confess that he had not acted alone, but with two (unnamed) others, and to claim that he had in fact defended Pasolini in the fight. For once, it seemed as though the hidden history or counter-history of one of the key *misteri d'Italia* was on the verge of being confirmed—Pasolini had indeed been assassinated—and perhaps, therefore, laid to rest. But in a familiar pattern, the resolved account dissolved into mystery once more (following an essential "rule" of postmodern paranoia and conspiracy theory): Pelosi's confession merely gave a further turn of the wheel to the multiplying stories, discourses, and representations of Pasolini's murder. Lawyers called for the case to be reopened (again), Oriana Fallaci's hypothesis returned, as did a new version from a frail Sergio Citti, and so on; but no definitive version emerged. Pelosi's "reality TV" revelation seemed to have confirmed the spiraling ironies of the textual play of high postmodernism: the man who was present at the scene in November 1975 offers as much and as little clarity and understanding as the imaginary web of event-narratives woven around Pasolini's death.

Notes

1. See, among many others, Barth David Schwartz, *Pasolini Reqiuem* (New York: Pantheon, 1992), 17–62.
2. E.g., in *L'Espresso*, November 9 and 16, 1975.
3. See Schwartz, *Pasolini Reqiuem*, 650–54, 671–84.
4. On Mussolini, see Sergio Luzzato, *Il corpo del Duce* (Turin: Einaudi, 1998); on Moro, see essays elsewhere in this volume; on Diana, see, e.g., *Mourning Diana: Nation, Culture and the Performance of Grief*, ed. Deborah Lynn Steinberg and Adrian Kear (London: Routledge, 1999). On JFK (as for the others), the literature and subculture is vast: in the context of Pasolini's work, it is worth noting the key role played by the famous Zapruder footage of the event in his reflections on film semiosis in *Empirismo eretico* (Milan: Garzanti, 1972). On literary deaths, see Martin Crowley, ed., *Dying Words: The Last Moments of Writers and Philosophers* (Amsterdam: Rodopi, 2000).
5. See Giuseppe Zigaina's remarkable sequence of four arcane books arguing that Pasolini foretold his own death and encoded the event into his work: see, e.g., Giuseppe Zigaina, *Hostia. Trilogia della morte di Pier Paolo Pasolini* (Venice: Marsilio, 1995). Traces of this idea remain in recent fictionalizations.

6. Emblematic in this regard was the response to the 1993 publication of Pasolini's collected poetry *Bestemmia*, ed. Graziella Chiarcossi and Walter Siti, vols. 1–2 (Milan: Garzanti, 1993); and in particular the debate launched by a review by Giovanni Raboni (*Corriere della sera*, December 23, 1993), explaining why Pasolini would never be a "classic" writer. See also Zygmunt G. Baranski, "The Importance of Being Pier Paolo Pasolini" in *Pasolini Old and New* (Dublin: Four Courts Press, 1999), 13–40, on the strange weakness of Pasolini's literary legacy.

7. On the hypocrisy of much of the response (not untypical of commemorative phases of mourning, of course), see Valerio Riva, "Ora tutti lo chiamano Pier Paolo," *L'Espresso*, November 16, 1975.

8. For a fuller analysis, see Robert S. C. Gordon, "Identity in Mourning: The Role of the Intellectual and the Death of Pasolini," *Italian Quarterly* 32, nos. 123–24 (Winter–Spring 1995): 61–74. Several articles are available at: http://www.pasolini.net/vita_sommario.htm (accessed August 10, 2005).

9. See Robert S. C. Gordon, *Pasolini: Forms of Subjectivity* (Oxford: Oxford University Press, 1996).

10. The most striking examples are *La divina mimesis* (Turin: Einaudi, 1975), which includes documents and photographs relating to his own (imagined) death by beating in Palermo and the self-immolation of the clearly autobiographical hero of his 1966 play *Bestia da stile*. In his film theory, he famously equated editing to death (and *vice versa*), both assigning meaning to otherwise indeterminate discourses (*Empirismo eretico*, 245).

11. The gay collective "Fuori!" issued a statement, "[Pasolini] was not killed because he was a man of culture, politics, poetry, but because he was homosexual". See also Roberto Polce, "Pasolini," *Re nudo* V (December 1975): 60–61.

12. Oriana Fallaci made very specific allegations in a famous article, "Pasolini ucciso da due motociclisti?," *L'Europeo* 46 (November 14, 1975); she was largely ignored.

13. See the massive Pier Paolo Pasolini, *Le opere*, ed. Walter Siti, vols. 1–10 (Milan: Mondadori, 1998–2003). For reasons of space, the intervening period of the 1980s and early 1990s is not treated here: see Golino, "Al di là della poesia."

14. See Eva Mazierska and Laura Rascaroli, *The Cinema of Nanni Moretti* (London: Wallflower, 2004).

15. Marco Tullio Giordana, *Pasolini: un delitto italiano* (Milan: Mondadori, 1994).

16. Dario Bellezza, *La morte di Pasolini* (Milan: Mondadori, 1981).

17. See Bellezza, *Poeta*, 12–13, for one example of many.

18. Quoted in Pier Paolo Pasolini, *Petrolio* (Turin: Einaudi, 1993), 569.

19. Davide Toffolo, *Intervista a Pasolini* (Pordenone: Biblioteca dell'immagine, 2002), 86–107.

20. Carlo Lucarelli, *Nuovi misteri d'italia. I casi di Blu notte* (Turin: Einaudi, 2004). On the *giallo*, see Luca Crovi, *Tutti i colori del giallo: Il giallo italiano da De Marchi a Scerbanenco a Camilleri* (Venice: Marsilio, 2002).

21. Alberto Garlini, *Fútbol bailado* (Milan: Sironi, 2004), 11–57; 427–55.

22. See Monica Jansen, *Il dibattito sul postmoderno in Italia* (Florence: Cesati, 2002). There has been a notable shift in recent work by so-called "postmodernist"

thinkers towards more realist and ethical and less relativist positions, which chimes with what is being suggested here; see, for example, Gianno Vattimo's *Nichilismo ed emancipazione* (Milan: Garzanti, 2003); or Eco"s turn to a more "closed" view of interpretation. I am grateful to Pierpaolo Antonello for his insights into this field.

23. See Jennifer Burns, *Fragments of* Impegno: *Interpretations of Commitment In Contemporary Italian Narrative, 1980–2000* (Leeds: Northern Universities Press, 2001).

24. Leonardo Sciascia, *L'Affaire Moro* (Palermo: Sellerio, 1978). See Robert S. C. Gordon, "A Neo-Rationalist Tendency in the Field of the Literary Intellectual in 1970s Italy: Vittorini, Sciascia, Ginzburg," *Journal of Modern Italian Studies* 6, no. 2 (Summer 2001): 249–64. Carla Benedetti, in her influential polemic *Pasolini contro Calvino* (Turin: Bollati Boringhieri, 1998), makes a related point by speculating on what Italian postmodern literature (Calvino, Eco) would have been like if Pasolini's postmodern apocalypse *Petrolio* had been finished and appeared alongside *Se una notte d'inverno un viaggiatore* . . . and *Il nome della rosa* in 1979–80.

25. Pino Pelosi, *Io, angelo nero* (Roma: Sinnos, 1995).

26. See various articles in *Corriere della sera*, May 8, 2005 and following. I am grateful to Stephen Gundle for sending me copies of these.

13

Making a Killing:
The "Monster of Florence" and
the Trial(s) of Pietro Pacciani

Ellen Nerenberg

The seven double homicides that took place in the Florentine hinterland between 1975 and 1985 offer a narrative of conspiracy that
plumbs public faith in organs of jurisprudence and is characterized by
mystery and jingoism. As Manlio Cancogni says in the introduction to the
summary of the case written by Francesco Ferri (who heard the case in
Florence's Court of Appeals and absolved Pacciani—a judicial sentence
later quashed), "Like most Italians, what I know about the Pacciani case is
based on hearsay."[1] Employing methods developed by the U.S. Federal
Bureau of Investigation (FBI), Italian law officials concluded the murders
were serial in nature and created an "identikit" to be used to build a list of
suspects. When Pietro Pacciani emerged as the prime suspect, organs of the
press were quick to call him *il mostro di Firenze* (the "Monster of
Florence"), a moniker used by the media to refer to the previously unidentified murderer. Pacciani was tried in 1994, found guilty, and sentenced. On
appeal, that sentence was vacated, and after another investigation, Pacciani
was accused once more; he was named co-conspirator to commit murder
with several others and was to have stood trial in 1998. He died awaiting his
second trial.

The narrative of the "Monster of Florence" is a story told in four parts
with significant built-in flashbacks. In chronological order, like that in the
précis I gave immediately above, these episodes date to 1951, 1974–85,
1989–94, and 2001. The "Monster Narrative," however, does not unfold in

linear fashion. Indeed, to retell the story in chronological order means accepting and endorsing the logical and "official" sequencing of events, something that in itself is problematic.

Structured more like a novel or film, the "Monster Narrative" contains both flashback and an epilogue indicating a future path of inquiry. Different from the compelling methodology Karen Pinkus makes use of in her exploration of the 1953 Wilma Montesi scandal, my examination *is* not a film but, instead, "is like" a film.[2] The difference this simile expresses is more than a matter of degree. Pinkus's project is admirably moored to its historical subject and uses cinematic technique and screenwriting convention to great success in unmasking the ways cinema and photography rendered everyday life in Italy of the early 1950s.[3] The re-presentation of the events I offer here does not privilege hindsight that imposes logic and order. Rather, this retelling of the Monster Story seeks to preserve its inconclusive essence.

Notes

In an eleven-year period, between 1974 and 1985, seven couples were murdered in the pastoral Florentine hinterland. The first double homicide took place in Borgo San Lorenzo on the night of September 9, 1974. The victims, Stefania Pettini and Pasquale Gentilcore, were killed in circumstances repeated in the six successive cases: they were shot to death in a remote area in their car, in a condition of partial undress, either at the beginning or the end of sexual activity, and in a state of obvious surprise. The following seven years in which no violence took place restored the bucolic serenity of the area, a peace ruptured in 1981 by another double homicide, radically similar to that of 1974. The "Scandicci Murders" took place on the night of June 6, 1981 in Bacciano, its victims Carmela de Nuccio and Giovanni Foggi. At the close of that summer, on the night of September 22, Susanna Cambi and Stefano Baldi were killed, again in highly similar circumstances, this time in Calenzano. The following June, the violence shifted to Montespertoli where, on June 19, 1982, Antonella Migliorini and Stefano Mainardi were murdered. Fifteen months later, on September 9, 1983, two German tourists, Horst Meyer and Uwe Rusch, were killed in Galluzzo. Although both victims were male (an aberration in the sequence of the murders until this point), the long hair of one led authorities to speculate that the killer had presumed the young man was a woman. The end of July of the following year brought the next murder supposed to be part of the series. In Vicchio, on July 29, 1984, Pia Gilda Rontini and Claudio Stefanacci were killed. The last murder to be attributed to this series took place thirteen months later, on August 9, 1985, the victims once more tourists, Nadine Mauriot and Jean-Michel Kraveichili.

Although the twelve murders I just listed all bore intense similarities, establishing the seriality of the murders was not without complication. While they occurred at close and regular intervals—the *sine qua non* of serial murder—the Borgo San Lorenzo homicides of 1974 fall outside the time frame. As well, for its shared characteristics, authorities wished to include the unsolved double homicide of Antonio Lo Bianco and Barbara Locci, which took place in Signa on the night between August 21 and 22, 1968, one of the flashbacks I alluded to above. Yet notwithstanding the temporal incongruity the 1974 murders presented with respect to the seriality of the other homicides, few experts doubted that the murders of the seven couples between 1974 and 1985 constituted a series.

The circumstances of death in all the murders share significant similarities: the victims died from gunshot wounds, out-of-doors in remote areas, and in their cars. In each case, the couple was killed with a .22 caliber Beretta that fired a Winchester Long Rifle Series H bullet. In a significant number of cases, the car's glove compartment was left open, and the female victim's purse left at the scene had been searched. All the DNA evidence recovered at the scene (in the form of semen or blood) belonged to one of the victims and thus could not be attributed to the killer. In a significant number of cases, the female victim's pubis had been sheared off with either a hunting knife or a surgical instrument. As well, in a significant number of cases the female victim's left breast had been removed, evidently by the same instrument. The media's spectacular display of the cadavers, a point I shall return to below, echoes Sciascia's "excellent cadavers," as well as the spectacular displays of deceased in other noteworthy cases (e.g., the Montesi case, Carlo Giuliani, the display of Claretta Petacci's body post-execution, etc.).

Not long after the police mobilized the *Squadra Anti-mostro* or the SAM (the Anti-Monster Team, though its ironic reference to the celebrated U.S. serial killer David "Son of Sam" Berkowitz is chilling), Pietro Pacciani emerged as a suspect. As will become clear, it was an unsurprising turn of events. However awful a person he was (and the demonstrated and repeated physical abuse of his wife, Angiolina, and the sexual abuse of his daughters for which he served a prison term in the late 1980s, supply ample evidence of his monstrousness), the state's case against Pacciani for the series of murders brimmed with lacunae, some not so serious, others that assailed the integral logic of the prosecution.

Real and material issues vexing to the Pacciani affair include some of the following questions: Where is the murder weapon? After a legendarily long

and thorough *maxiperquisizione* (search and seizure) of Pacciani's property, the *carabinieri* did not success in locating the Beretta used in the
crimes. Investigators recovered the handle of a revolver, wrapped in rags, in
a building on Pacciani's property, but its origin remained a mystery. Since
he was in prison at the time it was recovered, Pacciani could not have hidden it there himself, and the police could not determine who had. Moreover,
the recovery of a slip of paper with the word *coppia* (couple) and a license
plate number written on it proved similarly troubling. Investigators theo-
rized that it indicated a wider circuit of voyeurs who traded information
along with pornography and that could be involved. But the accumulation
of disturbing scraps of paper and rags does not end here. The provenance
of an anonymous letter implicating Pacciani and sent to the *carabinieri* was
never adequately explained. Could the authors have been Pacciani's own
daughters, retribution for the endless abuse they sustained at his hands?
The *maxiperquisizione* of the Pacciani property also unearthed a blank
notebook, manufactured in Germany and commercially unavailable in
Italy. Where did it come from? Could it have belonged to either Horst
Meyer or Uwe Rusch, killed in Galluzzo in 1983? Given the lurid aspects of
the case (incestuous sexual abuse of daughters, pornography, voyeurism,
and the like), one can see why an equally lurid tabloid, *Cronaca vera*, would
offer thorough coverage.

Cronaca vera indulged in precisely the sort of sensational details that the
Florentine daily *La Nazione* (not generally distinguished by its observance
of journalistic integrity) did not succumb to. When unable to publish
police photos, *Cronaca vera* staged its own photographic reenactments of
the crimes, their locales, and the bodies of the victims. And although
Cronaca vera is no more trustworthy than other exempla in the true crime
and gossip genre, the questions asked by its staff were often on point; in
fact, without the tabloid's coverage one would not be able to recover photographic spreads of the victims prior to their execution. To be sure,
Cronaca vera would have been grateful for the murders, which boosted its
sales that summer. They made a killing in more than one sense.[4]

The small, yet troubling, trail of paper and rags unearthed during the
investigation of the 1980s serial sex crimes recalls still other rags at the core
of confusion surrounding the Pacciani case. Sentenced for the 1951 murder of *cenciaolo* (ragman) Severino Bonini, Pacciani's criminal history
appeared vividly present in his 1994 trial. Although, most crimes of passion like Bonini's murder do not indicate a high risk of recidivism, in
Pacciani's case, the 1951 trial was interpreted as the necessary precursor to
the serial murders of the 1980s.

Chapter 2: Bringing a Monster to Trial

What were the steps leading to the trial, according to some legal experts largely misbegotten, of Pietro Pacciani for the series of double homicides in the Florentine outback? In 1984, following the Rontini-Stefanacci murders, the state's attorney (Procura della Repubblica di Firenze) solicited a report from criminological expert Prof. Francesco De Fazio, a forensic anthropologist who headed an institute for criminal investigation in Modena. These experts concluded that the murders appeared to have the same *modus operandi*, which established both seriality and a consistent author; that this person was a male who acted alone and according to his compulsions; that he was right-handed; that the excision of the breasts and pubises was sado-fetishistic; that he probably had semi-professional knowledge of firearms; that he was heterosexual but probably experienced serious setbacks in sexual encounters; and that he had no prior familiarity with the victims but was attracted serendipitously by the situations as they presented themselves. The State's Attorney also solicited the help of the FBI's behavioral science experts in Quantico, those who have now achieved notoriety (and primetime televised success) as "profilers." There was some talk of the "non-Italianness" of the crimes and their purported creator: as Carlo Lucarelli's fictitious detective sergeant claims in the novel *Lupo mannaro*,

> I've already told you what I think about your theory of a *serial killer*. . . . Look, do you see? Even the word is American and we're not in America here, we're in Italy. Here we call them *monsters* . . . not serial killers. We are in Modena, in Emilia![5]

In tandem with the Modenese experts and the FBI, the Deputy Chief of Police, Ruggero Perugini, appointed head of the newly constituted *Squadra Anti Mostro*, began assembling a computer-assisted screening, or profiling, program. For an unexplained reason, and contrary to the advice of the FBI, one of the limiting principles for the profile included subjects who had been in prison. The profile posited limits to age and timeframe as well: the parameters for the perpetrator's age were set at thirty and sixty years, and the timeframe was to end in 1989. The first screening produced sixty names, soon reduced to twenty-six suspects for reasons that have not been brought to light. Even though he was sixty-four years old at the time and therefore beyond the stated limits set by the criteria, and even though his arrest for the sexual abuse of his daughters came on May 30, 1987, fully one-and-one-half years after the 1985 homicides, leaving him, as a suspect in a series of murders, ample time to kill again, Pacciani's name was called up by the search. As Ferri meticulously observes, Pacciani's name probably should never have appeared on the list. In fact, Pacciani had been a free citizen for four years before the putative series of sex crimes began and eighteen months after it was believed to have concluded. A second screening again produced Pacciani's name among a field of eighty-two others. Ferri supposes that the appearance of his name on both lists led the team to identify Pacciani as the prime suspect. A warrant was issued to Pacciani on June 11, 1990, informing him that he would be investigated for possession of firearms, presumably the .22 Beretta. One-and-a-half years later, on October 29, 1991, a second warrant was issued, this time for the murders themselves. The *maxiperquisizione* was conducted April 22, 1992, and it was not until January of the following year that Pacciani was taken into protective custody.

Pacciani entered the collective consciousness of the investigators not because of results of scientifically rigorous methods of data collection so much as for the criminal history that left him open to suspicion. In fact, it was the events occurring in Tassinaia in 1951–52, that created a "monster" and led investigators to indict Pacciani.

Chapter 3: Flashback to the Deep Past/*passato remoto*

On April 11, 1951, in Tassinaia, in the Mugello area, Pacciani stabbed to death the traveling salesman Severino Bonini, whom he discovered *in flagrante delicto* with his (i.e. Pacciani's) fianceé, Miranda Bugli. The case was heard in Florence's Court of Assizes in late December and sentence handed down in January of the following year; in truth, however, the case had been opened and closed a hundred times by the popular performer Giubba, who recited his ballad, the story of Bonini's murder, in twenty quatrains, throughout the summer months at fairs and other public gatherings throughout the Florentine hinterland. Thus, even if the accounts in *La Nazione* were unavailable, or if a rural household lacked a radio, the story of Pietro, Miranda, and Severino was very widely-known:

Delitto a Tassinaia di Vicchio [6]

"Delitto a Tassinaia di Vicchio	"Crime at Tassinaia in Vicchio, [he] surprises
soprende la fidanzata con l'amante	his fianceé with her lover;
uccide il rivale a colpi di coltello."	and stabs the rival to death."
1.Un grande tragico fatto è avvenuto	A great tragedy has occurred

nel Comune di Vicchio nel Mugello
un giovanotto iniquo e fello
che a sentirlo ne desta pietà.

in the town of Vicchio in the Mugello,
[by] a youth so wicked and bad
That hearing of it arouses compassion.

2. Tal Pier Pacciani ha ventisei anni
che a parlarne il sangue si ghiaccia

lui sta a Paterno poder detto
    l'Aiaccia
oh sentite tutto quello che fa

This Pier Pacciani is twenty-six,
and to speak of it makes the blood run
    cold;
he lives at Paterno in a farm called
    Aiaccia;
oh, listen to what he does.

3. La ragazza si chiama Miranda
che è l'amante di Pier e ne dà
    la prova
lei sta a Villore detto Casanova
su il colle vicino a Maiol.

The girl is called Miranda
and she is Pier's lover and shows it;

she lives in Villore, called Casanova,
On a hill near Maiol.

4. A quattordici anni la pastorella
una sua avventura nel bosco
in lei niente c'era nascosto
prematura donna rendeva lei già.

At fourteen years this young shepherdess
had her own adventure in the woods,
and she hid nothing, for
She was already older than her years.

5. Da tanto tempo lui conosceva
così tanto era innamorato
che da breve si era fidanzato
alla giovane disse così.

For some time he knew
that he was so in love with her
that they were soon promised,
And so he said to her:

6. "Io ti amo così pazzamente
ed anche tu mi vorrai
    contraccambiare
quel che fu non ne voglio parlare
all'avvenire pensaci tu."

"I love you so wildly
[like] you want me to;

I don't want to talk about the past,
I'll leave you to plan the future."

7. E per breve trascorse l'amore
e da qui il fatto avviene ritroso
lui divenne tanto geloso
interi giorni la stava abbadar.

And their love was short-lived
and the deed now turns wayward;
he became so jealous that
he hung around her days on end.

8. L'undici aprile un sol di
    primavera
tal Severino venditore ambulante
di cenci e pelle da case tante e tante
anche da Casanova come il solito
    passò.

April 11th and a spring sun.

This Severino, traveling ragman
often passes many houses,
Including the one at Casanova.

9. I familiari della Miranda
son le tredici lo invitano a pranzare.
dopo pranzo via volle andare
a Poggiosecco si deve recar.

At one p.m. the family of Miranda
Invite him to eat,
and after lunch he wanted to leave,
for he had to get to Poggiosecco.

10. La sedicenne Miranda pastorella

il suo gregge nel bosco a pascolar
lui nel passar la volle chiamare
sbuca la macchia e la va vicin.

The sixteen-year-old shepherdess
    Miranda
takes her fold to the woods to graze,
and in passing he calls out to her,
starts through the thicket, and draws
    near.

11. Accanto a lei si mette seduto
per abbracciarla ne dà di piglio
e non sapeva che lì c'è un
    nascondiglio
il Pacciani che stava a sentir.

He sits down next to her
and moves to embrace her;
he didn't realize that through a

Peephole Pacciani was watching.

12. A questo punto Bonino Severino
non riesce a esser tanto audace
fa un tentativo e riesce capace
e la donzella alla gioia si dà.

Here Severino Bonino
isn't so bold.
he makes a move and succeeds,
And the young girl gives herself over.

13. Il fidanzato che più non resiste
inferocito sorte dal cespuglio
e vol far strage proprio nel cespuglio
disse "ambedue vi voglio ammazzar."

The fiancé can stand it no longer
he emerges enraged from the bush
and, wanting a bloodbath,
says to them both "I want to kill you."

14. Col coltello a serra manico
il sanguinario come fe' Caino
questo squilibrato paccianino
diciannove colpi su lui vibrò.

With a serrated blade,
in a bloodbath like Cain's,
this unhinged Pacciani
delivers nineteen blows.

15. Così lasciava il Bonino straziato
che di salto la ragazza afferrava

lei con questo suo udir si salvava
dice "Pierino presto ci sposerem."

Thus he leaves Bonino in pieces
and, bounding toward the girl,
    he grabs her;
she with these words saves herself:
"Pierino, soon we will be wed."

16. Lui rispose "se sposi saremo"
s'immutava e la volle abbracciare
"giura a nessuno di non rivelar
quel che è stato e nessuno lo sa."

"If we will be married," he says,
altering his mood and embracing her,
"swear to no one will you tell
what has happened here and no one
    will know."

17. Lui tornava dopo mezzanotte a caricarselo con le gambe al collo	He returned after midnight and took his burden, its legs around his neck,
come può fare la volpe a un pollo trecento metri così lo trascinò.	like the fox with a chicken, And in this way dragged the dead Bonino Three hundred meters.

18. La mattina a Vicchio era il mercato, lui tranquillo come a mene frego in una bottega di un certo Pellegro molti lo videro bere e giocar.	The next day was market day in Vicchio and he as carefree as Riley; many saw him drink and play cards in Pellegro's place.

19. Ma purtroppo la cosa s'inoltrava per Bonini ognuno era allarmato a Tassinaia viene ritrovato tra le foglie nascosto così.	But alas the deed developed and all were worried about Bonini; and he was found hidden in the thicket at Tassinaia.

20. Giovanotti all'amore voi fate è bene che ognuno abbia la fidanzata, ma se sapete che la donna è depravata come il Pacciani non dovete far.	You young folk, if you make love, it's good that every guy have his girl, but if you know she's perverted, Don't do like Pacciani did.

The ballad was published as a broadsheet by Florence's Vallechi Press; consequently, a city dweller unable to visit the fairs of the suburban hinterland had access to Giubba's opinion-forming song. The ballad rehearses each element of the crime, immortalizing it in the process. It publicizes Miranda's aborted pregnancy at age 14, two years before the murder. On the fateful day of the crime, Bonini is invited to lunch where Miranda catches his eye; he follows her as she takes her flock of sheep to graze and tries to make the most of a promising situation. However, Pacciani, as we read in quatrain 7 "divenne tanto geloso [e] interi giorni la stava abbadar" (became so jealous that he hung around her days on end) and, giving rein to his jealousy, begins to shadow Miranda's movements. Through an opening in the bushes, he watches as Bonini uncovers one breast and sees Miranda who, according to Giubba in quatrain 12, "alla gioia si dà" (the young girl gives herself over). Seized by jealousy, he crashes through the thicket like some animal "inferocito" or, made mad, as described in quatrain 13, and sets on Bonini wielding his serrated knife and stabbing him 19 times. At this point, Giubba describes Miranda's reaction as quick-witted and intended to save herself from Bonini's fate. "Pierino, presto ci sposerem," (Pierino, soon we will be wed) she says in quatrain 15 to dissuade him. Pacciani relents, and together, as Giubba describes, they decide to say nothing, rob the dead man, and leave him. Pacciani returns that evening and, as represented in quatrain 17, like the fox with a dead hen, drapes Bonini's legs about his neck and drags the body 300 meters into hiding. Stupidly, he spends the money the following day, just as news of Bonini's absence becomes public.

Composing the ballad before the trial was underway, Giubba conveyed his own opinions about the facts with impunity. Predictably, the ballad vilifies the teenaged Miranda, making *her* the reason for Pacciani's fall from grace and good standing. In quatrain 4 Giubba describes her as "prematura donna," (adult beyond her years), to whom Pacciani, in quatrain 6 entrusts the planning of their future. In quatrain 15 Giubba dwells on the near deceit of Miranda wishing to save herself—"lei con questo suo udir si salvava" (with these words she saved herself)—playing on Pacciani's helpless passion for her by saying they will soon be wed. Miranda, who is "depravata," as the last lines of the ballad attest, something I translate with the robust "perverted" to give a truer sense of its historical context, is at the root of the downfall of a stupid but otherwise harmless young man. As she testified at trial, Bugli did cry out to Pacciani, but before he had attacked Bonini, not after. The state's attorney successfully convinced the Court that Bugli had known Pacciani was witnessing the events. In this way the murder became a crime of passion, and while the court believed Pacciani reasonably had been drawn into homicidal rage, it did not find Bugli's claim of rape credible: after all, as Giubba's ballad had publicized, she was a "precocious" woman, and, to the opprobrium of all, had had an abortion. The court sentenced both Pacciani and Bugli in 1952. In early January, Pacciani was found guilty of *omicido colpevole* (homicide) and *furto aggravato* (aggravated theft), and Bugli was later convicted as accessory to Bonini's murder. She was sentenced to ten years, he to eighteen years and ten months, though he was paroled after thirteen (in 1964) for good behavior.

La Nazione, which had covered the 1951 case in exhaustive though decorous detail, opened wide the door to rumor more than four decades later with its coverage of the investigation of Pacciani for the murders attributed to the "Monster." Unsurprisingly, the editorial staff dredged up the reportage of the 1951 events. The image of Pacciani's homicidal rage was revisited and Giubba's ballad resurrected. The excised left breast of several of the female victims in the serial homicides was adduced as the somatization of Pacciani's supposed betrayal at witnessing Miranda's exposed left breast in the Tassinaia copse forty years earlier. The abuse of his daughters, his interest in pornography, and the unsubstantiated testimony of a witness claiming to have seen Pacciani in the vicinity of the Scopeti murders, all spilled out of the court building and into the adjacent streets in Florence's Santa Croce neighborhood.

In January 1994 Pacciani was informed he would stand trial for the eight double homicides attributed to the "Monster"; three months later, in April, the trial began. Despite the circumstantial nature of the evidence against him, even though one of the witnesses was later formally accused of involvement, despite the absence of a murder weapon or a confession, and despite the absence of a psychiatric evaluation for this putative sex criminal homicidal maniac, on November 1, 1994 Pacciani was found guilty for each pair of murders save the 1968 Lo Bianco-Locci murders.[7] He was sentenced to seven life sentences. Nearly a year later, Michele Giuttari, recently appointed head of the Florentine bureau of detectives, at the suggestion of the attorney general (Procura della Repubblica) began a systematic review of all of the evidence associated with the homicides and the Pacciani trial as the case progressed to the appellate phase, a trial that became known as *inchiesta bis* (the second iteration of a previous investigation). Pacciani's appeal was heard by the Appeal Section of the Court of Assizes in January of 1996. One month later, Mario Vanni, an old *compagno di merenda* (picnic buddy, as the group of voyeurs called themselves) of Pacciani, was arrested for his suspected role in the 1985 homicide of the French tourists Nadine Mauriot and Jean-Michel Kraveichili. The following day, February 13, 1996, the Court of Assizes absolved Pacciani of the crimes and nullified the sentence handed down by the lower court. However, in December of that year, on a technicality, the Court of Cassation vacated the decision of the Court of Appeals. In the intervening months, two other *compagni*, Giancarlo Lotti and Giovanni Faggi, were given notice they had become suspects. The trials were cut short, and it was ruled that Pacciani would stand in the defendant's box once more, for conspiracy to commit murder and not as the sole author of the murders, thus avoiding the constitutional stipulation against double jeopardy, "*ne bis in idem*." The trial was set for October 1998. However, in February of that year, called to Mercatale on another matter, the *carabinieri* found the lifeless body of Pietro Pacciani, who had succumbed to a major infarct, later ruled a wrongful death.[8] The day after Pacciani's body was found, the District Attorney for Florence asked that Lotti and Faggi be found guilty for the series of double homicides.

But the story of the Monster of Firenze is not coterminous with Pacciani's end. Like all good monster tales, it outlives the death of its protagonist.

Chapter 4: 2001 and After

In July and August 2001, fodder for still more beach reading, the story of the Monster, like the Undead, resurged once more into public view. Long after Carlo Lucarelli and Michele Giuttari's 1998 account *Compagni di sangue*—which built on Giuseppe Alessandri's shameless 1995 *La leggenda del Vampa* and followed the thoughtful accounts of both Nino Filastò, entitled *Pacciani innocente*, and retired jurist Francesco Ferri, *Il caso Pacciani*, published respectively in 1994 and 1996—the Monster narrative was put into public circulation.

Evidence of *mandanti* has appeared. It seems as though aristocratic, socially well-placed members of a Satanic sect could have (in fact, were likely to have) been involved in the crimes. As well, the disappearance of police funds earmarked for informants in the *Mostro* case comes to light. Further, a 1985 criminologist's report—never submitted to proper channels—appears; uncannily, this long-misplaced report includes theorizations of Satanic involvement. Finally, a *gola profonda* (a deep throat or confidential informant) comes forward to accuse eminent then–Procuratore di Firenze (and later named head of the Anti-Mafia task force) Piero Luigi Vigna of concealing evidence. Vigna, it is alleged, covered up the Sardinian link that joined the Lo Bianco-Locci murders to the series of double homicides in order gain leverage in kidnapping cases unrelated to the serial sex crimes.

The Monster Narrative's hold on the Italian public imagination has been strengthened as least as much by cultural expressions as by investigations by legal authorities or the media. Indeed, the "Monster of Florence" was nourished in the collective imagination in the way of all monsters: it was fed an admixture of "real" reportage and cultural representation. By word of mouth—or, as in the case of Giubba the troubadour, oral performance—the tale allowed rumor, as well as occasional and groundless notions of conspiracy, to prosper.

Notes

1. *Il Caso Pacciani. Storia di una colonna infame?* (Florence: Edizioni Pananti, 1996), v.
2. See Karen Pinkus, *The Montesi Scandal* (University of Chicago Press, 2003).
3. Pinkus rightly cautions scholars against the temptation to interpolate their own interpretation of the events in any recounting of those events, a practice that could easily give way to anachronizing. Such advice is prudent, and my aim here is to capture how, in the Pacciani case, anachronization played a key role in the presentation of the case to the public as well as to agents of the law and jurisprudence.
4. Indications of the trial are compiled from the following monographic sources, as well as reportage in *La Nazione*: Nino Filastò, *Pacciani Innocente* (Florence: Ponte alle Grazie, 1994); Giuseppe Alessandri, *La Leggenda del Vampa: la storia del mostro di Firenze* (Florence: Loggia de' Lanzi, 1995); Carlo Lucarelli and Michele Giuttari, *Compagni di sangue* (Florence: Le Lettere, 1998).

5. Carlo Lucarelli, *Lupo mannaro* (Rome: Edizioni Theoria, 1994), 33 (emphases original). This and all other translations are mine.
6. Reproduced in Alessandri, *La Leggenda del Vampa*, 30–31.
7. On the curious absence of a psychiatric evaluation of Pacciani, see Filastò, *Pacciani Innocente*, 102–3.
8. Pacciani was not a victim of violent crime (i.e., murder); rather, he suffered cardiac arrest due to a medication recently prescribed, a pharmaceutical counter-indicated by the other medications Pacciani, a relatively infirm man, had been taking.

14

Fashion Victims:
The Gucci and Versace Murders

Stephen Gundle and Lucia Rinaldi

The rise of Italian designer ready-to-wear in the 1980s was accompanied by an extraordinary increase in interest in the fashion industry. In contrast to the past, when designers and models had with few exceptions been known mainly within specialist circles, the fashion protagonists of the last two decades of the twentieth century became household names, superstars of a sort, who were regularly featured in the press with the stars of cinema, rock music and sports. The image that the fashion world projected of itself at this time was a supremely glamorous one.[1] Occasionally, some unpleasant event disturbed this fascinating façade. The death of a model due to an overdose or anorexia, the intrusion of a murder with a sexual motivation, the mysterious early death of a designer, tales of sexual exploitation, family feuds, professional rivalry, tax fraud and other similar events all briefly shook the dominant image. Such occurrences suggested that, behind the beauty and style, there was a sleazy dimension that was part of the permanently concealed structure of the fashion world.[2]

In the 1990s, two murders of men closely associated with the world of Italian fashion produced much speculation not only about why they had been murdered and by whom, but also about the wider subculture of fashion. The shootings of Maurizio Gucci in Milan in 1995 and of Gianni Versace in Miami in 1997 were front page news throughout the world. Although neither murder originated in the fashion sector, the press constantly related them to this. Coverage of Gucci's violent death evoked the history and the troubles of the dynasty. For his part, Versace was at the time of his death perhaps the best-known Italian designer in the world, the man who most symbolized the exuberance, excess, and sex appeal of modern fashion. For some observers, the high living and excess of the fashion community had somehow opened the way to the men's deaths. For others, the murders drew attention to the murky financial arrangements of the industry and its possible links to organized crime.

In this chapter, particular attention will be paid to the narratives that were woven around the cases. It will be shown that the Italian paradigm of the family feud was prominent in both cases, even though it was relevant only to one of them, while additional storylines highlighting crime, drugs, money, sex, and mass culture added spice and intrigue, turning the murders into real-life detective stories that lent themselves to evocation and fictionalization.

The Gucci Case

On the morning of March 27, 1995, Maurizio Gucci was shot dead in Milan, in the hall of the building where he had his office. He was killed before the eyes of the porter, who was also shot and injured when the fleeing killer realized that he had witnessed the murder. The *carabinieri* began their investigation into the shooting by looking into Gucci's business connections. He had sold his share of the family empire to Arab investors in the early 1990s and had embarked upon new projects. His new companies, which included investments in a chain of gambling casinos and the development of luxury holiday resorts, were all examined by the investigating magistrate, Carlo Nocerino, whose inquiries extended beyond Italy to several countries, including Switzerland and the United States. "Resorts and gambling, the inquiries point to business," ran a *La Repubblica* headline, while the Milan newspaper *Corriere della sera* announced on separate occasions possible trails in Switzerland and Majorca.[3] However, none of these leads produced any clue as to why he was killed or by whom.

Newspaper coverage of the murder dwelt at length on the fortunes and feuds of the Gucci family and of the fashion brand that, from relatively humble artisan origins in Florence, had become a worldwide symbol of luxury. At this time Gucci was once again a "hot" label. Its flagging fortunes were revived by the huge success of the American designer Tom Ford, who joined the company in 1990 and was appointed creative director in 1994. Under his leadership, the Gucci name once more resonated with wealth and luxury. This success indirectly reflected on Maurizio Gucci. As his life and business activities were picked over, an image took shape of a man who had many interests across Europe and beyond.

It was only by chance, almost two years later, that there was a breakthrough. At the end of December 1996, a bankrupt restaurant owner, who had recently returned to Italy from South America, called the police and claimed to have information about the murder. At that time the man, Gabriele Carpanese, was living in the low-budget Hotel Adry in Milan, where he had made friends with the doorman, Ivano Savioni. To the latter, Carpanese pretended to be a rich drug dealer who had fled from South America because he was hiding from the FBI. Savioni, fascinated by Carpanese's adventurous stories, candidly confided in him and admitted that he himself had been involved in something illegal: he had actively helped organize Maurizio Gucci's murder on behalf of the latter's ex-wife, Patrizia Reggiani. He also revealed that he and his accomplices were now dissatisfied with the payment they had received and intended to demand more from the wealthy widow.

After a few unsuccessful attempts to alert those in charge of the Gucci investigation, Carpanese managed to meet the chief of Milan's Criminalpol, Filippo Nenni, to whom he reported Savioni's story. From that moment, the Adry was kept under surveillance. As part of his collaboration with the police, Carpanese was to pretend to help Savioni and his gang blackmail Reggiani. The police discovered that Savioni had been contacted by Reggiani's close friend, a fortune teller named Giuseppina Auriemma (*la maga* Pina). Subsequently he had contacted a friend of his own, Orazio Cicala, a pizzeria owner ruined by gambling debts, who had agreed to hire a killer and drive the getaway car. All the suspects' telephones were tapped as was Savioni's car. On basis of the evidence they gathered from intercepted conversations, the police arrested Patrizia Reggiani on January 31, 1996, at 4.30 AM. She was at that time living in the luxurious flat in the Milan city center that, from 1994 up to his death, had been the home of Maurizio Gucci and his new partner, Paola Franchi. The police also promptly arrested the other four accomplices: Savioni, Cicala, Auriemma, and Benedetto Ceraulo, who was the hired killer.

Following her arrest and for years afterward, Reggiani constantly pleaded her innocence and accused Auriemma and her friend Savioni of having organized everything by themselves. They had then set about blackmailing her. Nevertheless, on November 3, 1998, she and her partners in crime were all found guilty of murder, a verdict whose announcement was so eagerly awaited that it was broadcast live on television. In 2001 Italy's highest appeal court, the Court of Cassation, confirmed Reggiani's guilt, while reducing her sentence slightly to twenty-six years. No account was taken of her family's plea of "mental infirmity" on account of brain surgery she sustained in 1990. Although attempts have been made to reopen the case, by the end of 2006 the original verdict had not been overturned.

The Versace Murder

On July 15, 1997, at 8.30 AM, Gianni Versace returned on foot to his luxurious villa on fashionable Ocean Drive in the South Beach resort of Miami, Florida. He had taken a brief walk to buy magazines and coffee at a nearby café. As he paused before opening the wrought iron gates to the property, two shots rang out that were heard in the area and inside the building. As Versace slumped to the ground on the steps outside the gates, people ran toward him while the gunman made off in haste. Although one man chased him, he gave up soon afterward and returned to the scene when the fugitive turned and threatened him with a gun. The killer, it was later established, took refuge in a parking lot, where he got into a red Chevrolet and changed clothes before once more fleeing on foot. Meanwhile, Versace's partner, Antonio D'Amico, had emerged from the villa and found him lying in a pool of blood. The police and an ambulance arrived, and the dying designer was conveyed to Miami's Jackson Memorial Hospital, where doctors pronounced him dead.

Witnesses to the murder spoke of a white man, approximately in his mid-twenties, having fired the shots. One bullet was fired into Versace's head from behind and another pumped into his body as he fell to the ground. The police investigation focused within hours on the person of Andrew Cunanan, a "gay serial killer" who had already murdered four men in three states since April. High on the FBI's most wanted list, Cunanan had been living in Miami for several weeks and had been seen, it transpired, on the south Florida club circuit. A university drop-out of Philippine parentage, born and raised in San Diego, he had become a glorified rent-boy, who had been maintained by a string of older, wealthy lovers. He is alleged to have begun his murderous spree by shooting Jeffrey Trail, one the closest friends of his lover, David Madson, on April 29, and then shooting Madson on May 3. Cunanan may have suspected that the two men had become involved. The spree continued with two further killings of mature men in Chicago and New Jersey. The first two and the last victim were all murdered with Golden Saber .40 caliber bullets, the same kind that killed Versace. The red Chevrolet pickup truck that was found in the South Beach garage had belonged to the previous victim. Cunanan, it soon emerged, had exchanged the license plates before reaching Florida.

A manhunt was launched with massive media coverage. It was expected that within days or hours Cunanan would be found and apprehended. In fact, he killed himself on a houseboat, just over a week later, after police had surrounded it and launched tear gas into its windows. It appeared that he had been planning to flee the country but the arrival of the police ruined his scheme. Rather than face capture and trial, he preferred suicide. For the authorities, this event brought an end to the hunt for the serial killer and also to the investigation into the Versace murder. Strangely, there appeared to be no connection at all between the designer and his killer. It was vaguely suggested that the two men may have briefly met in San Francisco in the early 1990s, when the designer was creating costumes for the city's opera house, but this claim was never substantiated. Rather it was assumed that Versace's celebrity and his well-known, if not widely broadcast, homosexuality had attracted the attention of a killer on the rampage who was targeting older men of his own sexual orientation.

The Family Narrative

Save for the method employed, the murders of Gucci and Versace could hardly have been more different. Yet certain common narratives characterized the treatment in the media. The first of these is the narrative of the family feud. Throughout the Gucci case, apart from the lengthy press articles about the investigation and accounts of arrests and trials, many pieces focused on the Gucci family. Articles often referred to the Gucci family tree, while the story of the fashion house was presented in a manner that highlighted details of the internal wars and feuds that had occurred during the 1980s and early 1990s as family members fought to gain control of the company. "The Guccis are known for their disputes, [they are a] family lacerated by accusations and trials over the share-out of the empire founded in 1923 by Guccio Gucci with a leather goods store in Florence," declared *La Repubblica* on November 3, 1998.[4] "For the Guccis," wrote *Il Giorno*, "their worst enemies have also been their relatives. First the brand and control of the company, then women. Hatred, grudges, jealousy, disputes."[5] The discovery that Maurizio Gucci's ex-wife was behind the murder plot reinforced the emphasis on the family feud and lent it validity. It transpired that Reggiani hated Gucci because he had deserted her in 1985 and since then she had no longer been able to live the glamorous and luxurious lifestyle to which she had been accustomed. She was concerned that Gucci would marry his new partner and bestow his fortune and properties on his new family. When the divorce was finalized in 1994, Reggiani decided to take action and called her best friend Pina for help, promising her and her accomplices a fabulous reward for the murder of her ex-husband.

As a first generation family company, the Versace fashion house was less rich with history than Gucci. Yet even though there was little obvious reason to resort to the family narrative to explain Versace's murder, it nonetheless featured prominently. The involvement in the business of the designer's brother and sister ensured that there was a similar overlap between family relations and business. While Gianni was in charge of the creative dimension, his sister Donatella was widely referred to as his "muse," and his brother Santo dealt with the financial side. In addition, Gianni's longstanding partner Antonio D'Amico and Donatella's husband Paul Beck played subsidiary roles. Originally from Reggio Calabria, the family presented a public image of unity and mutual support. The reality was somewhat different. Donatella was less than satisfied with her ornamental role and had pushed for more input. When Gianni fell ill with a serious health problem that was described as a tumor of the ear, she came more to the fore. She designed collections for the diffusion line Versus and was described in the press as a "growing power in Gianni's global fashion empire."[6] Just one month before his death, *Vanity Fair* ran a long feature on her that claimed to reveal the truth about "a brother-sister act that shifts between furious ego clashes and a serious case of mutual worship."[7] In some quarters this was read as a bid for power in a context in which Gianni's health was fragile and Santo, who was often derided and abused by his brother on account of his desire to rein in Gianni's penchant for lavish spending, might have asserted more influence.[8] Publication of Versace's will did nothing to stifle talk of family battles. Controversially, he named Donatella's daughter Allegra, then aged eleven, as his universal heir. Her brother Daniel received his art collection (which included several Picassos). D'Amico was given fifty million Italian Lira (approx. US$30,000) per month for life and the right to use all the designer's houses, although he subsequently renounced this in favor of a one-off payment. Neither Donatella nor Santo received anything. Both Santo and D'Amico released statements denying any acrimony, but few found this entirely persuasive.

Media coverage of the cases regularly employed words such as "heir," "saga" and "dynasty." Through language, family disputes were highlighted and real-life situations were brought closer to the realm of fiction. This was most marked in the Gucci case. The circumstances of the murder and the events leading to the culprits' arrest underlined this. Alberto Berticelli claimed in the *Corriere della sera* that the latter entailed "a plot worthy of a fictional detective story,"[9] while another journalist described the murder as "a crime that would have been to the liking of Agatha Christie."[10] The fictional quality of the whole affair was underlined by Leonardo Coen, who wrote, after the verdict was issued, of "the tragic and fundamentally exaggerated end of the Gucci saga, as if . . . a mysterious director had called 'Action!' for the last time in a film about the intrigues and events of a family in which fathers are against sons, brothers battle against brothers, and cousins plot against cousins."[11] Other journalists linked the case to the

Hollywood film about jilted ex-es, *The First Wives' Club*.[12] Some articles recalled the tropes of hard-boiled crime fiction and film *noir*. At the same time, they revealed a sharp moral judgment that, as will be shown in the next section, also marked coverage of Versace's murder.

Use of the term "dynasty" evoked the popular television series of the same name, which had a vast audience in Italy in the 1980s. The Guccis were perceived as being similar to the Colby family of the television drama and were constantly compared to it, with Patrizia Reggiani being likened to the *femme fatale* Alexis, played on television by Joan Collins. She was often described by the media as a "dark lady" on account of her (alleged) obsessive love of money and prestige at all costs.[13] References were also made to *Dallas*, another popular American television series in which two brothers (J. R. and Bobby Ewing) battled against each other and their half-brother Cliff Barnes for control of the family's oil wealth. The family dynamic of both television series helped them acquire a significant following in Italy due to the central role of family in the country's social and economic texture.[14] These associations spilled over into the Versace case, where the absence of a strong dynastic dimension to the story was compensated for by an emphasis on the close, seemingly quasi-incestuous, relations of Gianni and his siblings.

Luxury and Decadence

Undoubtedly one of the major sources of fascination of the two murders was the contrast they threw up between the less savory aspects of the lives of the victims and the extraordinary opulence of their lifestyles. The Gucci family and its "standard of living . . . [high enough] to make common mortals turn pale"[15] had long been endowed with glamour and prestige. Their story continually dazzled the public because they seemed to belong to a golden world and their privileged status inspired curiosity and envy. The coverage of the family's affairs, which increased in the 1990s as the fashion house grew in the world market, continued after the case of Maurizio's murder was solved.[16]

The banner headlines that Versace's murder attracted testified to the fame of the designer, who, after conquering Italy in the 1980s, had spread his fashion empire across the far east and Europe and then to the United States. Obituaries hailed him as "the king of glitz," the man who "combined beauty with vulgarity," and highlighted the way he "[welded] together high fashion with the very fabric of popular culture."[17] Versace owned four notoriously lavish houses, in Milan, on Lake Como, in New York and Miami, at which he hosted show business friends including Madonna and

Elton John. He had spent millions of dollars restoring the Miami villa to its 1930s glory, extending it and furnishing it in the most luxurious style imaginable.[18] The Casa Casuarina had originally been built by a wealthy gay couple and furnished with flamboyance, but it had fallen into disrepair. The Italian designer turned it into one of the most eclectically luxurious homes in the world. The Italian Renaissance was the main inspiration for the exteriors, including a marble mosaic-lined swimming pool, while references to Pompeii, ancient Egypt, and Gothic England marked the interior decor.

Two themes emerged in the coverage of the case that were both informed by a mixture of attraction and repulsion. The first of these was the idea of the fashion world as a terrestrial hell. While the designer's friends in the press talked of his sense of fun and color, his courtesy and friendliness,[19] those who were less enthusiastic about his siren dresses and the unabashed sexuality of his advertising took the opportunity to condemn them. This line was common in the foreign press. Versace "sold sex and glamour and he sold it with the gusto of the most garrulous second-hand car dealer" it was observed in one British newspaper.[20] "The shockingly violent and premature death of the designer most closely associated with rock and movie stars, Gianni Versace has—beneath the glitz and glamour—briefly illuminated a corrupt, sick and self-deluded world that is the reality of much of the fashion business," crowed Brenda Polan in the *Daily Mail*.[21] "The brutal death of Gianni Versace yesterday brought home an unpleasant, little acknowledged truth: that the fashion world, for all its glamour and pretty packaging, is a far murkier, and more dangerous, milieu than at first it seems," proclaimed *The Independent*.[22] Even the veteran fashion journalist Colin McDowell described the fashion business as "rotten to the core."[23]

Within this sort of coverage, the second theme emerged; that of Versace's homosexuality. Polan described the photographic books that appeared in his name as being "always uncomfortably semi-pornographic in a homoerotic way."[24] They "left little doubt as to Versace's sexual proclivities, if not to his actual private life." "His clothes too," she continued, "with their sadomasochistic themes, hinted at a lifestyle all too common among the hedonistic sensualists who are drawn to the world of fashion: that of gay bars, opportunistic cruising and dangerous encounters." The implication of this homophobic judgment was that Versace had somehow brought his death upon himself. D'Amico later admitted to the police that he and Versace had been in the habit of picking up male prostitutes at Miami Beach but he claimed that they had not done this for at least three years.[25] Speculation that, despite his long liaison with D'Amico, the designer had indulged in promiscuous unprotected sex, also fueled rumors that he had contracted

AIDS.[26] The family's decision to cremate his body in haste, before the 48 hours required by law had passed, and fly the ashes to Italy for the funeral added grist to this particular mill. Although it was relatively contained, speculation persisted that there were hidden aspects of the case that included possible closer connections between killer and victim.[27]

There was considerable comment that Versace had chosen, in his search for privacy, the most flamboyant house on the most well-known road in one of the most publicized resorts in America. His oft-voiced desire to lead a normal, simple life clashed blatantly with his professional thirst for celebrity, media coverage, and glamour. It seemed as if the designer was totally addicted to publicity and that this compulsion had inevitably drawn him into the realm of those who attract obsessive attention from fans, stalkers, and, in his case, a serial killer with only the most general of motivations. For this or some other reason, the fashion milieu appeared to have given rise to the climate in which one of its leading exponents could be senselessly murdered. Virtually unknown in Italy, save through fictional treatments and true crime documentaries, the phenomenon of the serial killer was seen as a product of the same universe of film and other mass cultural references that Versace had repeatedly employed in his work.

Crime and Retribution

In neither case was any involvement of organized crime established. Reggiani, it is true, did organize her ex-husband's death, but none of those she recruited belonged to one of Italy's more notorious criminal organizations. The magistrate Nocerino managed to trace a dubious transaction that Gucci had concluded with a notorious neo-fascist terrorist, but this had no bearing on his death. However, before the nature of the plot emerged, the killing appeared to have been a cold-blooded execution, a classic mob killing. Much the same was true of the Versace murder. "The hunt for the designer's assassin: vendetta or madness?" asked *La Repubblica*, while London's *Daily Mail* openly wondered in its title, "Did the Mafia kill Versace?"[28] The very rapid expansion of the Italian fashion industry in the 1980s and 1990s led to questions about the provenance of the capital that financed the development of some houses.

Three years earlier, in October 1994, *The Independent on Sunday* had run an article that explored the complex and secretive financial arrangements of the Versace empire. Published at a time when the Italian corruption scandals of the early 1990s had already brought down the old political elite, it reflected the growing interest in the role of bribery and tax evasion in the Italian fashion business. Fiammetta Rocco, the article's author, reported, "There are frequent rumours, as there are with most rich southern Italian businessmen, that Versace is somehow linked to the Mafia."[29] Finding it impossible to obtain business records for most of the companies in the group, she concluded that it was mostly a "front." Lawyers for Versace sued the newspaper for defamation and won and apology and undisclosed damages. This did not prevent stories of a similar nature being published in the immediate aftermath of the murder. The *Daily Mail* repeated the accusation that his business was linked to the Mafia and money laundering. Needless to say, the Versace family immediately countered such rumors by asserting that "only a madman could have killed him."[30]

Speculation continued mainly in the Anglo-American media about the possible role of organized crime in the killing. The efficient manner of the shooting and the absence of any substantiated connection between presumed killer and victim allowed various hypotheses to flourish.[31] The imaginative dimension was also significant here. Abroad, the popular image of Italy is not only the sunny and stylish one that most fashion houses deploy to promote their goods. It is also one of crime and violence. Only Dolce & Gabbana (Domenico Dolce is Sicilian) have dared, controversially, to harness the glamorous image of the dark-clothed, sunglasses-wearing mafia killer to their promotional machine. To say the least, others found the legacy of *The Godfather* and *Goodfellas* inconvenient.

Conclusion

Neither company was more than temporarily damaged by the killings and their *dénouments*. The fact that Gucci was no longer controlled by the family ensured that the commercial and critical success of the brand under Tom Ford was unaffected. The family drama unfolded on a separate plane. For Versace the problem was more serious since Gianni was not only the founder but also the creative force behind the brand. It was reported that, shortly after his death, banks fearful for the company's future demanded the repayment of loans. However, under Donatella's creative leadership, which was already present, according to some accounts, before her brother's death, the house recovered and prospered. Coverage of the designer's sister's trials, tribulations, and triumphs eclipsed talk of the past. However, this was not an entirely spontaneous process since the company intervened on more than one occasion to quash proposed publications on the life and death of Gianni, including a biography.

Walter Benjamin has observed that "fashion was never anything than other than the parody of the motley cadaver . . . and bitter colloquy with decay."[32] The association of fashion with murder has a certain attraction since glamour is never pure sunshine; it also has a dark and sleazy side. This dark allure has been explored in various books and films. Marco Parma's murder mystery set in the world of Milan fashion, *Sotto il vestito niente* (Under the Dress, Nothing),[33] was turned into a film in 1985 by the Vanzina brothers. The Versace killing itself inspired at least one fictionalized treatment, an exploitative film directed by Menahem Golan entitled *The Versace Murder*, in which the designer was played by veteran actor Franco Nero. The Gucci story, it was announced on several occasions, was to be turned into a film by *Goodfellas* director Martin Scorsese. Although the industry may find this interest in the dark underside of fashion distressing, risk and danger, as well as murder, are part of the fictional world of the movies and popular fiction. Since contemporary fashion has become part of the universe of mass communication, the boundaries between fact and fiction in its presentation are constantly transgressed. For this reason, fictional narratives easily structured reception and coverage of the two murders.

Notes

1. On the history and theory of glamour, see Stephen Gundle and Clino T. Castelli, *The Glamour System* (London: Palgrave, 2006). Specifically on Versace, see Reka C.V. Buckley and Stephen Gundle, 'Flash Trash: Gianni Versace and the Theory and Practice of Glamour' in *Fashion Cultures: Theories, Explorations and Analysis*, ed. Stella Bruzzi and Pamela Church Gibson, 331–48 (London: Routledge, 2000).
2. Two books treating the sleazy underside of fashion are Michael Gross, *Model: the Ugly Business of Beautiful Women* (New York: Bantam Press, 1995); and Mario Guarino and Fedora Raugei, *Scandali e segreti della moda* (Rome: Riuniti, 2001).
3. See Gianfranco Modolo, "Villaggi e case da gioco la pista punta sugli affari," *La Repubblica*, March 29, 1995; Danilo Taino, "L'ultima idea: punto sui casinò," *Corriere della sera*, March 28, 1995, p. 3; "Delitto Gucci, la trama è in Svizzera," *Corriere della sera* March 29, 1995, p. 1; Ranieri Orlandi, "Gucci, una pista porta a Majorca," *Corriere della sera*, March 30, 1995, p. 13.
4. "Dal delitto alla sentenza, le tappe dell'inchiesta," *La Repubblica*, November 3, 1998, this version downloaded from http://www.repubblica.it.
5. Lorella Capparucci, "Donne e colpi bassi nei litigi della dinastia," *Il Giorno*, February 1, 1997: 4. Another article amply dealing with the Gucci family's feuds is that by Leonardo Coen, "Oro e odio: Cent'anni di dinasty. Nemici di padre in figlio," *La Repubblica*, March 20, 1997, p. 3.
6. Cathy Horn, "La bella Donatella," *Vanity Fair* (June 1997): 118.
7. Ibid., 118.
8. Guarino, *Versace versus Versace*, 106.

9. Alberto Berticelli, "I killer di Gucci pensavano di essere in un film," *Corriere della sera*, February 4, 1997, p. 12

10. Diego Gabuti, "Amore, odio e miliardi. Proprio come un romanzo," *Il Giorno*, February 1, 1997, p. 1.

11. Coen, "Oro e odio," 3.

12. Natalia Aspesi, "Circe dell'alta società," *La Repubblica*, February 1, 1997, pp. 1–2; Vivian Kasam,"I tacchi a spillo fra le detenute; 'Il mio personaggio è di dark lady,'" *Corriere della sera*, February 1, 1997, p. 13.

13. Gian Antonio Stella, "Una compagnia di giro strampalata per un copione straordinario," *Corriere della sera*, November 4, 1998, p. 5.

14. On this, see Paul Ginsborg, *Italy and Its Discontents 1980–2001* (London: Penguin, 2001), chap. 3.

15. Capparucci, "Donne e colpi bassi," 4.

16. Gerald McKnight, *Gucci: A House Divided* (New York: D. I. Fine, 1987); Angelo Pergolini, Maurizio Tortorella, *L'ultimo dei Gucci: Splendori e miserie di una grande famiglia fiorentina* (Milan: Marco Troppa, 1997); Fabio Fox Gariani, *Il delitto Gucci: un'indagine criminologica completa* (Milano: Ulisse, 2003); Sara Gary Forden, *The House of Gucci. A Sensational Story of Murder, Madness, Glamour, and Greed* (New York: Perennial, 2001).

17. Tamsin Blanchard, "Versace: Very Sexy," *The Independent*, July 16, 1997, p. 12.

18. Charles Gandee, "Versace"s Castle in the Sand," *Vogue* (U.S. edition) (December 1994): 288–304.

19. Alexandra Shulman, "Versace and the power of fashion," *The Daily Telegraph*, July 16, 1997, p. 22.

20. Picture caption, *Sunday Telegraph*, July 24, 1994, p. 35.

21. Brenda Polan, "J'accuse," *Daily Mail*, July 19, 1997, pp. 10–11.

22. Andrew Gumbel and Steve Boggan, "Darkness behind the glamour," *The Independent*, July 16, 1997, p. 3.

23. Colin McDowell, "Depravity bites," *The Guardian*, Weekend Supplement, August 9, 1997, pp. 36–37. See also Guarino and Raugei, *Scandali e segreti*.

24. Polan, "J'accuse," 10.

25. Guarino, *Versace versus Versace*, 121–22.

26. See Michael McDonough and John Phillips, "Versace murdered in cold blood," *The Times*[London], July 16, 1997, p. 1.

27. For a full review of this and other theories, see Mario Guarino, *Versace versus Versace* (Rome: Fabio Croce, 2003).

28. *La Repubblica*, July 16, 1997: 1; *Daily Mail*, July 16, 1997, p. 1.

29. Fiammetta Rocco, "Gianni in Wonderland," *The Independent on Sunday*, October 23, 1994, suppl. p. 4.

30. *La Repubblica*, July 16, 1997, p. 3.

31. For one hypothesis, see Guarino and Raugei, *Scandali e segreti*, 175.

32. Walter Benjamin, *The Arcades Project* (Cambridge, MA: Harvard University Press, 1999), 63.

33. Marco Parma, *Sotto il vestito niente* (Milan: Longanesi, 1982).

15

Between True Crime and Fiction: The World of Carlo Lucarelli

Giuliana Pieri

Italian crime fiction, after a difficult inception in the 1930s and 1940s and steady but modest growth in the postwar period, has witnessed remarkable and unprecedented popular success since the early 1990s. The popularity of the homegrown *gialli*, sustained by a number of prestigious Italian publishing houses, television, and critical interest, has transformed the Italian literary scene into a realm of the *giallo* and the noir.[1] This phenomenon, which deserves further critical attention, has been characteristically undermined by literary critics, although, after the extraordinary success of the Sicilian detective writer Andrea Camilleri—who has been topping the Italian book charts since 1996—a lively and long-overdue debate on the merits of crime fiction has taken place, principally in national newspapers and magazines, which has both mirrored and fueled interest in this popular genre. Leading this new wave of Italian crime fiction is a considerable number of young writers, with the Bolognese *Gruppo 13* at the forefront of this literary phenomenon. *Gruppo 13*, with their postmodern ironic reference to the neoavanguardia of the *Gruppo 63*, is in fact a loose label under the umbrella of which one can find a group of Italian *giallisti* working in and around Bologna.[2] Luigi Bernardi, the co-editor of Einaudi's first series dedicated to crime fiction, *Stile libero noir*, noted, "Actually Gruppo 13 is as if it never existed: they are not thirteen and they have probably never met all together. The group is a media invention."[3] The media, as we shall see, certainly played a central role in the diffusion of knowledge of the new Italian crime writers, given that the cultural climate in Italy had traditionally been very hostile to this popular fiction and was particularly so in the early 1990s.

The marginalization of crime fiction by the Italian literary establishment has particular relevance if we shift our attention to Italian social and cultural history and look at crime fiction as an important but often misunderstood contributor to the postwar Italian tradition of social and political engagement (*impegno*) by intellectuals and writers, thanks to this genre's inherent, and often gritty, realism.[4] The literary critic Loris Rambelli dated the beginning of the social engagement of Italian crime fiction to the publication of Giorgio Scerbanenco's novel *Venere Privata* (Private Venus; Milan, 1966), the first of the noir series set in Milan in the post-Economic Miracle years, and suggested that *impegno* is an uninterrupted tradition that underpins most Italian crime fiction.[5] As Marco Sangiorgi has correctly highlighted, a number of critics and writers have recently engaged in a debate over the characteristics of Italian crime fiction and in particular its social and political role.[6] As Stephen Knight has argued in his study on *Form and Ideology in Crime Fiction* (1980), crime fiction can be viewed as the genre that more directly portrays the ideology of the society it is created by through its ideas about controlling crime, and law and order.[7] This ideological message, as I shall argue, is particularly evident in the themes and subjectivities that are portrayed and, more importantly, those which are marginalized or omitted from the narrative.

The new Italian noir writers have explored in the last decade a number of issues that are crucial to the understanding of the new social and political climate created in Italy after the end of the traditional party system and the corruption scandals of the 1990s.[8] Carlo Lucarelli is one of the most representative talents of this new generation of writers, and his work presents a stimulating interplay between real crimes and fiction in a way that has particular relevance when seen in the context of *impegno*. In this study, by looking at the fictional and real world of Lucarelli, I want to suggest that postmodern noir and detective writers in Italy, in common with the French *néo-polar* and many contemporary European crime writers, have taken it upon themselves to expose the evils of contemporary society, tackling issues such as immigration, the increasing violence of Italian society, social exclusion, and youth subcultures, together with the revision of the darkest periods of recent Italian history, with a particular focus on the Fascist regime, the rise of extreme right-wing movements, and the terrorism of the 1970s and early 1980s.[9] They appear and are often emphatically portrayed by the media as the new engaged writers, and *impegno* seems to be at the root of their writing and their extraordinary popular appeal.

Lucarelli, who was born in Parma in 1960, started his career with the publication of short crime stories in the early 1990s and was among the original members of the Gruppo 13.[10] His novels comprise three distinct series: a historical detective series set during the Fascist period,[11] one set in contemporary Bologna that focuses on serial killers,[12] and farcical detective novels set in contemporary Bologna that feature an incompetent, racist, sexist, and juvenile, but ultimately likeable, policeman, Coliandro.[13] Lucarelli has also been the host of popular late-night television series: *Mistero in Blu* (RAI 1998); *Blu Notte* (RAI 1999–2000), which examined unsettling and unsolved crimes; and, more recently, the *Blu notte: Misteri d'Italia* series (RAI 2001–02), which looked at some of the more illustrious and notorious unsolved crimes of postwar Italy. The last series looked at, amongst others, the deaths of Salvatore Giuliano, Wilma Montesi, Pier Paolo Pasolini, Giuseppe Alfano, and Paolo Borsellino, as well as the tragedies of Ustica and Bologna and two episodes on the "Monster of Florence."

In any analysis of the new Italian *giallisti* it is essential to be aware of the importance of the media and the way in which noir and crime fiction have been labeled and packaged. These writers, and this is the case of Lucarelli in particular, are extremely aware of the importance of the media and make extensive use of all the advertising vehicles at their disposal in the new web age. Lucarelli's official website, for instance, has an online discussion group and a chat room, as well as a detailed bibliography of the author and downloadable articles by literary critics and academics.[14] This is in itself very revealing, insofar as it is a deliberate attempt to construct a public persona of the author as both in dialogue with his readers—as any consumer-driven writer of pulp fiction may try to appear—and as an established writer with an extensive opus and critical literature dedicated to him.

A further interesting use of media manipulation and effective means of overcoming both critical hostility and attracting the interest of his readership is Lucarelli's conscious effort to present himself as both detective and historian; it is almost a denial of the simple image of the crime fiction writer in favor of the journalist-cum-historian-cum-real detective. This is particularly evident in Lucarelli's historical novels. The period analyzed in these novels—fascist Italy and the years that go from the Republic of Salò to the first postwar elections in 1948—is significant in the context of Italy's historical revisionism of the 1990s, when the debate on the historiography of Fascism led to the polarization of public opinion. In interviews with the author, and in essays and articles on Lucarelli's work, there are several references to Lucarelli's degree dissertation on Fascist police as an indication of the authenticity of the historical background of the novels. Lucarelli also talks openly about the similarities between the work and tools of the crime novelist with those of the historian: "There is an affinity between the narrative of the historian, historical methodology, and the method of those

who write crime fiction novels."[15] His analysis of the Fascist period is unde-
niably competent and creates a sense of historical authenticity in his fictional works. Yet what Lucarelli and his commentators have done so far is
to reinforce Lucarelli's persona as that of the writer as actual historian. The
equation between detective and historian is very important in the context
of any analysis of postmodern fiction, and in particular crime fiction, since
the detective is often also portrayed as a historian of the past.[16] Besides, as
Linda Hutcheon has argued, the function of narrative in a postmodern
context is a means through which posterity can access history, since the
textuality of history implies the historicity of literature.[17] The consequence
of this erosion of the divide between different types of narrative, and especially between fiction and reality, is particularly compelling in crime fiction
due to the social commentary implicit in the realistic portrayal of characters and events that typifies this genre. Lucarelli makes use of the detective formula in order to investigate neglected periods of Italian history,
responding to the actual historical and political debates that characterized
the 1990s. The equation in his case, however, is not of the fictional detective as historian but rather the author as historian in an interesting instance
of blurring the distinction between real crimes and fiction, a similarly
distinctive trait of Lucarelli's television work and real crime writing; this
blurring has wider implications in terms of the actual socio-political
engagement of his work.

Lucarelli's *impegno* is visible on many levels. His engagement with Italy's
changing social and political climate in the 1990s is very explicit in the
novels set in contemporary Bologna. In common with the new generation
of Italian *giallisti*, he focuses in particular on the scandals of *Tangentopoli*
(Bribesville), and the new political and cultural environment of the late
1980s and early 1990s. In *Lupo Mannaro* (Werewolf; 1994; 2001), the killer,
a highly successful businessman—whose speech mannerism punctuated
by the refrain "please allow me to . . ." is reminiscent of Silvio Berlusconi in
the early 1990s—commenting on the changes that are taking place in Italy,
pronounced: "the moral changes, detective inspector: new values, a new
constitution, a new republic, new objectives" (*Lupo mannaro*, 49). As
Lucarelli stated in an interview on the Gruppo 13 linking his work and that
of many of his Italian contemporaries with that of other European and
Mediterranean crime writers, crime fiction is the vehicle through which
one can tell the story/history of contemporary Italy: "Eco gave us the
example: one could use crime fiction as a vehicle. . . . Our critique, the sub-
terranean civic engagement, was filtered through the example of the
Mediterranean noir."[18] Eco, in the *Reflections* on *The Name of the Rose*
(1983) openly discussed the pedagogic intent of the postmodern novelist,

as well as writing what could be viewed as an apologia of the narrative strategy of detective fiction. It is thus not surprising that Eco should appear as the godfather of the new generation of postmodern crime writers who, following his example, were able to build upon the already established tradition of social commentary of Italian postwar crime fiction. Massimo Carlotto, Marcello Fois, and, more subtly, Camilleri, talk candidly about the social engagement of the new Italian crime fiction. Yet the ambiguity of the ideological stance of some of their works reveals the dangers of the rhetoric of *impegno*.

This is especially apparent in Lucarelli's overtly farcical series of Coliandro, which shows a high degree of social commentary implicit in the representation of the detective, who embodies to an exponential, and thus deeply ironic, level the characteristics of the average Italian.[19] Nevertheless, Mark Chu has carried out a convincing analysis of Lucarelli's novel *Febbre Gialla* (Yellow Fever) showing an underlying ambiguity in the novel's representation of social structures and ethnic minorities.[20] This ambiguity, I would like to suggest, is particularly evident in the treatment of immigration in the Coliandro series. In *Il giorno del lupo* (Day of the Wolf) for instance— the title is an open reference and tribute to Leonardo Sciascia's *Il giorno della civetta* (Day of the Owl)—references to immigrants are scarce; they are either the racist and superficial comments of Coliandro or they appear at the margins of the narrative like small details almost without importance. In the novel the fictional journalist Carlo Lucarelli informs his readers of an instance of arson in a pizzeria, and at the end of the article, which is reproduced on the page as if it were a newspaper clipping, he adds: "The Tunisian waiter, who at the time of the fire was sleeping in the kitchen, remains in a critical condition."[21] These few lines are significant as they hint at the conditions of illegal immigrants in Italy, their difficulty in finding employment and accommodation, exploitation at work, and illegal employment. This image conjures up all this, yet it is too marginal and marginalized in the narrative, ultimately pointing to a fundamental ideological ambiguity. Lucarelli, in common with other contemporary Italian crime writers, has repeatedly been recorded as claiming that his aim is a quasi-sociological analysis of contemporary Italy. Discussing in an interview the reasons for the success of the new wave of noir and crime fiction in Italy, for example, Lucarelli highlights the notion of commitment and social realism exemplified by these novelists: "we tell the truth, we invent but practice politics. Our stories resemble fiction but they are journalistic pieces, alternative investigations. Carlotto's books are novels but they tell the story of Italy's Northeast like sociology treatises. In a country full of questions without answers we find an ever increasingly passionate and numerous public."[22] This, however, makes the marginal representation of immigrants in Lucarelli's novels—and in the work of several other *giallisti* with the notable exception of Camilleri—difficult to interpret. One could argue that this is a sign of the actual marginalization of immigrants in contemporary Italian society, but this absence or marginalization is too systematic and recurrent in both Lucarelli and the many contemporary Italian crime writers. In such details lies the fundamental ambiguity surrounding the alleged sociological analysis of contemporary Italy in many of these works.

Alongside his fictional work and to accompany his broadcasting success, Lucarelli has also engaged in true crime writing, thereby continuing the Italian tradition of the link between fictional crime writing and investigative journalism inaugurated by Scerbanenco.[23] *Mistero in blu* is a collection of seven cases from the television series *Mistero in blu* and *Blu Notte*. These first television series and the book present a collection of unresolved murder cases.[24] With the exception of the case of Giuliano Guerzoni and Enrico Ughini, who were apprehended after a multimillion dollar robbery in 1996, these were all violent crimes; ordinary people were killed in their homes for no apparent reason and with no culprit ever found. Each case is presented by Lucarelli as a crime story in the style of a famous British or American detective or noir writer, and the narrative is full of the imagery of crime stories and films.[25] The cases are presented as an ideal anthology of crime and noir scenarios; the different social backgrounds of the victims and the particular style of the murders lend themselves to specific fictional styles from the British Golden Age to American thrillers and cinema. The common element that links the different narratives is the way in which Lucarelli always tries to connect the crimes to the cities where they were committed, looking for clues in the nature and culture of these places. Bologna, which is a central character of Lucarelli's narrative, is presented here, in common with his fictional crime novels, as a city of deception. It is the apparently placid small provincial town that conceals a capital of crime worthy of the urban metropolis of the best noir tradition:

> If you think about what is within the walls, Bologna is little more than a small provincial town, but if you look at it attentively, Bologna is a big thing which goes from Parma to Cattolica, part of a region splattered along the via Emilia, where people live in Modena, work in San Lazzaro and in the evening go dancing in Rimini. This is a strange metropolis of 2000 square kilometers and two million inhabitants, which grows like an oil stain between the sea and the Apennines and does not have a real center but a widespread periphery, which is called Ferrara, Imola, Ravenna, or the Romagnola Riviera. [26]

This is a city, Lucarelli tells us, in which, within the medieval walls, the past seems to have been kept intact, but that is in fact a miniature Tokyo or Los Angeles.[27] This image of Bologna as a big, sprawling metropolis is a common refrain in Lucarelli's novels.[28] The passage above, for instance, is reworked almost verbatim from his novel *Almost blue*.[29] It is also a clear echo of Scerbanenco's description of Milan in his noir trilogy[30] and is ultimately an homage to noir literary and filmic conventions and the closest disclosure of Lucarelli's masters and models.

In *Blu notte: Misteri d'Italia*, Lucarelli tackles some of the darkest pages of Italy's recent history, and by retelling these unsolved mysteries and giving space to witnesses and the family and friends of the victims, he shows how the pain for those left without closure is still raw. The series reinforces the image of the Italian political and defense officials as unable and/or unwilling to find the truth and is a clear indictment of the establishment. The episode of the death of Pasolini is the most revealing. Lucarelli here uses original footage and interviews with the writer to highlight Pasolini's aesthetics and his engagement with political and social issues. Lucarelli pays tribute here to the figure of the *intellettuale impegnato* and arguably to the most committed intellectual of all in postwar Italy. In this episode he shows his pedagogic intentions, which characterize the entire series, by providing a simple introduction and tribute to Pasolini's place in the cultural history of postwar Italy and by inviting his viewers to continue their own investigation into both the murder case and Pasolini's oeuvre by providing an essential bibliography with the end titles of the program. All Lucarelli's television series can be, and indeed have been, viewed as examples of a new *impegno* in which a writer-turned-journalist is fighting against the loss of historical memory and the general, real or alleged, apathy of the public.

Lucarelli is a talented writer who, as Guido Bonsaver has showed in his analysis of Lucarelli's historical series and *L'isola dell'angelo caduto* (The Island of the Fallen Angel) in particular, also very consciously uses his literary masters—the influence of Consolo is especially manifest.[31] Yet Lucarelli frequently publicly denies his literary credentials and puts forward his investigative-journalistic persona. He consistently talks about his novels as investigations, emphasizing the importance of his research into the technological developments of forensic science, eagerly trying to create a fiction of authenticity surrounding all his work. In addition, he continually strengthens the focus on his social and civic *impegno*. In *Mistero in blu*, explaining what compelled him to relate these unsolved stories, he talks about the sheer horror of the crimes as: "something that should not happen, that should not be forgotten but that needs to be told and continued to be recounted so long as it remains unsolved."[32] This points to the importance of memory and the moral imperative of the writer. Nevertheless, the journalist-cum-detective Lucarelli consistently refrains from getting personally involved with his investigations. While offering alternative hypotheses to the official (lack of) explanation of the crime, he does not support any, and ultimately his exercise is rather anodyne from the point of view of real crime investigation, though from a fictional point of view Lucarelli is a master of suspense and his plots work perfectly.

Massimo Carloni, a great supporter of the new *giallisti*, described Lucarelli's television series as an attempt: "at Sciascian-journalistic ascendancy, to penetrate into the mysteries that the daily chronicle offers and that the forces of order are unable to disclose."[33] The reference to Sciascia is significant, because what is lacking in Lucarelli is precisely what constituted the core of Sciascia's detective novels, such as *Il contesto* and *Todo Modo*, which turned the formula of detective fiction into an acute critique of contemporary Italy while also questioning "the nature of things beyond specific issues of historical justice and injustice, trying to get at some absolute truth underlying man's obsessive desire for power."[34] Carloni believes in the mimesis of contemporary Italian society displayed by contemporary Italian crime writers, who "in many cases have mirrored better than many 'serious' novels the tormented national situation of the past fifteen years."[35] Carlotto, another chief exponent of the new Italian noir writers, explains in an interview the similarities that can be found among many contemporary Italian crime writers in terms of the peculiar culture of the generation that grew up in the 1970s: "Our generation of writers comes from the 1970s; we all seek to do what at the time used to be called counter-information. Our novels resemble the old fashioned investigations, which newspapers do not do anymore, fearing litigation and because of the obstacles created by the transformation of the world of the media."[36] Because of its realism and the writers' overt declarations of *impegno civile*, contemporary noir fiction is of great interest in the study of the emergence, circulation, and cultural representations of those subjectivities that were previously marginalized and suppressed by highbrow literature. Yet, as I have suggested above, at least in the case of immigration, arguably the biggest issue facing Italy in the 1990s and in the twenty-first century, this representation is often problematic and frequently also ideologically ambiguous.

The critical ethos of Italian noir and detective writers in the 1990s, which in its complexity is outside the remit of the present study, is a literary and cultural phenomenon worthy of note and deserving further scrutiny. The critical reception of these writers and their popularity casts an interesting light on the need for a realistic portrayal of contemporary Italy and the recent history of the country, as well as on the appetite of Italian readers for stories that very closely reflect current social and political affairs. However, I would ultimately question whether *impegno* characterizes the way in which Lucarelli and many of his fellow crime writers portray contemporary Italy with its social and political problems. Contemporary postmodern writers make common use of the rhetoric of *impegno*, which is, however, frequently open to ambiguities and leaves one wondering whether they display a real social conscience or, as Burns has pointed out, their commitment is a "cynical cashing-in on the *Zeitgeist*."[37] The answer is partly to be found in the role played by the media, since media attention has increased these writers' sales and, consequently, influenced their relationship, creating a mutual courtship. The media have also been keen to present these writers as historians of the past and investigators of the present, blurring the boundaries between their fictional crimes and the real mysteries of contemporary Italy. Many writers, however, have supported and actively promoted their image as new paladins of *impegno*. What they have done, and Lucarelli is a very significant example, is to reinforce and/or create new personas for themselves—the crime writer as serious historian, and the crime writer as investigative journalist—rather than leaving these roles to their fictional heroes. The game, however, is often too literal and risks diluting the power of this type of fiction that has realism and the portrayal of social issues at its core.

Notes

1. Massimo Vincenzi, "Da Camilleri a Lucarelli l'Italia si colora di giallo," in *La Repubblica*, August 3, 2001, http://www/repubblica.it/online/cultura_scienze/noir/portante/portante.html (accessed September 14, 2006).
2. They comprise among others Carlo Lucarelli, Marcello Fois, Andrea G. Pinketts, Pino Cacucci, and Massimo Carloni. See *I Delitti del gruppo 13: Antologia illustrata dei giallisti bolognesi*, ed. Massimo Moscati (Bologna: Metrolibri/Granata Press, 1991).
3. Luigi Bernardi, "Un questurino nella città che non è come le altre città," in *Fiori alla memoria*, ed. Loriano Macchiavelli, 167–78 (Turin: Einaudi, 2001), 177.
4. For an analysis and bibliography on postmodern *impegno* see Jennifer Burns, *Fragments of Impegno. Interpretations of Commitment in Contemporary Italian Narrative, 1980–2000* (Northern Universities Press, 2001).
5. In an interview in *Il resto del Carlino* (October 11, 2001) on the occasion of the republication of the novels of Scerbanenco, Rambelli stated, "From that moment, the *giallo*, in Italy, can be considered a novel about society."

6. Marco Sangiorgi, "Introduction," in *Il giallo italiano come nuovo romanzo sociale*, ed. Marco Sangiorgi and Luca Telò, 15–23 (Ravenna: Longo, 2004).

7. Stephen Knight, *Form and Ideology in Crime Fiction* (London: Macmillan, 1980).

8. See *The New Italian Republic: From the fall of the Berlin Wall to Berlusconi*, ed. Stephen Gundle and Simon Parker (London: Routledge, 1996); and Paul Ginsborg, *Italy and its Discontents: Family, Civil Society, State 1980–2001* (London: Allen Lane, 2001).

9. On French noir fiction see the excellent study by Claire Gorrara, *The Roman Noir in Post-War French Culture. Dark Fictions* (Oxford: Oxford University Press, 2003).

10. For a bibliography of Lucarelli up to 1996 see *Dizionario bibliografico del giallo*, ed. Roberto Pirani, Monica Mare, and Maria Grazia De Antoni, 3 vols. (Pontassieve: Pirani bibliografica, 1994–98), II, ad indicem. For a detailed but not exhaustive bibliography, see also Lucarelli's official Web site: http://www.carlolucarelli.net.

11. Ibid.

12. Ibid.

13. *Falange Armata* (Milan: Hobby and Work, 1993); *Nikita* (Bologna: Granata Press, 1994); *Il giorno del lupo* (Bologna: Granata Press, 1994; repr. Turin: Einaudi, 1998).

14. http://www.carlolucarelli.net and http://www.misteriditalia.com.

15. Carlo Lucarelli, "Il giallo storico ambientato durante il fascismo," in Sangiorgi and Telò, *Il giallo italiano*, 153.

16. See Claire Gorrara, "Tracking down the Past: the Detective as Historian in texts by Patrick Modiano and Didier Daeninckx," in *Crime Scenes. Detective Narratives in European Culture since 1945*, ed. Anne Mullen and Emer O'Beirne, 281–90 (Amsterdam: Rodopi, 2000).

17. Linda Hutcheon, *A Poetics of Postmodernism* (London: Routledge, 1988).

18. Cinzia Fiori, "Lucarelli: alla ricerca dello spirito irrazionale del noir," *Corriere della Sera*, June 25, 2000.

19. I am grateful to Lucia Rinaldi for this reading of Coliandro in her PhD thesis on *Postmodernity, Identity and Representation in Contemporary Italian Crime Fiction* (Royal Holloway, University of London, 2007).

20. Mark Chu, "Giallo sarai tu! Hegemonic Representations and Limits of Heteroglossia in Carlo Lucarelli," *Spunti e Ricerche* 16 (2001): 45–58 (45).

21. Lucarelli, *Il giorno del lupo*, 31.

22. Vincenzi, "Da Camilleri a Lucarelli l'"Italia si colora di giallo."

23. Lucarelli's television series were all accompanied by books: *Blu notte* (Turin: Einaudi, 1999), *Misteri d'Italia. I casi di Blu notte* (Turin: Einaudi, 2002), *Nuovi misteri d'Italia. I casi di Blu notte* (Turin: Einaudi, 2004), and the special episode of *Blu notte* on Mafia crime that began 1992, *La mattanza. Dal silenzio sulla Mafia al silenzio della Mafia* (Turin: Einaudi, 2004). Other books of true crime writing by Lucarelli comprise Carlo Lucarelli and Michele Giuttari, *Compagni di sangue* (Milan: Rizzoli, 1999) on the *Mostro di Firenze*; Carlo Lucarelli and

Massimo Picozzi, *Tracce criminali. Storie di omicidi imperfetti* (Milan: Mondadori, 2006); and by the same authors *Scena del crimine: Storie di delitti efferati e di investigazioni scientifiche* (Milan: Mondadori, 2005).

24. They comprise the case of Francesca Alinovi, a young art critic and lecturer at DAMS in Bologna, who was killed in her flat in June 1983; Antonella Falcidia, killed in Catania in December 1994; Massimiliano Iorio, killed in Rimini, in March 1997; Alessandra Vanni, killed in Castellina near Siena in August 1997; Count Alvise di Robilant killed in Florence in January 1996; Domenico, Gemma and Angela Santangelo, killed in their flat in Naples in October 1975.

25. Some cases, Lucarelli claims, may have been written by Agatha Christie, Patricia Highsmith, Cornell Woolrich, J. D. Carr, James Elroy, E. A. Poe, or Stephen King; others develop like a film by Hitchcok, Kubrick and Tarantino.

26. Lucarelli, *Mistero in blu*, 24–25.

27. "A small Tokyo made of glass towers, lights, and concrete," *Mistero in Blu*, 25. "It looks like a sleepy provincial town lost in a medieval dream but it is a small Los Angeles lit up and as big as an entire region." *Mistero in Blu*, 27.

28. See, for example in *Lupo Mannaro*, when the narrator talks about Emilia Romagna: "One can see this region like a single big city which goes from Reggio to Cattolica . . . a kind of Los Angeles with a few million inhabitants and an extensive surface and the via Emilia on the road" (37–38).

29. See Carlo Lucarelli, *Almost blue* (Turin: Einaudi, 1997), 100.

30. "There are still people who don't realize that Milan is a great cosmopolitan city. They have failed to notice that the scale of things has altered. They talk about Milan as though it ended at the Porta Venezia. . . . Mention Marseilles, Chicago or Paris, and everyone knows you're talking of a wicked metropolis, but with Milan, it's different. Surrounded as they are by the unmistakable atmosphere of a great city, there are still idiots who think of it in terms of local color. . . . They forget that a city of two million inhabitants is bound to acquire an international flavor," Giorgio Scerbanenco, *Duca and the Milan Murders*, trans. E. Ellenbogen (New York: Walker, 1966), 108–9.

31. Guido Bonsaver, "Storia, libri e carnazza. Il romanzo di Lucarelli tra fondali storici, intertestualità e ricette narrative," in *Nuova Prosa* 38 (2003): 45–56.

32. Lucarelli, *Mistero in blu*, 72.

33. Massimo Carloni, "L'arcobaleno narrativo di Carlo Lucarelli," *Delitti di Carta* 8 (2001): 83–84.

34. Mullen, "Leonardo Sciascia's Detective Fiction and Metaphors of Mafia," in *Crime Scenes*, 92.

35. Massimo Carloni, "Storia e geografia di un genere letterario: il romanzo poliziesco italiano contemporaneo (1966–84)," *Critica Letteraria* 46 (1985): 171.

36. Massimo Vincenzi, "Carlotto: 'Cerchiamo la verità e la gente si appassiona,'" in *La Repubblica*, November 3, 2001.

37. Burns, *Fragments of Impegno*, 184.

Part VI

The Legacy of Anarchism

16

The Anarchist Assassin and Italian History, 1870s to 1930s[1]

Carl Levy

This chapter will present an overview of the effects of anarchist assassinations and assassination attempts on the political, social and cultural history of Italy from the 1870s to the 1930s. Assassinations carried out by anarchists had a significant effect on the politics and the political culture of modern Italy, especially during the 1890s and the middle 1920s. I will examine how the intended and the unintended effects of these acts shaped the liberal and fascist states. This will be followed by a discussion of the effects of these acts on Italian culture and particularly on the culture of the left. This will include an examination of the social and cultural contexts of the assassins or would-be assassins themselves. Finally, the conclusion examines the mysteries, the serendipity, and the maze of competing narratives surrounding their acts.

Anarchist Assassinations: A Historical Overview

Two eras of *attentati* (assassination attempts) mark the history of the history of European and Italian anarchism in the late nineteenth century—the late 1870s/early 1880s and the 1890s. They also are markers in the evolution of the Italian liberal state and shadow the life and death of the king, Umberto, who presided over Italy. The first attempts in the late 1870s and early 1880s can be placed within the context of a series of assassinations and attempted assassinations throughout Europe.[2] In Italy on February 9, 1878, a bomb was thrown in Florence at a procession honoring the late King Vittorio Emanuele. On November 17, 1878, during a tour of Naples,

King Umberto was attacked by a young man armed with a hidden knife that bore the inscription "Death to the King, Long Live the Universal Republic, Long Live Orsini." The day after, in Florence, a bomb was thrown into the crowd, killing four bystanders, and on November 20 in Pisa a similar event was the scene of another terrorist bombing, this one with no fatalities.[3]

The 1890s have been characterized as the era of anarchist assassinations, and the Italians took a particularly prominent role in English, French, and Spanish anarchist circles.[4] There were some failed attempts: in June 1894 an anarchist carpenter, Paolo Lega, took a shot at Prime Minister Crispi. In April 1897 an unemployed blacksmith, Pietro Acciarito, with marginal ties to the anarchist movement at best, lunged at the king's carriage with an awl with little effect. But other attempts were deadly. Sante Caserio stabbed to death Sadi Carnot, President of France on June 24, 1894. On July 1, the Livornese journalist Giuseppe Bandi was stabbed to death by an anarchist because of Bandi's polemic in the local press about Sante Caserio's deed. (Earlier, in February 1889, in a sectarian feud, two anti-organizationalist anarchists, Luigi Parmeggiani and Vittorio Pini, stabbed, though not fatally, an ex-Garibalidino and Internationalist, Celso Ceretti, in Mirandola; they were on their way to attack the socialist reformist Camillo Prampolini when they were intercepted by the police.[5]) Michele Angiolillo shot Cánovas, Prime Minister of Spain, on August 8, 1897. Luigi Lucheni, in what was perhaps the most senseless assassination, stabbed to death the innocuous Elizabeth of Austria on September 10, 1898. King Umberto I was finally assassinated by an anarchist, Gaetano Bresci, on July 29, 1900.[6] The number of heads of state and government and monarchs was unprecedented, but as Richard Bach Jensen observes, outside of Spain anarchist terrorism "killed relatively few people" before 1914.[7] The violence was spectacular, occurring in the heart of great urban centers (Paris, Rome, Zurich, London, Barcelona), and magnified by the emergence of mass journalism hungry for lurid headlines.[8]

The next significant spate of anarchist attempts or attempts claimed to be anarchist inspired occurred between 1924 and 1926. Earlier, an Italian anarchist plot to kill Mussolini when he visited London in December 1922 was thwarted by Scotland Yard and MI5. Anarchists exiled in Paris and so-called Garibaldians and members of *Italia Libera* plotted or were entrapped by *agents provocateurs* in a plan to assassinate Benito Mussolini.[9] In a well-planned attempt by the anarchist exile network, however, Gino Lucetti threw a bomb at Mussolini's automobile in Rome on September 11, 1926; it would have certainly killed him if it had struck its target, but it exploded harmlessly nearby.[10] On October 31, 1926, a crowd in Bologna lynched Anteo Zamboni (the adolescent son of an ex-anarchist) after he, too, apparently tried to kill Mussolini.[11] Michele Schirru in 1931 and Angelo Sbardellotto in 1932 were executed by firing squad after they were accused of planning to make attempts on the life of the *Duce*.[12] In 1933 Vincenzo Capuana arrived back in Italy from Pittsburgh, Pennsylvania, to kill Mussolini but was tracked down by the police after he was betrayed by an imprisoned anarchist.[13] From London Emidio Recchioni helped sponsor a series of plots that never got off the ground.[14] Camillo Berneri, the anarchist intellectual, was involved in a series of plots to kill the *Duce* between 1927 and 1932 as he was trailed and deported from one European country to another; one of these plots may have included collaboration with Carlo Rosselli's *Giustizia e Libertà*.[15] Attempts by Leonida Leoni and Pio Turroni in 1938–39 were unsuccessful.[16]

Anarchist Assassinations as Turning Points in Liberal Italy

The anarchist or anarchist-related attempts in the late 1870s effectively caused the outlawing of the First International in Italy. Indeed the attempt by the left under Zanardelli and Cairoli to pass more liberal legislation on the right of association was stopped by the more restrictive approach of pre-empting "political crimes." Emergency legislation was approved in June 1894 that lasted until December 31, 1895. This banned all the "subversive" newspapers and parties. Three thousand anarchists were sent to penal islands, and hundreds of others fled abroad. But the socialists were also hard hit. The next turning point was the assassination of Umberto by Bresci. If the 1890s was the era of authoritarian mobilization, the era of Giolittian liberalization, so it is argued by historians and contemporaries alike, was ushered in by the gunshots at the Monza Race Track.[17] The laws against the *malfattori* promulgated over twenty years previously were mitigated by a new approach by another generation of liberals. The anarchist firebrand Galleani argued that new exceptional laws could never be passed because of the "emboldened crowd." But aside from this sectarian grandstanding, his assessment did mirror the standard interpretation of reconciliation and a new openness following the repression of the 1890s and its dramatic finale at Monza.

The final turning point, in 1926, returns us to a repressive conclusion. In the wake of the supposed attempt by Zamboni on his life on October 28, 1926, Mussolini issued exceptional degrees (the "Rocco Laws") which killed off for good liberal Italy. All "anti-national" parties and newspapers were suppressed. Passports were canceled, and severe penalties were put in place for clandestine expatriation. The Special Tribunal for the Defense of the State was established. The death penalty was announced for those guilty of seeking the assassination of the king or the head of government.

Anarchist Assassins as "Social Types"

Who were the men who carried out the *attentati*? Giovanni Passanante was a twenty-nine-year-old-shepherd, servant, and cook from the village of Salvia near Potenza.[18] Paolo Lega was a Romagnole carpenter from Lugo.[19] Sante Caserio was a semi-literate, twenty-one-year-old baker from a poverty-stricken family who lived in the village of Motta Visconti near Milan.[20] Pietro Acciarito was a twenty-four-year-old destitute blacksmith from the village of Artena near Rome.[21] Michele Angiolillo was a twenty-six-year-old printer from Foggia who had a technical school education.[22] Luigi Luccheni was born in Paris of Italian migrant parents.[23] He lived in an orphanage as a child and had been a soldier in Abyssinia, a free spirit who traveled around the capitals of *Mitteleuropa* and at the time of his crime a hand-to-mouth laborer. Gaetano Bresci was thirty-one, born on the same day as his victim's successor.[24] He hailed from a lower-middle-class family from Prato down on their luck. His family had owned a farm, and his brother was an officer in the army. He was an industrious and highly-skilled silk weaver.[25] Gino Lucetti was twenty-six, from Avenza, and had been orginally a marble worker in the Carrarese and then a stone mason in France and Belgium.[26] He had been an *ardito* (commando) during the war and had connections with the *Arditi del Popolo* (an anti-Fascist militia) in the early 1920s. He had wanted to kill Mussolini since reading about the *strage di Torino* (the massacre of Turin) of December 1922, in which a number of anarchists and communists were brutally murdered by local Fascists. Anteo Zamboni was a fifteen-year-old youth from Bologna with some education but who worked in the family printers at the time of his lynching.[27] Michele Schirru was a thirty-two-year-old Sardinian from Padria.[28] His father had been a customs official, and he had some education, but the family could not afford to send him to secondary school in Cagliari or Sassari. After serving in the Italian army as an *ardito* (commando) during the First World War and witnessing the antiwar uprising in Turin in 1917, he emigrated to the United States and lived in the New York borough of the Bronx for several years, earning a living as a wholesaler of bananas. Angelo Sbardellotto was a twenty-five-year-old miner and mechanic from Mel in Belluno who had migrated to France and Belgium.[29] Thus in many senses the assassins or would-be assassins were a cross-section of liberal Italy's working and artisan classes.

Passanante, Sante Caserio, and Lucheni used daggers, Acciarito an awl. Lega, Angiolillo, Bresci, and Zamboni (apparently) employed revolvers. Lucetti threw a SIPE bomb (a hand grenade). Schirru and Sbardellotto never had a chance to employ weapons because they were arrested with the *intention* of killing the *Duce*. Appropriating Lombrosian-like terms (Cesare Lombroso identified: the political assassin—Bresci; criminally insane assassins—Passanante and Acciarito; and the passionate killer— Sante Caserio) these anarchists can be placed in three categories.[30] The spontaneous anarchists and "patsies" were Passanante, Lega, Acciarito, Lucheni, and Zamboni. The real role of Zamboni in the attempt in 1926 is not at all clear, and we will return to him shortly. The other four were the voices of "misery, a desperate misery" and not formally associated with any anarchist group.[31]

Sante Caserio, Angiolillo, and Bresci were loners. They were associated with the anarchist movement as acolytes, such as Sante Caserio, who visited the Milan offices of the anarchist journalist, lawyer, sociologist, and poet Pietro Gori.[32] Bresci was active in anarchist meetings and was part of the anarchist movement in Paterson, New Jersey. Indeed he saved Errico Malatesta, by successfully tackling an enraged individualist anarchist who took exception to a speech Malatesta was giving. During the week Bresci lived as a boarder in Bertoldi's Hotel in Paterson and then returned to his family in nearby West Hoboken on the weekends. He was not part of a plot, and there is only "unsafe" evidence (more on this later) to suggest that he was being sent by the Paterson anarchists to kill "King Machine Gun," as they called Umberto after the massacre of demonstrators in Milan in 1898. He bought his seven-dollar revolver in a hardware store in Paterson and did target practice on his days off.[33]

Only three anarchists can be associated with proven plots that were either in the final stages of execution or carried out: Lucetti, Schirru, and Sbardellotto. And of these three, the only clear-cut case is that of Lucetti.[34] The case of Gaetano Bresci is far more difficult to discern, and this leads us to a discussion of the elusive quality of forensic evidence, personal testimony, newspaper reports, and "social facts."

All That Is Solid Melts into Air

The role of the anarchist assassin in the history of liberal and fascist Italy has been incorporated into historical narratives chiefly in two ways. I have already discussed the convenient deployment of anarchist assassinations and attempted assassinations by commentators to mark major political turning points in the history of Italy from the 1870s to the 1920s. The other approach is to assimilate these acts into the social history of the anarchists, the left, and *sovversivismo*.[35] I have hinted at this when detailing the social backgrounds of the assassins. The assassin played a key role in shaping the culture of the anarchists and gave this culture a historical pedigree found in the self-sacrifice of the heroes of the *Risorgimento*. Thus the assassination attempts on leading state figures were played out within a well-known cyclical script of revenge and/or tyrannicide. Sbardellotto was inspired to assassinate Mussolini at least in part to avenge the execution of Schirru.[36] But the anarchists' enemies could employ similar rhetoric. Thus the priest Guiseppe Volponi was sentenced to eight months' imprisonment and a thousand lire fine after he was reported to have commented from the pulpit of Rome's San Sebastiano church, "The atheist Bresci was an instrument of divine vengeance against a dynasty that has deprived the Popes of their temporal power."[37]

The assassination attempts on Mussolini between 1924 and 1926 permitted him to don the mantle of the man of providence. But the police also reported that after Lucetti's near miss, one Luigi Melandri was arrested in a Roman bar after saying that "If he had killed him, I would have paid for everybody's drinks."[38] Regional pride could also be detected in other comments collected after the execution of the Sardinian Schirru, when a citizen of a small town in Sardinia was arrested shouting "*Viva Michele Schirru!*" or merely "*Viva La Sardegna!*"[39]

The aftershocks of assassination attempts might also rub the Italian public the wrong way. Thus, after the blacksmith Acciarito was sent to solitary confinement, the queen demanded that the government discover the "plot" behind Acciarito's lone act. Thus the "usual anarchist suspects" were duly rounded by the police in Rome and one, Romano Frezzi, was beaten to death in his cell; the police, setting a precedent for the "accidental death of the anarchist Pinelli" more than a half century later (see the chapter by Foot), claimed it was suicide.[40] Furthermore, an informer was put in Acciarito's cell and threatened to implicate Acciarito's family if he did not name names. But these clumsy moves by the government merely mobilized large demonstrations and sacrificed the sympathy the king had won and led to a decade of controversial, if inconclusive, trials (again strangely foreshadowing the Pinelli affair).[41] Even under the fascist regime Mussolini could overplay his hand.

Although Sbardelloto's family was hounded by the local fascist hierarchy of Mel, and Beluno Mussolini took a personal and strangely benevolent interest, leading interventionists and fascists "of the first hour" (Arpinati, Rocca, and Gioda) had been individualist anarchists who had praised "propaganda by the deed." And Mussolini himself had written in praise of

Orsini, Angiolillo, and Bresci before the war in the socialist *Lotta di Classe* on the anniversary of Umberto's assassination.[42]

The anarchist assassination and assassin thus had become part of the subversive second culture of the Italian left of liberal Italy. Competition over who would seize the cultural memory in the diaspora also spurred on the New York and New Jersey anarchists. Thus after Umberto's assassination the monarchist newspaper of New York, *L'Araldo Italiano* raised a thousand dollars for a stone wreath to be placed on Umberto's tomb, but the anarchists of Paterson raised the same amount of money more quickly to support Bresci's wife and family. In their *Nickel-protesta* postcards the image of Bresci was superimposed over the Statue of Liberty.[43]

The trial, execution, and memorialization of the anarchist assassin became an integral part of the anarchist subversive culture. Sante Caserio was cast in the role of secular saint. The anarchist intellectual Pietro Gori and the Italian socialist Filippo Turati pictured him as a semi-literate "convert" whose miserable life was given order by his new faith. Thus, for Turati, Sante Caserio (the boy Catholic) was no longer religious but still devoted. He refused to drink alcohol or have sexual relations: "I have married an idea not a woman," Pietro Gori claims he said in his Milan law offices.[44] The courtyard execution scene was always an important trope in this melodrama, as in the cases of Sbardellotto and Schirru, which moved Mussolini. And thus when Angiolillio was garrotted by the Spanish state for his assassination of Cánovas, he shouted "Germinal," the seventh month of the French Revolution's calendar and the title of the novel by Zola dear to the hearts of anarchists and socialists.[45] At his last meal, the casual diner who shared his table in Monza remembered Bresci calling himself Caserio. Bresci, unlike the lost souls Passanante, Lega, and Acciarito, was something of a dandy: he dressed for the occasion, including his silk suit and cravat. When he shot Umberto, he cried out that he had not killed the man but "I have killed a sovereign. I have killed a prince."[46] Sbardellotto picked a symbolic moment to carry out his attempt. Apparently he had decided to strike on October 28, 1931, the ninth anniversary of the March on Rome and then moved the date to June 2, 1932, when the ashes of Anita Garibaldi were brought to Rome to be laid to rest.[47]

But the burials of the anarchists were equally significant for their followers and adversaries. Some of the assassins or would-be assassins were buried in obscure plots after going mad in prison (Passanante and Acciarito). But others were memorialized. In some cases the battle over a contested memory was crystallized around burial and remembrance. The plaque in Bologna that remembered Anteo Zamboni was controversial.

Was Zamboni one of the first heroes of the Resistance or an innocent "patsy" of internal fascist skulduggery? His father, an anarchist turned Fascist, sponsored the first interpretation, not least to distance himself from Arpinati, his former patron and fascist *Ras*, who was assassinated at the end of the war under rather mysterious circumstances.[48] With the controversy continuing in the aftermath of the war, his father complained that his son had been murdered twice: once physically by the fascists and then spiritually by certain elements of the Resistance who lacked due respect for his son's sacrifice.[49]

There has always been a school of thought that classified some of these acts as indirect suicides, and evidence is at hand. Luigi Lucheni was given life imprisonment by the Confederation of Switzerland but asked in a letter addressed the authorities to be executed and was found hanged in his cell in 1910.[50] Passanante proclaimed, to the authorities, "I was tired of living so I tried to kill a sovereign."[51] He, Lega, and Bresci were found dead in their cells, although in all these cases the authorities may have "assisted" their suicides.[52]

The role of the police and *agents provocateurs* cannot be discounted. Thus fascist police spies entrapped anarchists, republicans, and members of *Giustizia e Libertà* in Italy, France and Belgium. Both Ricciotti Garibaldi and the police spy Menapace ensnared them in a series of plots, plots to blow up the royal family in Milan in April 1928, to kill Alfredo Rocco in Brussels, to bomb the train of the Spaniard Princess Maria José carrying her to her fiancé Umberto of Savoy, and to assassinate Dino Grandi at the Geneva headquarters of the League of Nations.[53] It seems clear that, for example, in other assassination attempts, Mussolini did set up his own assassination. Thus the PSU, the reformist socialist party of the martyred Matteotti, was outlawed after Tito Zaniboni's 1925 attempt to assassinate the *Duce* on the anniversary of the victory of 1918 had been blown and the plotter arrested.

Plot and counter-plot inhabit territory also claimed for serendipity and bad timing, especially for those unfortunates found in the company of the assassin in the period leading up to an attempt. In the case of Bresci, the Italian state enlisted the dead and the living to prove that Bresci had been sent by the anarchists of Paterson to assassinate Umberto, even though an investigation by the Supreme Court of New Jersey discovered no plot.[54]

Conclusion: Four Mysteries

Angiolillo, the lone murderer of the Prime Minister of Spain, was long thought to be part of a plot. Were Cuban nationalists, engaged in a vicious and bloody war of independence against the Spanish, involved in financing his venture? It was claimed in various accounts that he was given a thousand (or five hundred) francs by the Cuban nationalist junta in Paris. But there is no evidence of a connection between Angiolillo's plot and the junta and even the other anarchists.

Was Bresci murdered in prison? And to what extent was he part of a plot involving a group of anarchists mainly from Paterson, silk weavers, hailing for the most part from Prato, Vercelli, and Biella? After his sentencing, Bresci followed the same route as Passanante: he was placed in the same prison, Portolongue and kept in isolation, first in the "Passanante Tower" and then in a special cell in the island prison of Santo Stefano. In 1901 he became an obsession for Giolitti, who believed that Maria Sofia had been in cahoots with the anarchists of Paterson, New Jersey.[55] And Giolitti's spies claimed that the exiled Queen of Naples, Maria Sofia, was busy plotting with the anarchists and particularly the Neapolitan anarchist Errico Malatesta, to "spring" Bresci on May 18, 1901. This was part of a wider plan, in which the Bourbon Queen would neutralize "reactionaries" in the South in a common goal to rid Italy of the House of Savoy.[56] Now it is certainly true that *La Grande Vecchia, la reine aux anarchistes*, as Marcel Proust called her, did invite anarchists to her "court" at Neuilly, even though her own sister Elizabeth, Queen of Austria, had been murdered by Lucheni![57] Malatesta certainly dined with her on March 23, 1901, and unpublished letters do show that he received some money from her.[58] But how they were going to spring Bresci from his island prison was never explained: in any case Bresci was found dead, hanging from a cell window by a towel, even though he was under constant surveillance. There was a four-day gap between the death and the actual autopsy, and it had been argued that the man in charge of the Acciarito affair and soon after appointed as the superintendent of Italian prisons, had carried out a "wet job" on Bresci.[59] Case unsolved.

The Zamboni case raises the question of how a teenaged boy of rather low intelligence, a boy his family called "potato" and "chubby", became an assassin. The murder weapon was never found, and some of the evidence seems highly suspect. For example, a notebook found in his bedroom, filled with phrases and mottoes from the ancients and moderns on the subject of carrying out justice against tyrants, doesn't seem to match his handwriting or his educational or intellectual capacities.[60] The family was a suitable candidate for a setup. The father had been an anarchist, but like the *Ras* of Bologna, Arpinati, he had converted from anarchist individualism to Fascism. Indeed, the boy's name had been changed from it original Ateo to Anteo after his father's conversion. The family was largely dysfunctional and perfect to be condemned in a court of law.[61]

So what are the alternative interpretations?[62] One is that Zamboni did do it. Another is that the family, as the state originally claimed, did it. That is, Zamboni and his family had not left their anarchism in fact. Another is that Zamboni was an innocent bystander. Several eyewitnesses identified a man in a gabardine suit as the shooter: it was claimed that he covered his tracks by drawing the lynch mob on the boy. Another is that Arpinati and the Zambonis did it. Arpinati was being transformed from an accomplished torturer to a "liberal" fascist or authoritarian conservative and feared Mussolini's quest for a personal dictatorship.[63] Finally, and most likely, other dissident fascists from Milan and the Veneto did it. Farinacci and Grandi were behind the plot to discredit Arpinati and also to send a warning to Mussolini himself: the Second Wave of fascism would not be halted. Arpinati was driving Mussolini's car slowly through the throng, so this would naturally put him in an awkward position if anything did happen.[64] Certainly, Mussolini used these events to discredit Arpinati when he mounted a dissident campaign in the 1930s![65]

The strange case of Michele Schirru is melodramatic and was used for Lina Wertmüller's film, *Amore e anarchia*, which is dealt with by Dana Renga in the next chapter.[66] He certainly received funds from the anarchists of New York and Recchioni in London, and probably also Emilio Lussu. But he seemed to be closely shadowed by operatives of Arturo Bocchini (Mussolini's chief secret policeman) on both his journeys to Italy in April–June 1930 and January–February 1931. Indeed fifty thousand photos of him were distributed around Italy. But he failed to carry out his deed and frittered his money away on an affair with a Hungarian ballerina in Rome. Rounded up from a bordello to have a compulsory examination for venereal disease, he discharged a pistol in the police station and the plot was revealed. But had the plot collapsed, and was Schirru's execution a form of suicide in which Mussolini, for his own reasons, was complicit?[67]

At the trial of Gaetano Bresci, his defense lawyer, Francesco Saverio Merlino, explained why Italy and the Italians had become identified with the political assassination. This former anarchist and author of one of the first insightful analyses of Liberal Italy, argued that Italy had a weak political culture that had fostered the hero worship of kings. But the criminalization of the anarchists in the 1880s and the left in the 1890s had called up its murderous opposite. A free civil society and the decriminalization of ideologies would weaken the hold of the assassin on the minds of the Italians.[68] Thus Merlino follows the route of the social and political historian employed in the first part of this chapter, where I examined the turning points in the history of Liberal Italy. And yet serendipity, the mysteries of the Italian state and the mysteries of human motivation make these stories ever more complicated and fascinating.

Notes

1. I would like to thank Professor Benedict Anderson for his useful comments, kind suggestions and merciless proofreading of an earlier version of this chapter.

2. For an in-depth overview of the entire period see, R. B. Jensen, "Daggers, Rifles and Dynamite: Anarchist Terrorism in Nineteenth Century Europe," *Terrorism and Political Violence* 16, no. 1 (2004): 116–53.

3. Nunzio Pernicone, *Italian Anarchism 1864–1892*, (Princeton, NJ: Princeton University Press, 1993), 147–54.

4. Pier Carlo Masini, *Storia degli anarchici italiani nell'epoca degli attentati* (Milan: Rizzoli, 1981), 23–54, 107–20, 145–61; Carl Levy, "Malatesta in London: The Era of Dynamite," in "A Century of Italian Emigration to Britain 1880–1980s five essays," ed. Lucio Sponza and Arturo Tosi, *The Italianist, Supplement* 13 (1993): 25–42.

5. Pernicone, *Italian Anarchism*, 240–41.

6. "Carnot's murder was the first assassination of a French head of state since 1610 and Humbert's the first of a member of the house of Savoy in 700 years" (Jensen, "Daggers, Rifles and Dynamite," 134).

7. Jensen, "Daggers, Rifles and Dynamite," 116.

8. Ibid., 116, 125, 134, 140–42.

9. Alfio Bernabei, *Esuli ed emigrati italiani nel Regno Unito, 1920–1940* (Milan: Mursia, 1997); Alfio Bernabei, "The London plot to kill Mussolini," *History Today* 49, no. 4 (1999): 2–3; Lucio Sponza, *Divided Loyalties. Italians in Britain during the Second World War* (Bern: Peter Lang, 2000), 33–34; Luigi Di Lembo, *Guerra di classe e lotta umana. L'anarchismo in Italia dal biennio rosso alla guerra di Spagna (1919–1939)* (Pisa: Biblioteca Franco Serantini, 2001), 175–78.

10. Riccardo Lucetti, *Gino Lucetti: L'Attentato contro il Duce 11 settembre 1926* (Carrara: La Coop. Tipolitografica, 2000).

11. Brunella Dalla Casa, *Attentato al Duce, le molte storie del caso Zamboni* (Bologna: Il Mulino, 2000).

12. Di Lembo, *Guerra di classe e lotta umana*, 181; Charles F. Delzell, *Mussolini's Enemies* (Princeton, NJ: Princeton University Press, 1961), 33–39, 106–8; Michele Corsentino, *Michele Schirru e l'attentato anarchico* (Catania: Anarchismo, 1990); Giuseppe Fiori, *Vita e morte di Michele Schirru, l'anarchico che pensò di uccidere Mussolini* (Bari: Laterza, 1990); Giuseppe Galzerano, "Attentati anarchici a Mussolini," in *Atti del congresso su l'antifascismo rivoluzionario tra passato e presente*, by Luigi Di Lembo et al. (Pisa: Biblioteca Franco Serantini, 1992), 77–98; F. Berti, "Per amore della libertà," *A rivista anarchica* 38, no. 268 (2000–2001): 1–14; Giuseppe Galzerano, *Angelo Sbardellotto. Vita,*

processo e morte dell'emigrante anarchico fucilato per l'"intenzione" di uccidere Mussolini (Casalvelino Scalo: Galzerano Editore, 2003).

13. Di Lembo, *Guerra di classe e lotta umana*, 185–86.

14. References in footnote 10 and the detailed account of Recchioni's activities, in Giuseppe Galzerano, *Angelo Sbardellotto*, 376–423; Pietro Dipaola, "Emidio Recchioni," in *Dizionario biografico degli anarchici italiani*, vol. 2, ed. Maurizio Antonioli et al. (Pisa: Biblioteca Franco Sernatini, 2005).

15. U. Marzocchi, "Carlo Rosselli e gli anarchici," in *Giustizia e Libertà nella lotta e nella storia d'Italia*, by Carlo Francovich et al. (Florence: La Nuova Italia, 1978); Francisco Madrid Santos, *Camillo Berneri. Un anarchico italiano (1897–1937): Rivoluzione e controrivoluzione in Europa (1917–1939)* (Pistoia: Archvio Famiglia Berneri, 1985), 200–220; Santi Fedele, *Il retaggio dell'esilio: Saggi sul fuoriuscitismo antifascista*, (Soveria Mannelli: Rubbettino, 2000); Di Lembo, *Guerra di classe e lotta umana*, 182–87.

16. Di Lembo, *Guerra di classe e lotta umana*, 181.

17. See for example, Martin Clark, *Modern Italy 1871–1995*, 2nd ed. (London: Longman, 1996), 136; Fulvio Cammarano, *Storia politica dell'Italia liberale 1861–1901* (Bari-Rome: Laterza, 1999), 507–8; M. Degli Esposti, "Il regicidio, l'opinione pubblica e gli esiti della crisi di fine secolo," in *Cheiron* 38, nos. 35–36, 292–93. For the general context see, Umberto Levra, *Il colpo di stato della borghesia: La crisi politica di fine secolo in Italia 1896–1900* (Milan: Feltrinelli, 1975). For a recent evaluation of the effects of the assassination see "La morte del re e la crisi di fine secolo," ed. Maria Malatesta, *Cheiron* 28, nos. 35–36.

18. Pier Carlo Masini, *Storia degli anarchici italiani da Bakunin a Malatesta* (Milan: Rizzoli, 1974), 152. For a detailed account of his life before his attempt on the king see, Giuseppe Galzerano, *Giovanni Passanante* (Casalvelino: Galzerano Editore, 1997), 5–51.

19. Masini, *Storia degli anarchici italiani*, 36.

20. Ibid., 40–41.

21. Ibid., 108.

22. F. Tamburini, "Michele Angiolillo e l'assassinio di Cánovas del Castillo," *Spagna Contemporanea* 4, no. 9 (1996): 102–4.

23. Masini, *Storia degli anarchici italiani*, 117–18.

24. Ibid., 142; Arrigo Petacco, *L'anarchico che venne dall'America. Storia di Gaetano Bresci e del complotto per uccidere Umberto I* (Milan: Mondadori, 2000), 13–29; Giuseppe Galzerano, *Gaetano Bresci. Vita, attentato, processo, carcere e morte dell'anarchico che giustiziò Umberto I* (Casalvelino Scalo: Galzerano Editore, 2001), 111–28.

25. For the rather unusual context of the skilled "North Italian" (as the American immigration authorities termed them) silk weavers of Paterson, New Jersey, where Bresci emigrated see, Franco Ramella, "Un caso di emigrazione. Gli operai italiani a Paterson, New Jersey," in *Tra Fabbrica e Società. Mondi operai nell'Italia del Novecento*, ed. Stefano Musso, *Annali Feltrinelli* 33 (1997): 741–75.

26. Lucetti, *Gino Lucetti*, 63–77; Lorenzo Del Boca, *Il dito dell'anarchico. Storia del'uno che sognava di uccidere Mussolini* (Casale Monferrato: Piemme, 2000), 81–82.

27. Della Casa, *Attentato al Duce*, 102–9.

28. Galzerano, "Attentati anarchici a Mussolini," 88–93.

29. Ibid., 93–96.

30. Masini, *Storia degli anarchici italiani*, 157–58.

31. Ibid., 117–18.

32. Ibid., 41–43.

33. G. W. Carey, "The Vessel, the Deed and the Idea: Anarchists in Paterson, 1895–1908," *Antipode: A Radical Journal of Geography* 10, no. 3 (1979): 47.

34. In his European survey Richard Bach Jensen argues that: "In France and Italy, at least, the anarchist assassin or bomb thrower was usually a lone individual. An accomplice or two, as in the case of Ravachol, might assist the anarchist bomb thrower or assassin but usually he received little more than emotional support and meager financial assistance from a few friends and sympathizers" (2004, p. 137).

35. On the concept of *sovversivismo* see, Franco Andreucci, "'Subversiveness' and anti-fascism in Italy," in *People's History and Socialist Theory*, ed. Raphael Samuel, 199–204 (London: RKP, 1981); Carl Levy, "Italian Anarchism, 1870–1926," in *For Anarchism: History, Theory, and Practice*, ed. David Goodway, 26–78 (London, New York: Routledge, 1989); Tobias Abse, *Sovversivi e fascisti a Livorno: Lotta politica e sociale, 1918–1922* (Milan: Franco Angeli, 1991); Carl Levy, "'Sovversivismo': The Radical Political Culture of Otherness in Liberal Italy," *Journal of Political Ideologies* 12, no. 2 (2007): 147–59; Antonio Sonnessa, "Working Class Defence Organization, Anti-Fascist Resistance and the *Arditi del Popolo* in Turin, 1919–22," *European History Quarterly* 33, no. 2 (2003): 183–218.

36. Galzerano, "Attentati anarchici a Mussolini," 93.

37. Petacco, *L'anarchico che venne dall'America*, 59.

38. Galzerano, "Attentati anarchici a Mussolini," 80–81.

39. Delzell, *Mussolini's Enemies*, 108.

40. It has been claimed that the unfortunate bricklayer Trezzi was perhaps the first prisoner in the history of Italy to be "suicided." See Maria Malatesta, "Magistrati, Politici e Diritti Umani in Italia e in Francia. Un'Ipotesi di Ricerca," in *Cheiron* 38, nos. 35–36 (2001): 72–73. For other accounts see, Alessandro Coletti, *Anarchici e questori* (Padova: Marsilio, 1971), 51–78; Massimo Felisatti, *Un delitto della polizia? Morte dell'anarchico Romeo Frezzi* (Milan: Bompiani, 1975); Marcello Santoloni and Nicola Marucci, *Gli ingranaggi del potere: Il caso dell'anarchico Acciarito attentatore di Umberto I* (Rome: Ianua, 1981); Ferdinando Cordova, *Alle radici del malpaese: Una storia italiana* (Rome: Bulzoni,1994), 7–15, 50–53, 161–71. For the anarchists and the Italian legal system in the late nineteenth century, see Romano Canosa and Amedeo Santosuosso, *Magistrati, anarchici e socialisti alla fine dell'Ottocento in Italia*

(Milan: Feltrinelli, 1981); and Ferdinando Cordova, *Democrazia e repressione nell'Italia di fine secolo* (Rome: Bulzoni, 1983).

41. Masini, *Storia degli anarchici italiani*, 110–14.
42. See Mussolini's article "Il Caso Manfredi," *L'Avvenire del Lavoratore*, February 6, 1904, and also *Lotta di classe*, July 16, 1910. Also see Stephen B. Whitaker, *The Anarchist-Individualist Origins of Italian Fascism* (New York: Peter Lang, 2002), 31–54; Pierre Milza, *Mussolini* (Rome: Carocci, 2000), 49–137; Richard Bosworth, *Mussolini* (London: Arnold, 2002), 56–99. In general, see, Philip V. Cannistraro, "Mussolini, Sacco-Vanzetti, and the Anarchists: the Transatlantic Context," *Journal of Modern History* 68 (March 1996): 31–62; Galzerano, *Gaetano Bresci*, 74
43. Masini, *Storia degli anarchici italiani*, 171–73.
44. Ibid., 41–2; J. C. Longoni, *Four Patients of Dr. Deibler. A Study in Anarchy* (London: Lawrence & Wishart, 1970), 197.
45. Masini, *Storia degli anarchici italiani*, 116. Professor Benedict Anderson in a very helpful e-mail also pointed out to me that Germinal "was the first month of spring, when seeds dormant in winter start to come alive. Zola picked this up with the meaning politically that after the winter of repression would come the spring of resistance. March 21, 2005.
46. Petacco, *L'anarchico che venne dall'America*, 35.
47. Galzerano, "Attentati anarchici a Mussolini," 91–92.
48. Whitaker, *The Anarchist-Individualist Origins of Italian Fascism*, 179–84.
49. Dalla Casa, *Attentato al Duce*, 251–72.
50. Masini, *Storia degli anarchici italiani*, 118.
51. Antonio Parente, *Giovanni Passanante, anarchico o mattoide?* (Rome: Bulzoni, 1989), 14.
52. Petacco, *L'anarchico che venne dall'America*, 151–62.
53. Madrid Santos, *Camillo Berberi*, 200–222; Di Lembo, *Guerra di classe e lotta umana*, 184–87. And in general for the provocative activities of Mussloni's secret police see, Mimmo Franzinelli, *I tentacoli dell'OVRA. Agenti, collaboratori e vittime della polizia fascista* (Turin: Bollati-Boringhieri, 1999).
54. Carey, "The Vessel, the Deed and the Idea," 50.
55. Petacco, *L'anarchico che venne dall'America*, 145–46. The sources of this "information" were two former anarchists and now his secret agents, Ennio Belelli ("Virgilio") and Enrico Insabato ("Dante"): both had vivid imaginations and had to earn a living by making themselves invaluable.
56. Masini, *Storia degli anarchici italiani*, 165–69; Petacco, *L'anarchico che venne dall'America*, 135–49. The go-between was Angelo Insogna, Maria Sofia's trusted aide, biographer of Frances II, variously Bourbon, anarchist and con artist, who in 1908 swindled a large amount of cash from a British merchant bank in an affair tied to the reconstruction of the devastated city of Messina, recently struck down by a horrendous earthquake.
57. Masini, *Storia degli anarchici italiani*,168–69; Petacco, *L'anarchico che venne dall'America*, 145–46.

58. L. Gestri, "Dieci lettere inedite di Cirpriani, Malatesta e Merlino," *Movimento operaio e socialista* (October–December, 1971).

59. Petacco, *L'anarchico che venne dall'America*, 151–62.

60. Dalla Casa, *Attentato al Duce*,102.

61. Ibid., 77–113.

62. For a review of the various interpretations see Dalla Casa, *Attentato al Duce*, 43–75.

63. Ibid., 63–64. For Arpinati's transformation into a Fascist dissident, see Whitaker, *The Anarchist-Individualist Origins of Italian Fascism*, 131–63.

64. Dalla Casa, *Attentato al Duce*, 163–66.

65. Ibid., 251–253; Whitaker, *The Anarchist-Individualist Origins of Italian Fascism*, 165–71.

66. For Schirru see Fiori, *Vita e morte di Michele Schirru*; Galzerano, "Attentati anarchici a Mussolini," 88–93.

67. Delzell, *Mussolini's Enemies*, 107–8.

68. Petacco, *L'anarchico che venne dall'America*, 117–24. For his study of Italy after the *Risorgimento* (originally published in French) see, Francesco Saverio Merlino, *L'Italie telle qu'elle est* (Paris: Albert Savine, Editeur, 1890).

17

Failed Anarchists and Anti-Heroes in Lina Wertmüller's *Amore e anarchia*

Dana Renga

I would like to stress my horror at these attempted assassinations. These acts are both evil and stupid as they harm the cause that they are meant to serve. . . . But those assassins are also saints and heroes. . . . When their extreme gesture is forgotten, we shall celebrate the ideal which inspired them.

—*Errico Malatesta, as cited in* Amore e Anarchia

Lina Wertmüller is keenly interested in exploring power dynamics. She has taken on fascism, Nazism, the mafia, chauvinism, labor unions, big business, and so on. Her critique of power during historic fascism is readily apparent in the complete title of the film dealt with in this chapter: *Film d'amore e d'anarchia, ovvero stamattina alle 10 in via dei Fiori nella nota casa di tolleranza* (*Film of Love and Anarchy, or This Morning at 10 a.m. in Via dei Fiori in a Well-known House of Prostitution*). This title (typically wordy for Wertmüller) combines love, anarchy, and the suppressed account—at least within the narrative of the film—of the failed attempted assassination of Benito Mussolini. The words from the title, "or This Morning at 10 AM in Via dei Fiori in a Well-known House of Prostitution" begin the "official" report of main protagonist and would-be anarchist Tunin's death at the end of the film, omitting his name and altering the description of his death. Of course, the viewer knows the truth: after his arrest as a result of declaring "I wanted to kill Mussolini," Tunin stands up to Spatoletti, the chief of police and hyper-masculine icon of fascist

Italy/Mussolini by exclaiming "long live anarchy!" and refusing to offer any information regarding his involvement with the anarchists. As a result, he is brutally assassinated for his newfound loyalty.[1] From the onset, Wertmüller warns that the personal (love) informs the political (anarchy).[2]

In *Love and Anarchy*, as the title implies, the emotional is continuously interrupted by the political and vice versa. Wertmüller focuses on dissonant images—including but not limited to love/anarchy, mother/prostitute, city/country, and hero/coward. A clear example of her "politics of polarity" is present in the final citation of the film, where the famous Italian anarchist Errico Malatesta is quoted as suggesting that the anarchist is both murderer and villain, hero and martyr: "I want to repeat my horror at these attempts that are both evil and stupid as they harm the cause that they should be helping. . . . But those assassins are also saints and heroes . . . and they will be celebrated when the brutal fact will be forgotten, and only the ideal that enlightened them and their martyrdom will be remembered." *Love and Anarchy* challenges traditional definitions of "anarchists," "martyrs" and "heroes" while offering novel perspectives on the politics of gender and power often debated in the cultural arena of the 1970s. This period is particularly fascinating, as many Italian filmmakers insisted on returning to and re-reading the twenty years of fascist rule as they felt unsatisfied with previous interpretations of the era that were simplistic or hermetic. Rather than confidently celebrating the collapse of historical fascism, exalting the partisan "heroes" and then welcoming the emergence of many popular leftist organizations in the early 1970s, Wertmüller, for one, continues to resist totalitarianism on all levels. She is a child of the Resistance, part of a generation acutely interested in unmasking the continual sway of power in Italy.

In returning to the subject of fascism, and treating a failed anarchist, she critiques and dismantles the authoritarianism intrinsic to her own era, as she explains in an interview with Peter Biskind: 'I would like to take myth away from history. . . . It frightens me when the face of power is presented with seriousness.'[3] Wertmüller posits that the present-day individual must continue to contest fascistic discourses of power, even long after historical dictators appear to be dead and buried. She positions the individual as responsible for his/her global community, explaining the exigencies of a post-fascist society: "I am interested in the time *after* the moment of revolt, the period in which a social structure must be established which nurtures human beings who embody a certain kind of harmony—a harmony in disorder. . . . In order to prepare us for this harmony, we must realize that each one of us reflects and is responsible for the shape of our society."[4]

Wertmüller's "harmony in disorder" is essentially non-hierarchical and anti-authority.[5]

Love and Anarchy clearly privileges anarchy, a philosophy whose tenets are at odds with traditional historiography and the oppressive regimentation of fascist politics. In presenting an anarchist vision, the film unties that which binds the figurative fasces of government and gives voice and vision to previously tacit members of society. In foregrounding anarchy—whose etymology implies "without government" or, more specifically, "without a leader"—Wertmüller condemns not only organized governments, but the political and administrative systems that they perpetuate, whether they be fascist, communist, socialist, Christian-democratic and so on. The role of anarchy in Wertmüller's film is readily apparent: Tunin, after witnessing the murder of father-figure Michele Scarravento, an *engagé* anarchist on his way to assassinate Mussolini, enlists with the cause and attempts to take Michele's place. The narrative then treats Tunin's arrival in Rome, his involvement with the anarchist/prostitute Salome and love affair with the prostitute Tripolina, ending with his violent murder at the hands of the fascists. To further historicize the film, Wertmüller references several historical anarchists and would-be assassins such as Anteo Zamboni, Michele Schirru, and Angelo Sbardellotto. The name for Salome's teenage boyfriend, who was stabbed to death at a fascist rally in Bologna in 1926, is taken directly from Zamboni, and Tunin is based loosely on a combination of Schirru and Sbardellotto. Interestingly, if one believes the widespread story that Zamboni never fired at Mussolini and instead was scapegoated on the spot, like Tunin, these three were condemned to death without even attempting to take Mussolini's life. (Schirru and Sbardellotto were sentenced to die in front of the firing squad for only *intending* to kill the dictator.)[6]

This film is concerned with the very philosophy that historical Fascism stifled when it came to official power in 1922; as we know, during the "red two years" of 1919–20, anarchism, communism, and socialism encouraged numerous strikes and protests throughout Italy. Spatoletti, in fact, makes specific reference to the early fascists' attack on anarchists in referring to the "good old days" of nighttime roundups, castor oil treatments and beatings. The tripling of assassination attempts in the recent past ironically negates Spatoletti's resolute belief that "everyone loves the Duce." In returning to the topic of anarchy and affirming its active presence during the fascist period, Wertmüller gives cinematic space to a philosophy of anti-power in a decade, the 1970s, fraught with conflicting centers of jurisdiction.

Throughout the film, Tunin and Michele repeatedly express their hope for a "free society." Their thoughts on anarchy approximate Ernst Bloch's utopian sensibility, defined as a space of "happiness, freedom, non-alienation, the Eternally-Female . . . *where the whole world* [is in] *a rapport with total perfection*."[7] Wertmüller's anarchist hero Michele echoes Bloch's interpretation in describing the "ultimate goal" of anarchism: "There we will be at peace with one another, sharing, in harmony. We were created as equals, and we must therefore live as equals."[8] The anarchist utopia is a free space, where altruistic ideologies flourish in a classless society with communal ownership, and where humanity is feminized and lives in harmony with nature. Throughout the film, Tunin, Michele, and Salome underline a fundamental utopian value: the freedom of the individual.[9] Tunin, a feminized male anti-heroic character intimately bound to the natural world, embodies such an idea of an "impossible utopia."

At several points in *Love and Anarchy*, Tunin has significant interactions with urban and rural environments. The urban metropolis represents nationalist expansion, domination, and death, while more natural spaces come across as egalitarian, ruminative, and nonbelligerent. *Love and Anarchy* presents a male anti-heroic character who is feminized and intimately bound to the natural world. Tunin embodies and reflects a utopian metaphysics that resists authoritarianism. Profoundly influenced by the anarchist Michele, Tunin is most at ease in natural surroundings lacking audible discourse.

Tunin is a conflicted character, and his ambiguous construction evidences a dichotomy between "traditional" gender associations of "male" and "female." Wertmüller's film proposes that identities of gender and their subsequent interpolations into cultural and political arenas are socially constructed, perpetuated, and disciplined. Not only does the film promote this concept, but it also self-consciously presents the viewer with the textual strategies needed to dismantle such facile constructions. Although Tunin attempts to assert such conventional "masculine" qualities as honor, heroism and aggression, his character is feminized through being consistently—and very comfortably—associated with nature, romantic love, and anarchy. Here too, as in her representation of the brothel, Wertmüller is using cultural and gender stereotypes inherent to fascist ideology and deeply rooted in patriarchal culture (woman represents nature and the romantic) only to ironize and subvert such clichés. Although Tunin is victimized by fascism, he twice rejects fascist authority as embodied by Spatoletti. I would like to point out that Wertmüller's creation of Spatoletti is so self-conscious that the viewer cannot help but laugh at his claims of sexual prowess and world domination.[10]

Tunin is often the source of the film's comedy; for example, he is the butt of many jokes at the brothel. He is frequently feminized through his physical presentation: his freckled and expressive face is shown in close-up at an angle and both soft music and low-key tonality lighting regularly enhance his presence, a representation that strongly diverges from the boisterous depiction of Spatoletti. In addition, Tunin resists masculinist/authoritarian systems, demonstrating instead a strong affinity with the space of the brothel as well as the natural and the animal world—he is shown with chickens and cows and even adopts a kitten.

Tunin's anti-heroism is demonstrated during his execution, constructed to be diametrically opposed to another famous cinematic execution: that of the Partisan Manfredi in Rossellini's *Rome Open City* (1945). Of course, the example par excellence of the vaunted "maleness" associated with the heroism of the resistance is Rossellini's Manfredi. During this renowned sequence, Manfredi is shown in close-up, at low and straight angle with bright lighting, and his visual presentation is accompanied by a cataclysmic score as Don Pietro views his beaten body and curses the Nazis for their inhumane crimes. Wertmüller, however, does not ask that the viewer consider Tunin's resistance as a technique to condemn the fascists, therefore attesting to the downfall of the regime and its violent stance. Unlike Manfredi, Tunin's features are barely made evident. Instead, a sack covers his head and he is framed by a long shot at high angle in the shadows, so that he almost becomes invisible, as he blends into the prison wall. There are no witnesses to his death, save the viewer, who is left with a sense of contradiction and incredulity, and, as the upbeat circus music accompanies his torture, the ironic contradiction between the visual shot and the musical score is brutally apparent. No one vindicates Tunin's death. As Marcus explains: "By representing the sad plight of Tunin, Wertmüller is fulfilling the neorealist mandate of memorializing Resistance activists who died a traceless death."[11] The viewer, then, is implicated in the process of signification, as he/she is prompted to take responsibility for the action on the screen. *Love and Anarchy* implies that, in order to imagine a world without violence, we must reaffirm our intellectual power and realize our responsibility to our civilization, as Wilhelm Reich explains: "The fall of our civilization is inevitable if those who work . . . should not become conscious of their enormous responsibility quickly enough."[12]

In several of the film's most salient narrative moments, Tunin's feminine qualities are poignantly illustrated while he is allowed fleeting visions into utopian environs. The textual implications of Tunin's presence in the fascist new-town Sabaudia, for example, assist in dismantling hierarchical cultural formations of sexual and political power. These associations blur stereotypical impressions of "city" as representing social integration, nationalist expansion, domination, and death while the natural is a feminized space corresponding with silence, pre-expression, and utopian longing. Here, buildings are less reminiscent of colonial ambition and monetary gain. Instead, as narrative focus turns from edifice to individual, sense is evoked through the protagonists' interactions with urban space.

In the following scenes to be analyzed, Salome makes a date for a Sunday outing with Spatoletti, bringing along Tunin and Tripolina so that Tunin may scope out the upcoming fascist rally in Sabaudia and prepare for the upcoming assassination. Sabaudia is both an extraordinary example of urban planning and a perfect emblem for the colonial aspirations of *Il Duce*. Along with the *Esposizione Universale di Roma* and the towns of Pontinia, Aprilia, Pomezia, and Littoria (now Latina), Sabaudia orients the Roman traveler from the eternal city toward the ocean and beyond, in the direction of the multiple countries possibly reached by the Mediterranean on a journey of Mussolini's much hoped for, yet never obtained, imperialist expansion.[13] The city is meant to seamlessly blend political ideology (colonial ambitions, legitimization of fascist projects) and town planning.

The Sabaudia sequences reinforce Tunin's discomfort in the urban environment, a discomfort introduced minutes into the film at his arrival in Rome. In this earlier scene, a series of seven shots evokes how the fascist state desired to capitalize on the glory of the Risorgimento while simultaneously dominating the modern city: the militaristic music accompanying the montage, the fascist march "All Hail, Country of Heroes," weds martial architecture with political ambition as a series of low-angle medium shots of the statue of Vittorio Emanuele II, the first king of Italy after the country was unified, are followed by a medium shot of Mussolini's balcony in Palazzo Venezia, where it was believed that the dictator worked all night and never slept. The camera then returns to the statue, zooming out and panning left to illustrate that much of the city of Rome, including the Vatican, can be seen, and supposedly controlled, from within the walls of the Vittoriano. This montage is followed by an extra-long shot in high-angle of Tunin as he enters the city of Rome for the first time. A sound bridge is employed as the camera zooms in on a medium-long shot of Tunin looking quite ill at ease, suggesting that the same governing powers of the previous shots attempt to control his actions.

The theme of governmental control over visual space is furthered by the initial presentation of Spatoletti on his way to Sabaudia. Here he is shown in close-up on his motorcycle, and the quick paced music of Rossini's *The Silken Staircase* suggests melodrama, speed, and pursuit. Spatoletti dominates the country setting with his oppressive physical presence and his fascist salute to a passing vehicle. The film then cuts to a montage of shots of the city of Sabaudia, introduced by a close-up of a fascist mural depicting farmers cultivating wheat—alongside Mussolini—that is tied into the symbolic fasces. The rapid pace of the editing complies with the musical motif, as shots of Spatoletti lecturing to a group of fascists presents the city as a series of closed-in spaces, controlled and dominated by the officers. The only anomaly within the sequence is the presence of a Fellini-esque horse.

When Tunin later re-enters the city of Sabaudia alone, a musical motif reminiscent of the score written by Ennio Morricone for Sergio Leone begins, suggesting the discomfort, suspense, and circumspection typical of the climate shortly before a western shoot-out: it is composed of an octave that steadily repeats as Tunin peruses the assassination site. In this way, the soundtrack externalizes his fear. The scenes concerning Tunin's visit to Sabaudia and subsequent escape to a country field are exemplary of Wertmüller's ability to manipulate sound and image, creating a beautifully constructed and poignant aesthetic representation without the inclusion of dialogue. The restricted and organized visual space associated with fascist control is liberated by Tunin's presence, as a series of long shots depicting the protagonist within the environment of the city opens up previously closed spaces, introducing fresh perspectives on a space formerly dominated by the performative fascism of Spatoletti. The empty and silent piazza is reminiscent of many of Giorgio De Chirico's early paintings, and the broad, round tower present in eight of the scene's fifteen shots specifically evokes his *La tour rouge* (1913), a metaphysical painting of a red tower in an empty piazza flanked by buildings.[14]

The only movement within the painting is suggested by an equestrian statue on the right, reminiscent of the horse in the Spatoletti sequence, and the unsettling silence and immobility of space implies that motion is not perpetually absent, only temporarily concealed as if on the verge of awareness. The equestrian image in the painting evokes anarchy, madness, and artistic creation as well in that the statue references a monument to King Umberto in Torino (assassinated in 1900 by the anarchist Gaetano Bresci), which stood at the end of the street "where Nietzsche had lived while writing *Ecce Homo*."[15]

As Tunin wanders through the town, the absence of natural sound and lack of movement eerily intimate his predicament without the necessity of verbal explanation. Angela Dalle Vacche calls Sabaudia "a city of the mind"[16] and, similar to Freud's analogy in *Civilization and Its Discontents*, where he chooses the city of Rome as a representation of the psyche's past,[17] Sabaudia stands for the foundations and products of fascism. Similar to De Chirico's painting, the Sabaudia sequence evokes absence rather than presence and expectation over action. In turning Mussolini's planned urban environment into an empty and silent canvas pregnant with anticipation, Wertmüller brushes aside fascist colonial ambition and violence.

The Sabaudia sequence culminates in a close-up of Tunin, and as he closes his eyes out of apprehension, the music mirrors his consciousness as a melody begins that includes the soft, emotionally charged tune and female voices often associated with the protagonist. As Tunin surveys for the final time the balcony from which he is to shoot the dictator, the music builds, and the western motif is transformed into a melody accompanied by female voices. With this transformation of perspective, commonplace images of patriarchal rule over unfettered space apparent in films like *Camicia nera* ([Black Shirt], Giovacchino Forzano, 1933) become depriviliged and conventional fascist phallic icons of male power and virility such as machinery—for example, Spatoletti's motorcycle—and towers lose their traditional signifying power.

The film then cuts to an extra-long shot of Tunin in a large field. Upon his arrival in the natural setting, the music and female voices steadily increase in volume, working in harmony with the editing to frame Tunin within the natural environment. This narrative framing is accomplished by a variation of both camera angles and distance from subject, as the gradual shift from high-angle extra-long shot to straight-on angle close-up welcomes Tunin into the field, and the depth of focus creates a symmetrical relationship between subject and milieu. Tunin's obvious air of comfort and peacefulness as he surveys the landscape contradicts earlier sentiments of distress. A series of shots complete Tunin's homecoming as he is shown lying down in the pasture, as Wertmüller explains, "pre-establishing a contact with mother earth."[18] He is alternately depicted twice from a straight-on angle and twice from high angle, and as he falls into a deep sleep the viewer is asked to reflect on the ontological implications of the two spaces—one artificially constructed, the other natural—that Tunin has just visited. Tunin's presence in both topographies is quite fascinating in light of the architectural significance of the so-called "Pontine towns." Built originally on the reclaimed land of the Pontine marshes, Sabaudia is said to represent a perfect collective of productive land and urban dwelling. Rather than dominate the natural space, these towns are "inconceivable outside the agricultural organization that supports them and that they support."[19]

Ultimately, Tunin's feminization proposes a narrative cinema that does not stop at mocking and disputing traditional modes of representing male subject-hood (i.e., the caricature Spatoletti and the hyper-masculine war machine that he embodies); furthermore, and more importantly, Wertmüller succeeds in feminizing cultural spaces traditionally associated with a masculine point-of-view. Tunin's cinematic presentation acutely diverges from conventional modes of cinematic gender representation. Whereas the principal male protagonist typically creates cinematic action, dominating and controlling the film's spaces,[20] Tunin's presentation self-consciously deconstructs the possibility of male-dominated and transfigured distance. In Wertmüller's presentation of Sabaudia as a city of the mind, liberated at least from fascist colonial aspirations and connected to the natural space of the field by means of a sound bridge, distinctions between the restricted signifiers of "male" and "female," culture (city) and nature, become blurred, and possibilities of narrative interaction are heightened.

What Wertmüller attempts here is a "cinema of poetry"—to borrow Pasolini's terminology. She juxtaposes shots and points of view to create a psychologically charged space surpassing the visual image, connecting Tunin's perspective with her own. Much like the language of poetry, where sense is evoked not from the words themselves but from their interplay and combination within the text, meaning in this film is created through its visual style.[21] Through her use of "free indirect discourse," the combination of shots suggests a transcendent metaphysical space where the static emptiness of the town of Sabaudia is emblematic of the futile undertaking of fascist cultural imperialism. Invested with a sense of the weightlessness of the ahistorical moment, Tunin is unencumbered by the oppressive presence of Spatoletti and the regime he represents.

Love and Anarchy opens with a question: as a child, young Tunin asks his mother, "What's an anarchist?" His mother quickly responds that anarchists kill royalty and are then hanged. The final scenes of the film offer another, yet not so straightforward, answer to Tunin's query: Anarchists give their life for a cause and, in exchange, are remembered for what Malatesta describes as "the ideal that enlightened them." *Love and Anarchy* concludes by presenting dissonant images and thematics: personal concern for Tunin wins out over Salome's political activism, Tunin is both anti-hero within the film and martyr to the viewer, the violently tragic finale is accompanied by a burlesque score, and anarchists are stupid and crazy but are also worthy to be considered martyrs. In sum, within the narrative of the film, anarchy prevails; nothing is centered, wrapped up, or orderly (in the sense that "order" is one of the mantras of fascism). As Tunin, a man in disorder, reconnects city with country, anarchy as a political ideology is dis-invested of its violent aspect, and what remains is a de-masculinized subject who would forsake violence and advancement for ontological contemplation.[22]

Notes

1. One critic argues that Tunin's death has no witness: "Beaten to a pulp for what essentially was no more than an intention, his very life and death are hushed up for political expediency. No one will ever know him as an anarchist." Although within the narrative of the film it is true that only Salome, Tripolina, and the fascists know that he is an anarchist, it should not be forgotten that he is certainly memorialized for the spectator as such. Grace Russo Bullaro, "'What's an Anarchist?': Exploring the Boundaries of the Personal and the Political in Wertmuller's 'Love and Anarchy,'" *Forum Italicum* 35, no. 2 (2001): 470.

2. The title sequence furthers the critique of power inherent in the title; it is composed of a series of close-ups of black and white stills of Mussolini's eyes and face, cross cut with images of the masses at a fascist rally. The montage is accompanied by a voice-over of one of Mussolini's speeches backed by the approval of the crowds and the intermittent beating of war-drums that stress the bellicose nature of the dictator's speech. Although this montage focuses on oratory skill and physical presence—qualities that assisted in wooing the masses into passive submission—it simultaneously suggests that the regime is as impotent as the motionless photographs. A script follows the sequence, declaring Tunin's motivations: "His outrage compelled him to act." Once again, the emotional and the political are intimately entwined.

3. Peter Biskin, 'An Interview with Lina Wertmüller,' in *Women and the Cinema: A Critical Anthology*, ed. Karyn Kay and Gerald Peary (New York: Dutton, 1977), 330.

4. Gina Blumenfeld and Paul McIsaac, "You Cannot Make the Revolution on Film: An Interview with Lina Wertmüller," *Cineaste* 7, no. 2 (1976): 9.

5. The notion of "harmony in disorder" is a central theme that recurs in many of Wertmüller's films, in particular *the Seduction of Mimi* (1972), *Seven Beauties* (1975), and *Swept Away* (1974). The Spanish anarchist Pedro from *Pasqualino settebellezze* is the most obvious mouthpiece for Wertmüller's attitude in that he describes a new "man in disorder" necessary to overcome the regimented rhetoric and politics of fascism.

6. For a history of anarchy in Italy (in addition to the comprehensive chapter in this book by Carl Levy) see Mauro De Agostini, *Prisoners and Partisans: Italian Anarchists in the Struggle Against Fascism* (London: Kate Sharpley Library, 1999); Giuseppe Fiori, *L'anarchico Schirru: condannato a morte per l'intenzione di uccidere Mussolini* (Milano: Arnoldo Mondadori, 1983); Giuseppe Galzerano, *Angelo Sbardellotto: vita, processo e morte dell'emigrante anarchico fucilato per l'intenzione di uccidere Mussolini* (Scalo: Galzerano, 2003); and Richard Hostetter, "Anarchism Versus the Italian State," in *The Anarchists*, ed. Irving Louis Horowitz, 390–418 (New Brunswick, NJ: Aldine Transaction Publishers, 2005).

7. Ernst Bloch, *The Principle of Hope*, vol. 3 (Oxford: Basil Blackwell, 1986), 1192.

8. *The Screenplays of Lina Wertmüller*, trans. Steven Wagner (New York: New York Times Book Company, 1977), 92.

9. Errico Malatesta explains the importance of such an awareness: "The subject is not whether we accomplish Anarchism today, tomorrow or within ten centuries, but that we walk toward Anarchism today, tomorrow and always." Errico Malatesta, *A Talk Between Two Workers* (Oakland: Man!, 1933), III. Wertmüller believed that "Malatesta was a wonderful human being. He was the philosopher of an impossible utopia. But within his utopian dream is the core of a very important principle—that of the freedom of the individual," Blumenfeld and McIsaac, "You Cannot Make the Revolution on Film," 7.

10. For a treatment of Spatoletti's performative sexuality see Millicent Marcus, "Wertmüller's 'Love and Anarchy': The High Price of Commitment," in *Italian Film in the Light of Neorealism* (Princeton, NJ: Princeton University Press, 1986), 328–29, 334–37.

11. Millicent Marcus, 'Film d'amore e d'anarchia,' in *The Cinema of Italy*, ed. Giorgio Bertellini (London: Wallflower, 2004), 184.

12. Wilhem Reich, *The Mass Psychology of Fascism*, trans. Vincent R. Carfagno (New York: Farrar, Straus and Giroux, 1970), xvi.

13. In 1925 during a speech appointing Filippo Creminosi as the first fascist governor of Rome, Mussolini discussed his dreams of nationalist expansion beyond the walls of the Eternal City: "The third Rome will spread itself onto other hills, along the banks of the sacred river, to reach the shores of the Tyrrhenian Sea. A straight line—the broadest in the world—shall carry the fury of the *mare-nostrum* from arisen Ostia to the heart of the city where the Unknown Soldier stands guard." Joanne Basso Funigiello and Philip J. Funigiello, "EUR, 1936–1942: Town Planning, Architecture and Fascist Ideology," in *The Canadian Journal of Italian Studies* 4 (1981): 86.

14. In the screenplay, Wertmüller points out that Sabaudia is reminiscent of the Italian metaphysical school of painting. She describes "the surrealistic atmosphere which was perhaps the very same that inspired the artists De Chirico and Savinio." *Amore e Anarchia*, in *The Screenplays*, 116.

15. Paolo Baldacci, "De Chirico and Savinio: The Theory and Iconography of Metaphysical Painting," in *Italian Art in the 20th Century: Painting and Sculpture 1900–1988*, ed. Emily Braun (Munich: Prestel, 1989), 63.

16. Angela Dalle Vacche, *The Body in the Mirror: Shapes of History in Italian Cinema* (Princeton, NJ: Princeton University Press, 1992), 232.

17. Sigmund Freud, *Civilization and Its Discontents*, trans. James Strachey (New York: W. W. Norton, 1961), 17–19.

18. Wertmüller, *Amore e Anarchia*, in *The Screenplays*, 123.

19. Henry Millon, "Some New Towns in Italy in the 1930s," *Art and Architecture in the Service of Politics*, ed. Henry Millon and Linda Nochlin (Cambridge: Massachusetts Institute of Technology Press, 1978), 333.

20. Laura Mulvey, *Visual and Other Pleasures* (Bloomington: Indiana University Press, 1989), 20–21.

21. Pier Paolo Pasolini spells out what is meant by a poetic language of cinema: "La formazione di una 'lingua della poesia cinematografica' implica dunque la possibilità di . . . una prosa d'arte, di una serie di pagine liriche, la cui soggettività è

assicurata dall'uso pretestuale della 'soggettiva libera indiretta': e il cui vero protagonista è lo stile" (the formation of a 'language of cinematographic poetry' therefore implies the possibility of creating ... an aesthetic prose, a series of lyrical pages, whose subjectivity is assured by the pretextual use of 'free indirect discourse' whose true protagonist is style), Pier Paolo Pasolini, "Il 'cinema di poesia.'" in *Saggi sulla letteratura e sull'arte* (Milano: Arnoldo Mondadori editore, 1999), 1485.

22. *Love and Anarchy* approximates Teresa De Lauretis's definition of "women's cinema" as the film's "visual and symbolic space" is constructed to create diegetic flashes that resonate and make sense to the extra-diegetic female-engendered viewer. Teresa De Lauretis, *Technologies of Gender: Essays on Theory, Film and Fiction* (Bloomington: Indiana University Press, 1987), 133.

Index